THE
WEHRMACHT
LAST WITNESSES

THIS IS AN ANDRE DEUTSCH BOOK

Design copyright © Carlton Books/Edgehill Publishing
2001, 2010
Text copyright © Edgehill Publishing 2001
Pictures © Cromwell Productions Limited 2001

This edition published in 2010 by André Deutsch
A Division of the Carlton Publishing Group
20 Mortimer Street
London
W1T 3JW

Previously published as *Servants of Evil*

This book is sold subject to the condition that it shall not, by
way of trade or otherwise, be lent, resold, hired out or
otherwise circulated without the publisher's prior written
consent in any form of cover or binding other than that in
which it is published and without a similar condition
including this condition, being imposed upon the
subsequent purchaser.

All rights reserved.

A CIP catalogue record for this book is available from the
British Library.

ISBN 978 0 233 00295 8

THE
WEHRMACHT
LAST WITNESSES

First-hand accounts from the survivors
of Hitler's armed forces

BOB CARRUTHERS General Editor
Foreword by **DR SIMON TREW**
of The Royal Military Academy, Sandhurst

ANDRE
DEUTSCH

Contents

FOREWORD BY SIMON TREW.................................... vii

INTRODUCTION ix

CHAPTER ONE
The Blitzkrieg Era 1939–1941 1

CHAPTER TWO
The Germans in Russia 33

CHAPTER THREE
The U-Boat War: Days of Success 1939–1942 67

CHAPTER FOUR
The Luftwaffe: Eagles Ascending 1939–1942............... 101

CHAPTER FIVE
The U-Boat War: Days of Failure 1943–1945.............. 135

CHAPTER SIX
The Defeat of the Luftwaffe 1943–1944 163

CHAPTER SEVEN
The Closing Battles: From Stalingrad to Berlin 1943–1945... 191

CHAPTER EIGHT
Prisoners 225

BIBLIOGRAPHY 263

INDEX... 265

Foreword

During the dramatic decade that began in 1935, Hitler's Germany mobilised over twelve million of its citizens for war. Many went willingly enough, enthused by Nazi propaganda and a desire to right the perceived wrongs of the peace settlement that ended the First World War. Others were more reluctant crusaders for the Nazi cause. However, under Germany's harsh regime, they had little choice but to take up arms when ordered to do so. Whichever the case, three million of them would die by May 1945. Most of the rest would carry the physical and mental scars of the catastrophe they witnessed for the rest of their lives.

Unsurprisingly, the second half of the twentieth century saw an avalanche of English-language literature on the Second World War. Most of this came from British and American sources, but a reasonable proportion originated "on the other side of the hill". In particular, the 1950s, '60s and '70s saw a steady flow of books written by senior participants in the German war effort. Some of these – for example, Albert Speer, Hitler's Armaments Minister – were important political figures. Others were high-ranking staff officers such as Walter Warlimont or Reinhard Gehlen, or military commanders such as Erich von Manstein, Heinz Guderian and Otto Skorzeny. The air force and navy also had their representatives, among them Adolf Galland, chief of the Luftwaffe's fighter arm, and Admiral Karl Doenitz, who led Germany's U-boat offensive throughout the war.

Although their works added greatly to our understanding of strategic and operational matters, they said little about the wartime experience of millions of ordinary Germans. Most of the generals and admirals seemed to be concerned mainly with shifting the blame for Germany's defeat towards Hitler, and with justifying and excusing (and sometimes apologising for) their own actions. To their credit, some authors – notably Cornelius Ryan and Paul Carell – did use interviews with the Wehrmacht's rank and file as a central part of their research. However, few front-line memoirs or personal accounts of any quality emerged in the English language. Unfortunately, perhaps the most famous of those that were published, Guy Sajer's *The Forgotten Soldier*, is now widely thought to be a work of fiction.

Yet throughout these years, a massive resource remained largely untapped, in the shape of the personal memories of Wehrmacht war veterans. Although old comrades' associations flourished, and numerous journals and unit histories were produced, the audience for these works consisted mainly of the veterans themselves. This was not surprising, for their often self-pitying tone and politically unreconstructed, self-censored content provoked hostility within West Germany, and made them appear unsaleable abroad. Indeed, only recently have small quantities of such works emerged in translation. Consequently, a significant gap remains in our understanding of the German experience of the Second World War.

Servants of Evil, produced in conjunction with Cromwell Productions' television series of the same name, is intended to help fill this gap. Based on recent interviews with army, air force and navy veterans, it provides new perspectives on a range of issues large and small. Some of its content makes unpleasant reading, but given the subject matter, this is inevitable. Other parts are enlightening, providing insight into personal motivation and attitudes, and into the Wehrmacht's tactics. There are even some humorous episodes. But throughout, the emphasis is on the experience of the ordinary German soldier, sailor and airman, told in a candid and straightforward fashion. The result is a thought-provoking and readable account of some of the most important events of the twentieth century.

DSC Trew
Sandhurst
May 2001

Introduction

For most people alive at the time, the Second World War is a distant, if painful, memory. For very many more, it is just history, something that happened before they were born and made no impact on their lives or their recollections. However, for those who served and survived, the recollections are as vivid as they were at the time they occurred, and nearly 60 years later they remain vivid down to the last fine detail.

Until recently the picture has been somewhat incomplete. The generals and politicians have written their memoirs, the regimental histories have found their way into print, some of the participants have set down their experiences, the films, the videos, the documentaries have been made. It is, however, the victors who write history, and the Second World War has been no exception. Now, a group of German veterans who have kept silent for nearly 60 years have come forward with accounts of their own war.

In their youth they served the Third Reich and their Führer for the six years the war lasted and came away with impressions and memories of the conflict from the sharpest of sharp ends – the early halcyon days of the blitzkrieg, the hazards and rigours of the Russian campaign, the discomforts of the U-boat war, the war in the air and the last days of Berlin in 1945 as the "1,000-year Reich" went down in the blood, flames and destruction of total ruin.

The Third Reich had many faces, and the German veterans who tell their stories in this book came to the Second World War from different and sometimes surprising perspectives. For example, Detlef Radbruch, who fought with the Luftwaffe, had little time for Hitler and actually came from an anti-Nazi family, but, as a soldier, he still believes "you have to do your duty". Hannau Rittau, who served in a Luftwaffe anti-aircraft unit, says much the same thing: "We had to defend our home and we had to defend our country, and that's what we tried to do."

Heinz Reiners joined the Kriegsmarine because his father had served in the German navy during the First World War: "So his son had to do the same in the Second! But it wasn't just that. We were young, we were enthusiastic. The propaganda we heard told us that only the Germans were worth anything, all the others were nothing. That's the way we were brought up in our youth."

For Karl Born, a volunteer who joined the Luftwaffe, his war service was a natural continuation of his training as a glider pilot, which began when he was only 13, in 1936:

> At that time the first flying groups had been set up in the Hitler Youth. We were supervised by the German Air Sport Association, which had been founded after the First World War by former airmen. They had been forced to switch to gliders because Germany wasn't allowed to build planes with engines any more. I took various glider-pilot exams in this Hitler Youth Flyers [Flieger-Hitlerjugend] group and after that the air-pilot licence for gliders, which permitted me to fly gliders loaded with up to 10 people.

Born found it all a great adventure, though this feeling was afterwards tempered by his war experiences:

> I volunteered when I was 17 and when I was 20, in 1941, I went on my first mission. Flying was enormous fun, and I was full of enthusiasm for it. If we were asked to fly somewhere, anywhere, I always volunteered straight away. Of course, it was a good feeling to survive aerial battles, but in retrospect, later, when you reviewed it all, you had to say that it was all madness. The war, every war, shooting at men you'd never seen before... I must say that, today, I wouldn't want to volunteer.

Wolfgang Reinhardt was another volunteer for whom the war was just an extension of peacetime activity. Reinhardt belonged first to the Jungvolk and then to the Hitler Youth, and that meant that between the ages of six and 16, before he volunteered, he was preparing for war and knew little else:

> I was a recruit in the Army NCO school, Potsdam-Reiche, the elite school in Germany. Whoever went through its doors could be proud to have been there, you could walk three centimetres taller. All the training was geared to war. We were trained on mortars and machine guns; and made mock attacks on bunkers, although it wasn't all that much of a pretence because live rounds and shells were used. The training was tough. We had to face all the dangers of real battle, and its discomforts, too.
>
> I'll give you an example. There was a river in East Prussia called the Liebe, a small river perhaps one metre deep. We were ordered to about-turn and march into the Liebe, about-turn and march out of the Liebe, about-turn back into the Liebe again, holding rifles and machine guns up so that they didn't get wet. We had to put up with the cold, too. Potsdam in winter was ice-cold, lousy cold.
>
> As a training exercise, we were ordered to attack a town. We had hardly started when the command came to stop. "Artillery, change of positions, you must dig yourselves in." And we sat there for hours in that cold in the snow before the word came that we could continue and the change of positions was over.
>
> It went to extremes. We had to run around the training areas with full pack and equipment, not walking, but running over three or four kilometres of the training areas, including the field packs we had. Later the field pack was replaced by a storm pack. We had to climb over walls, over barbed wire, through a pipe, over the wall again, and that went on for an hour or more.

Eckhart Strasosky was a leader in the Hitler Youth before he joined the Wehrmacht on December 1, 1939, and he later fought in Yugoslavia and Russia. At 18, Strasosky had already commanded a group of young 14- to 18-year-olds and was destined for the officer corps from the start:

I was an officer at 22. At that time, once the war had begun, every boy of the right age volunteered to join the Wehrmacht. I was one of them. But I didn't really understand anything about politics and there were many others like me. Before the war, when we were 10 or 14 years old, we didn't even realize that we were being prepared for war, through military fitness training or sporting achievements. We weren't told what the end of it all was going to be.

Hajo Hermann, later to become a famous Luftwaffe ace, approached the war from a predominantly political point of view. The Treaty of Versailles of 1919, which ended the First World War, had reorganized areas of Europe in such a way that German minorities found themselves severed from Germany and placed under the rule of two new countries: Czechoslovakia and Poland. In both countries, or so Hitler claimed, they were suffering discrimination.

Millions of resentful Germans, including Hajo Hermann, believed him. They were mollified when the problem of the German "exiles" in the Sudetenland of Czechoslovakia was solved at Munich in 1938: the agreement made there by Britain, France, Germany and Italy transferred the Sudeten districts to the Third Reich. In 1939, however, the Germans in Poland had yet to be rescued. When Germany precipitated the Second World War by attacking Poland on September 1, 1939, Hermann was firmly convinced that it had been a great wrong to consign a predominantly German population to the Poles:

That had to be redressed. Hitler's suggestion, to hold a referendum, was refused by the Poles, who were unfortunately supported in their decision by the British and Americans. And that led to the conflict. At any rate, I participated in that war and I always said to myself that we did what we just had to do, what Germans had to do. If we had accepted the injustice, then we would have been the worst idiots ever.

I was a bit older than most, 25 or 26, when the war began in 1939, and I'd studied history, listened to my teachers talking about the First World War, the Treaty of Versailles and that shameful Paragraph 231, which blamed Germany for the war. So after Hitler took power, we could say, "Thank God, now we have an army again, now we can put things right and get back the land that has been taken away from us."

Others, though, saw the political imperative that fuelled the policies of Hitler and Nazi Germany from a different angle, as the workings of a dictatorship that punished dissension with death. Benedikt Sieb was one of them. He was a 19-year-old apprentice in Hamburg when his life was changed by the Nazi diktat:

> My apprenticeship ended in 1941, after two years, not because of anything I had done, but because in the factory where I worked, someone had been discovered listening to English radio programmes. He was sentenced to death. I became involved because the Gestapo wanted me to make a statement as an eyewitness. I refused to do it. The next thing I knew, the Gestapo demanded that I sign up for the Russian front or they'd send me to a concentration camp and my parents would be shot. So I signed up.

Rudolf Oelkers was in an even more invidious position, as the son of a social democrat. Democrats, socialists, communists, trades unionists and other political opponents had been the first targets of the Nazis after Hitler came to power in January 1933. Many were imprisoned in concentration camps, many were executed. Oelkers's father was more fortunate: he was given a choice. Rudolf Oelkers still has the documents in which his father's choices were spelled out:

> My father was told, "Either you keep quiet or you'll be put into a concentration camp." He decided not to go to the concentration camp, but he also decided not to keep quiet. We lived in a country village, so everyone knew about my father. It was very uncomfortable – probably dangerous – because there were members of the SS in the village. Everyone knew me as "the red", the "communist" son of a "communist" father. I wasn't the only one. There were many more, but for their own safety, maybe, they all joined up.
>
> I wanted to do the same. Fortunately my father stopped me from volunteering for the Waffen-SS. I was only 16 and had no idea what

the SS, the Waffen-SS or the whole Nazi business was going to mean. Eventually I was in Russia with the 18th Panzer Division, the division commanded by Colonel-General Guderian himself. But afterwards I was glad we lost the war. Can you imagine what would have happened if Hitler had won?

Heinz Friederich, who was born in 1928, was in uniform for only the last three months of the war, but he remembers very well how he was forced to enlist:

We were suddenly told at school that we had to register voluntarily. We were put under duress, we weren't allowed to leave the room until we had signed up. Two or three weren't at all willing, but they were physically forced to sign by their relatives. Probably the relatives had been threatened with something bad. After it was all over, it was said that we had registered voluntarily, of our own free will. What a farce!

There were subtler ways of binding recruits to the Nazi cause. Some might call it economic blackmail. However, before the war, Helmut Benzing, who trained for the Kriegsmarine but ended up seeing the destruction and capture of Berlin in 1945, feels he had had good cause to be grateful for the generosity of the Nazi state and with that, good cause to serve it in war.

I knew the time when unemployment was rife, so when the Nazis came and suddenly my father got work and everyone got work, I was convinced it was for the best. We didn't know anything else, or rather what we did know wasn't good – hunger, unemployment and so on.

We were very young, of course, and we didn't have any contact with the outside world. We could only see and believe in what was happening in front of us. There was no television and no one who could tell you about different ways of doing things. Whether or not those ways – the Nazi ways – were right or wrong, we couldn't judge, that's the truth. I say again that we were much too young and we didn't hear any contrary opinions about what was going on with the Nazis.

Leo Mattowitz, who served in Russia during the war, had also known some very hard times before Hitler came to power:

> In 1933, when Hitler took power, I was 11 years years old. In the Ruhrgebiet, where I lived, there was abject poverty. I went to school with a small piece of bread, my father was out of work, everyone was out of work, it was a time of great poverty. We had no shoes, only clogs, and I had to walk four kilometres to school even in the winter through the snow. I got my first shoes from Adolf Hitler. All of a sudden my father was given work, the neighbours got work and I was delighted to wear proper shoes for the first time. So of course we all supported Hitler. He had rescued us from a terrible situation.

What Mattowitz did not realize as yet was the even more terrible situation he was going to find when he was serving in Russia. Neither did another Russian veteran, Edmund Bonhoff, though he soon came to learn that once he was in the army there was no turning back:

> We grew up as Nazis. The Hitler Youth made us into Nazis. That was their whole aim. I was quite enthusiastic about the Hitler Youth. I was born in 1920, so I was 13 when Hitler came to power – far too young to see all that Nazism really meant. Today, of course, I can see it differently, but then I know so much more. So much I wish I didn't know.
>
> Even so, I must say that we are all guilty, very guilty, because of what the Nazis did. But the ordinary soldier as such, he just did his duty. All of us had to, because we'd have been punished otherwise. If any one of us had said, "We don't want to fight any more" or something like that, we'd have been shot immediately. We all knew that. We all knew about others who been shot. They did that often enough.

Whatever the personal path that led them to war – whether it was duty or enthusiasm, whether they were pressured into it or believed their cause was just – for everyone the Second World War was a time of excitement and boredom, frantic action and waiting for action, facing death or escaping it, watching comrades die while others survived, and celebrating triumph or swallowing defeat. These German veterans saw it all and tell a sometimes fascinating, sometimes moving, often horrific tale of the long-ago war they fought and lost, but a war they can recall as if it happened yesterday.

CHAPTER ONE

The Blitzkrieg Era 1939–41

THE BLITZKRIEG THAT EXPLODED across Germany's border with Poland on September 1, 1939 was a new kind of warfare, more destructive, more terrifying, more shocking in its speed and power than any form of warfare previously known. Overnight other armies were made to look antiquated now that the forces of Nazi Germany had demonstrated for the first time what motorized infantry, tanks and aircraft could do when they acted in concert. The use of the term "blitzkrieg" – lightning war – coined by the Allies early in the war, was fully justified. As the hapless Poles soon discovered, blitzkrieg struck hard, it struck fast and it struck decisively.

The attack on Poland was the point at which the appeasement policy previously followed by Britain and France finally broke down. They had allowed the forces of Nazi Germany to march into the Rhineland in 1936. They had protested, but did nothing, in 1938 when Adolf Hitler announced the Anschluss: this union of Austria and Germany had been forbidden under the Treaty of Versailles at the end of the First World War. They had given in when Hitler demanded the Sudetenland of Czechoslovakia, ostensibly to protect the rights of the German minority there. They had also failed to react effectively when, contrary to his word, Hitler absorbed the rest of Czechoslovakia into the German Reich in March 1939. At that juncture Poland was the next obvious target on Hitler's list of territorial demands and Britain and France promised the Poles their support if they were attacked.

On September 3, 1939, two days after Hitler's forces invaded Poland and refused all demands to withdraw, Britain and France, together with Australia and New Zealand, declared war. By then the Germans were well on their way to an easy victory and, despite the promises, the Poles were left to fight on their own. The British, the French and the world could only watch as the German armoured columns sliced through Poland, backed by the Luftwaffe, which plastered Polish airfields and destroyed runways, hangars and fuel stores. Railways and communication lines were systematically disrupted.

With no armoured divisions, few anti-tank or anti-aircraft weapons and a largely obsolete air force, the Polish army had little chance. Enveloped by a double encirclement, its power to fight back was virtually eliminated and the last major Polish defence, at the battle of the River Bzura, ended with the surrender of 100,000 Poles. Although Warsaw managed to hold out until September 27 and the last organized resistance did not cease until October 5, the Germans had prevailed in less than three weeks. Soviet Russia, then an ally of Nazi Germany, had invaded two days earlier and ultimately Poland was dismembered and most of it shared out between them.

Hajo Hermann, holder of the Knight's Cross with Swords, who later became a famous bomber ace, scoring nine victories, flew over the border with Poland on the first day of the invasion. The German forces, always the focus of Josef Goebbels's inventive propaganda department, had been told that they were making a defensive move: the Poles were going to invade Germany and so deserved to be attacked. Hermann, who was to become a famous night-fighter pilot, had his own ideas about that. He believed that the Poles had invited retribution through their ingratitude towards Germany after the First World War:

> We liberated Poland in the First World War. At the time, it was a province of Russia. We made it independent and said, "You can have your kingdom again!" But were the Poles grateful? Not a bit of it! After the war the Poles acted against us and took western Prussia away from us, and Upper Silesia. That was a very great injustice. When you think of September 1, 1939, you have to bear this in mind. When you flew against the Polish enemy remembering how they betrayed us, you feel very patriotic, there's no mistaking it. If nowadays, someone says, "How could you have done that? That's how the war began!", that's nonsense, nothing began on September 1. The war started only when Britain and France declared war on us two days later.

Hans Lehmann, who was with the invasion troops on the first day, had a less virulent view of the Poles:

> No. I didn't hate them. As far as I was concerned they were human beings, not that I loved them, you understand. It's simply that they were a foreign people, that's all, but I didn't feel that I had to exterminate them, or whatever, I can't say that. That was true of only a very few people. It's also true, though, that men become brutal when they are at war for too long; it gets easier and easier to shoot a person the longer you are out there.

Strictly speaking, the German campaign in Poland was not true blitzkrieg. It was basically a conventional offensive with certain blitzkrieg elements. Those elements were decisive, though. The most important was the element of surprise, which was why there was no formal declaration of war by Germany. The Polish government knew an attack was coming, but many Polish soldiers were caught completely off guard. Hans Lehmann remembers how unprepared they were:

> The Poles hadn't expected to be invaded and we really did take them by surprise. We were able to just walk in at first. Then the first troops arrived and by that time the Poles knew what was happening. They started firing, but it wasn't very effective. In comparison with ours, the Polish weapons were so out of date that they couldn't do anything. We fired back, of course, and some of the Poles were shot. The others either ran away or surrendered. Afterwards the whole Polish army realized they were helpless and capitulated.

Blitzkrieg theory had no place, either, for the extensive preliminary artillery bombardment which had been regular practice before major battles in the First World War. Instead, the Germans delivered swift-striking attacks from the air. One of the Luftwaffe's major players was the Junkers-87 "Stuka" dive-bomber, which had already shown its paces during the Spanish Civil War of 1936–39, when it was used by the German Condor Legion to bring a new and previously unimagined brand of terror to warfare. The Ju-87, capable of a top speed of 255mph and armed with two 7.9mm MG81 and two 7.9mm MG17 machine guns, carried a bomb load of around 2,000lb, but it created panic and confusion on the ground even before any of these weapons came into play.

Ugly and angular, the Ju-87's gull-wings gave it a thoroughly sinister appearance. The dive-bombers swooped down like birds of prey, giving off a chilling screaming sound. This sound was produced by the sirens the Germans fitted to the wheel covers. Colloquially they were called the "Trumpets of Jericho", with all the promise of utter destruction that biblical reference implied. Hans Lehmann remembers the effect as the Ju-87s dived on their victims below: "The Stukas – they dived on to the enemy lines and the moral state of the adversary was so depressed because of the terrible sound it made. They had already begun to run the moment they heard it. They weren't going to wait for the bombs to fall!"

In Poland, tanks as well as aircraft appeared in a new guise. Like the military aircraft, the tank had been a newcomer to war in 1914–18, but the requirements of blitzkrieg had helped to transform it from the metal "lozenge" designed to lumber across the muddy First World War terrain to a faster, much more mechanically reliable vehicle.

The tank and the Germans' use of it in Poland and later, in western Europe, epitomized a long-held tenet of the Prussian military system: the value of mobility. The fighting in the First World War had been the antithesis of mobility and restoring it to its proper place in warfare played an important part in searching analysis undertaken after 1918 by Germany's keenest military minds. They were determined to avoid a repetition of the essentially static nature of the First World War, with its futile battles of attrition and costly effort for the sake of little gain. Never again, they resolved, would Germany be brought to her knees by a long-drawn out war or starved into submission by blockade. It was unthinkable, too, that the horrors of trench warfare should ever be repeated. Future wars were going to be won by swift and decisive action.

One of the most acute and perceptive of German military minds was Heinz Guderian, who became the legendary German tank commander of the Second World War. Guderian's aim was to create Panzer Divisions, all-arms formations that could range over the battlefield at will, causing maximum damage and doing it fast by not being tied to the speed of infantry formations.

The future tank force, as Guderian saw it, would be concentrated in these Panzer Divisions, not dispersed in small numbers. They would be spearheads of a unified formation which also included aircraft, artillery and mechanized infantry. Tank commanders would not remain in positions far in the rear, like the generals of the First World War, but would operate near the front, responding instantly to changing situations and issuing orders by radio directly to their units.

Making the most efficient use possible of available technology was only part of Guderian's plans. He also had a clear understanding of the value of proper training, and the fact that it was vital to encourage drive and initiative even in the lowest ranks. The German army as a whole was an army of incomparable standards, but the men of the tank force were to be trained to an even higher pitch of excellence.

Guderian was regarded as something of a maverick among the German "top brass" and, as he stated in his memoirs, his concept of warfare was too revolutionary for the ultra-conservative General Staff. As a result, Guderian claimed, they blocked his ideas for many years. All the same, in the mid-1930s Guderian's theories appealed where it mattered most in Nazi Germany: the Führer himself approved.

Hitler had his own, political, use for swift, decisive war as envisaged by Guderian and others of like mind. During the late 1930s Hitler appeared to be just a cynical risk-taker, dangling British and French politicians like puppets and relying on their fear of another war to force concessions out of them. This did not mean he was unaware of realities. If he were to make his strike in his long-planned campaign in eastern Europe, then he would have to do it quickly. If he waited, Britain and France could become too strong for him and there might never be another opportunity.

The chance Germany would be taking in another war was already known even outside Germany, as Georg Lehrmann discovered when he heard a chilling prediction from a Czech prisoner. The prediction was remarkably accurate, and its conclusion was that Germany would lose:

> In Czechoslovakia, we were based in a small town 10 kilometres from the German border. We had a Czech prisoner who spoke perfect German, so that we were able to converse very easily. He told us, "Listen, you can start a war with us, but don't start on the others because then you have had it." I said, "How is that possible?" and he replied, "I know it. First of all, you'll probably march on France and then on Russia and then you'll get it in the neck." That is what the Czech said before the war had even begun

The Czech prisoner was, of course, right about Russia. What he could not take into account was the extent to which blitzkrieg was going to move the goalposts of warfare. For a start, the Luftwaffe's first purpose was to seize control of the air. To do that, they hoped to destroy the Polish air force on the ground. However, although most Polish planes escaped – they had been moved to new locations – the Luftwaffe's numerical advantage was so great that the Poles were unable to prevent it from using its aircraft wherever and in whatever manner it wished.

This was the first demonstration in the Second World War of a truism: the fact that superiority in the air was the ultimate superiority. From then on, what little hope the Poles might have had vanished completely.

Once the German air force had taken care of the preliminaries, the tanks and other motorized units moved in and sliced a swathe of destruction across Poland, the like of which had never been seen in war before. Hitler himself was astonished by the havoc when he visited his Panzer forces soon after the invasion.

A communiqué issued by the Germans at this time was naturally triumphalist in tone, but at the same time largely accurate:

> In a series of battles of extermination, of which the greatest and most decisive was in the Vistula curve, the Polish army numbering one million men has been defeated, taken prisoner or scattered. Not a single Polish active or reserve division, not a single independent brigade, has escaped this fate. Only fractions of single bands escaped immediate annihilation by fleeing into the marshy territory in eastern Poland. There they were defeated by Soviet troops. Only in Warsaw, Modlin and on the peninsula of Hela in the extreme north of Poland are there still small sections of the Polish army fighting on and these are in hopeless positions.

However futile the Germans considered their position to be, the manner in which some Poles fought back was savage. It should not be fogotten that the level of casualties suffered by the German forces in Poland would exceed those in all other theatres until the Russian campaign. Hans Lehmann was an eyewitness:

> There was hand-to-hand fighting in Poland, man against man. There were fanatics on both sides. It's either you or it's me and to the death, they were saying. Forget about being taken prisoner. You feel hatred perhaps for a moment if someone has been shot beside you, you feel great hatred of the opponent…

Individual reprisals were not unusual. Hans Lehmann became involved in one such incident after a young Pole was arrested:

A company commander said to me, "He had a knife on him, you must shoot him!" A Polish man, a young Polish man, he could have been only about 21 years old. Because I had known the commander for some time, I said, "You're off your head. I won't do it." Fortunately I got away with it because I knew him. If it had been an officer I didn't know, then he would have shot me straight away. Experiences like this made me very, very sad. But then for us it was to a greater or lesser extent depressing anyway. Some men, young men mostly, took it all quite lightly, but others took it very badly. Some of our comrades, when it began in Poland, actually messed their pants.

Eventually, after some three weeks, the battle for Poland resolved itself into a last desperate struggle for the capital, Warsaw. For a time the defenders refused all demands to surrender and were subjected to day after day of bombing and shelling. By September 26 it was reported that the city's business centre was in flames. Over 1,000 civilians were reported killed, and four churches and three hospitals filled with wounded were destroyed. According to the German communiqué, there were no longer any buildings in Warsaw remaining intact, and not a house in which there had not been a victim of bombs or shells. Within the previous 24 hours some 100 fires had broken out following the launching of a hail of incendiary bombs.

On September 21, six days before the surrender of Warsaw, the city's Lord Mayor, M. Starzynski, issued his own statement. It was a bitter comment on what the Nazis had labelled "a humanitarian war":

I want the whole civilized world to know what the Nazi Government means by humanitarian war. Yesterday, in the early hours of the morning, seven of our hospitals were bombed, among many other buildings, with terrible results. Soldiers wounded on the battlefield were killed in their beds. Many civilians, among them women and children, were killed outright or buried under the ruins. But the most barbaric crime was committed against the Red Cross Hospital, which had the Red Cross flags flying from the windows. Several hundred wounded Polish soldiers were there.

Despite brave words and the defiance of Warsaw, many Poles yielded to the logic of the situation without too much of a struggle. Hans Lehmann belonged to a platoon that was put in charge of 400 Polish prisoners. "They were glad the war was over for them. It all happened so fast that they were completely overrun before they knew it. You see, if a man realizes there's no prospect of changing a situation, then he surrenders, he wants to protect his life."

Similarly, on the march into Poland, Lehmann passed through whole villages where there was no appreciable resistance:

If a village didn't have any soldiers, then the men didn't bother to take up arms. There was one village now and again where we were fired at, but on the whole the civilian population remained very calm, in order to protect their property and possessions. They knew that at the moment when foreign soldiers arrive, it could cost them their lives if they rebelled against them.

Polish resistance nevertheless cost the Germans dear, both in men and materiel. According to Hans Lehmann, the casualties had begun at the border on the first day:

When we marched into Poland there were corpses all around. Many of them were Germans. They lay around and no one bothered about them. I was so upset that I couldn't eat for three days. Later on, almost the whole company was destroyed, and our armoured cars too. If they'd been put out of action, we had to leave them. If the caterpillar tracks were hit, then you were unable to move even if the whole vehicle hadn't been destroyed. Some of the caterpillar tracks were blown clean off, so you couldn't drive any more. On one occasion there were 10 or 11 of us, together with a second driver, when we were hit.. They were all injured – and very badly – except for me.

The German triumph in Poland was so speedy that, ironically, it made trouble for Lehmann. His platoon was ordered to take their 400 Polish prisoners to Danzig and then rejoin their unit. It did not work out that way:

We couldn't get back, so instead we returned to our headquarters in Harburg. The next thing we knew, we were being threatened with a court martial as deserters! It was all sorted out in the end, but the reason we hadn't been able to follow orders and rejoin our unit was that the campaign in Poland was over so quickly. Before we could catch up with them, our unit had moved out and returned to Germany!

After Poland, hostilities on land settled down into what contemporary journalists termed the Phoney War or, among the Germans, the Sitzkrieg, or Twilight War. Sitzkrieg did not mean inactivity, but two important factors governed this outwardly quiet time that was so much of a contrast to the shock and drama of the Polish campaign.

The first was the defensive attitude of the French. The German High Command feared the military strength of France and had objected to Hitler's reoccupation of the Rhineland in 1936 in case this prompted the French to use this strength against them. When France and Britain had declared war on Germany, the Germans had been appalled at the idea of confronting this apparently strong power they fancied lay across their western frontier. What they did not take sufficiently into account was that the French military concept of the time was predominantly defensive. During the Phoney War the French confined their operations to occasional patrols, a few probing missions and intelligence forays, but basically they sat behind their infamous Maginot Line awaiting events.

The Germans, for their part, held back from attacking the French at this juncture because they had only 23 divisions on their western frontier, to France's 100. The rest of the German army had been used in Poland and time was needed to deploy and refit their forces for future action. However, future action, when it came, did not occur in the direction the troops had come to believe. Reinhold Ründe of the Luftwaffe air signal corps was one of many who believed that the next target of attack would be Britain: "We all had the feeling after the Polish campaign that we would be going to England. All of us in the Luftwaffe thought we'd be off to England one way or another. No one dreamed that it would be Denmark and Norway."

At that time Norway and Denmark were neutral, but their geographical position posed a danger to the vital supplies of iron ore that came to German north-coast ports from Sweden. The route for these supplies ran from Narvik, the ice-free port on Ofot fjord, through the Norwegian fjords and on to Germany. The Royal Air Force, flying from Britain, could easily disrupt this supply line, so that securing the two Scandinavian countries under German control became imperative.

Norway had particular attractions, with its long coastline indented by a mass of fjords. In German hands, that coastline could help prevent the chance of a British blockade, deny Britain control of the trade routes and put a stop to any threat it could pose by occupying bases there.

The Danes were the first victims of this next German campaign. Denmark was invaded on April 9, 1940. It was all over within a day. The Wehrmacht met nominal resistance from the Danish Royal Guard before the Germans took charge and Luftwaffe aircraft circling overhead obliged a very reluctant King Christian X to cooperate. King Haakon VII of Norway was in a better position. He refused the German demand to accept a government led by the collaborator Vidkun Quisling and, with the support of his ministers, resolved to resist.

By then the German land, sea and air invasion was already under way.

On April 7, the same day the British decided, after much hesitation, to mine the Norwegian Leads, Reinhold Rïnde was on board ship as vehicles from the air intelligence battalion and flak guns were being loaded into the holds:

> Another ship anchored in front of us was loaded with dismantled plane sections, flak and artillery. The next night we were instructed that we had to leave the deck, and go below because we were about to sail through sovereign Danish waters between the Danish islands in order to get to the Skagerrak.

These precautions were necessary because Denmark was still neutral and uninvaded at that juncture, though not, of course, for long, and the German ships had to avoid detection by the Danes. They were lucky.

> Though they prowled around, the Danes didn't notice that the ships were loaded with war material. Merchant ships often sailed this route and I suppose they assumed that ours were the same. It was only

when we had left sovereign Danish waters in the direction of Skagerrak that we were able to stop and get together with the rest of the invasion fleet: 13 heavy transport ships, torpedo boats and minesweepers. We had to be careful of mines, so one ship sailed behind the other with the minesweepers and torpedo boats between them.

In the early morning hours on April 9 we saw in front of us, approaching from the west, the heavy cruiser Blücher, which was supposed to be unsinkable, and the small cruiser Emden. We were in the second ship behind the Blücher and we were able to see that there were nurses and heavy flak on the deck. At around 0500 hours the convoy slowly got under way. Just before we entered Oslo fjord, all the ships were stopped and torpedo boats drew up alongside each one and handed the ship's officers a document roll.

Ründe and his comrades were about to be informed that they were going to occupy Norway as friends, not enemies. The author of this fiction was Adolf Hitler:

We were all ordered out on deck. The Führer's orders were read to us, saying that we had to occupy Norway as a protection for the Norwegians – and ourselves – against Britain and France. In the event that the Norwegians didn't understand this, and tried to resist, they had to be crushed without consideration. And so we sailed on into Oslo fjord. The entrance to the fjord was very wide, with Sweden on one side, Norway on the other.

Then suddenly the Blücher started firing shells towards the shore, but we couldn't see exactly where they were aimed. At that moment some tactical Luftwaffe aircraft roared over our heads in the dawn light, heading towards Norway. All of a sudden there was an explosion on the Blücher and we saw clouds of smoke.

The fourth ship behind Ründe's was hit, with devastating consequences for the Germans on board.

The tanker was hit by torpedoes and sank, leaking its oil over the water. The sea caught fire – we saw it burning – and we heard men screaming and screaming, such horrible screams! It wasn't possible to save them, that was evident. No one from the German fleet, neither the navy command nor anyone else, took any notice of the men swimming in the oil or attempted to rescue them. The order was straight ahead, straight ahead, straight ahead.

We continued sailing, and we could still hear the Blücher's guns firing. But clouds of smoke were belching out. The Blücher was going down. The ship was listing to port and soldiers were jumping off the decks into the sea. Before long, we saw the Blücher sinking at the bows and gradually take everything and everyone left on board down into the depths. Soldiers were swimming on the surface; the temperature of the water was below freezing point at the time.

The Blücher had been hit by 11.2-inch and six-inch guns fired from the shore and later by torpedoes. Although her captain, Heinrich Woldag, managed to get her anchored onshore in the hope of repairing her turbines, successive explosions defeated the effort. She had to be abandoned at 0700 hours and at 0723 she capsized and sank. Reinhold Ründe watched:

We noticed a low, throbbing noise in the ship, several throbbing noises. We knew something was wrong and we were all up on the deck. Suddenly the Blücher was firing again. We saw muzzle flashes from her starboard side. She was firing towards Oslo fjord, but she had started to list to port. We saw soldiers and also nurses sliding down the deck into Oslo fjord, the list was so pronounced that they could no longer hold on and it didn't take long before we saw that the stern of the Blücher was rising up into the air. The bow was pressed downwards.

At that moment German tactical planes roared over our heads and bombed fortifications to our left which turned out to be the Oskarsborg fortifications. We didn't know it then, but the fortress was armed with torpedo emplacements. The exterior of Oskarsborg was quite badly damaged, we could see that. Several waves of planes flew in but during this raid by German planes the Blücher was sinking more and more, and then disappeared, bow first into Oslo fjord. It happened quite quickly. It was certainly all observed from both the Swedish and Norwegian shores, because shortly afterwards fishing boats came out and tried to save the men swimming around in the water.

More and more of them arrived. Our ships were now stationary, beside the sinking Blücher, waiting for the rescue to begin. No one from our ship took part in the rescue operation, it was all done by civilians, Norwegians and Swedes. The Swedish navy also came out with ships and searched for survivors. There were rocks sticking out of the water, and some of the people from the Blücher tried to cling to them. But they were so slippery that they couldn't get a handhold and slid into the water and drowned. Some were saved at the last minute by the Norwegians and Swedes.

There was nothing to do now but sail on towards Oslo. But the Blücher was given one last salute by the German ships. "After this terrible disaster, all soldiers were assembled on deck, standing to attention as we sailed over the sunken Blücher towards Oslo. It all went smoothly. The Norwegians didn't attack and we reached Oslo without trouble."

Meanwhile the Wehrmacht's units had gone ashore and fought their way into the Norwegian capital as far as the city's airport. The Norwegian planes parked there had been destroyed from the air and Luftwaffe bombers had landed on the runway. One of the German pilots was Hajo Hermann, whose war almost ended there and then:

We had been sent to Norway because the British had landed a corps in Bergen and it was our job to attack their landing areas and support ships. When we arrived we found the airfield was stuffed full with German planes. Then I spotted one runway that was relatively clear. I flew in – I had a lot of bombs on board – and touched down, but then the plane rolled and rolled and rolled. Either the runway was too short or I did it wrong. Anyway, our plane smashed into this narrow path at the end of the strip. My crew leapt out in a tremendous fright, but I stayed sitting in the plane and they screamed, "You're going to explode! You're going to explode! Get out of there!" However, my mood was that of a ship's captain who wanted to go down with his ship. Fortunately there was no explosion, but it was a very nasty moment for me.

After Reinhold Ründe's ship had berthed at Oslo, the vehicles were unloaded. The reception the Germans received as they drove through the capital was muted:

> The people of Oslo stood on both sides of the street and followed the passing convoys with their eyes. No shots were fired, we were able to march safely through. Some of the Norwegians even waved to us. They didn't seem all that angry and there was no resistance, but their faces were serious. We supposed that the radio stations had been taken over by Quisling, who ordered the Norwegians to remain calm.

From Oslo, the convoy drove to Hamar. Several of the vehicles had crews of 10, all armed with rifles and machine guns. The country was mountainous and the German vehicles proved to be too wide and too high for the narrow roads, so progress was slow. The convoy passed through wooded country and the Germans were fired on by Norwegian soldiers hidden in the trees. No one was hit, Ründe remembers, but the Germans prepared to fight back: "We got out of our vehicles now and again and set up firing positions. But we hardly saw an adversary, there was snow and ice everywhere, everything was covered, the passes and the roads too. Sometimes we had to get out and shovel snow before we could drive on."

The task assigned to Ründe's unit was to repair telephone lines to airports and command posts. When they reached Trondheim, where the lines had been damaged by the Norwegians, the two German battle cruisers Scharnhorst and Gneisenau were in harbour after participating in the German landings at Narvik. During the war the British made several attempts to destroy the battle cruisers to stop them preying on Allied convoys in the Atlantic. The Gneisenau was crippled by mines, but the Scharnhorst was sent to the bottom by naval action in December 1943. Three years earlier Reinhold Ründe had witnessed an early British attempt to sink the commerce raiders which were such a danger to them:

> Two days after we arrived in Trondheim, there was a British air raid on the Scharnhorst and Gneisenau. The Scharnhorst was slightly

damaged by bombs exploding on deck, a gun barrel was smashed and the decking suffered damage. Three days later we sailed from Trondheim and visited the two ships. Our job in the signal corps was to inspect the air-raid damage and make an official report.

Ründe and the rest of the signal corps moved on to Steinkjer, and, along the way, witnessed the Luftwaffe and the Royal Air Force in action:

Now and again during our journey from Trondheim to Steinkjer, British planes flew over the Trondheim fjord and were fought off by German fighters, Some were shot down, and British soldiers who had landed north of the Trondheim fjord were captured by the Germans. They were taken to the fortifications at Trondheim, where they were treated as German POWs according to the provisions of the Geneva Convention.

Ründe remembers ruefully how well these British prisoners were treated compared with their German counterparts:

They were sent packets from England. They were allowed to buy food. They had regular postal contact and cards from the International Red Cross. These prisoners even received civilian visitors and had visits from other captured British units. That was all possible for them, but it was denied to us Germans in other countries during the war.

When the Norwegians finally surrendered, on June 9, 1940, Ründe's unit was in Namsos, which had been evacuated by British forces several weeks earlier, on May 3. The Norwegian army were allowed to hand in their weapons, remove their uniforms if they wished to and then went home, or rather they were supposed to go home. Having lost the regular war, many later resorted to irregular warfare and became partisans. Ründe encountered them:

There were Norwegian soldiers up in the mountains. They fired at us and we only saw them as they ran off across the snow and ice among the trees. We had to get out of our cars, use them as cover and then fire our rifles. I myself carried the P38 sub-machine gun. Our cars were quite heavily armoured – a rifle bullet wouldn't have penetrated them – and the Norwegians were firing rifles, rather old-fashioned rifles as we later discovered. They had long barrels and looked like weapons we had seen in museums. I think they came from the First World War. The Norwegians didn't have modern weapons, like the latest machine guns. They used water-cooled MGs and they were ineffective.

By the time the Norwegians surrendered, another fighting front had been opened up by blitzkrieg, this time in western Europe when the Germans invaded Belgium, the Netherlands, Luxemburg and France on May 10, 1940. This was the blitzkrieg which obliged the British to finally withdraw their troops from Norway and return home to defend their own country. King Haakon and the Norwegian royal family went with them and spent the rest of the war as exiles in Britain. From there, Haakon, an exemplary monarch provided the inspiration for the Norwegian resistance to the Germans.

The blitzkrieg in the west was a shock, despite the first demonstration in Poland. The shock had an extra edge because the Germans did what many military experts had considered impossible. The Maginot Line had stood as an impregnable barrier on the Franco-German border ever since it was completed in 1935 after five years' construction. The gap where it ended in the north, at the Belgian frontier, was covered by the Ardennes forest, a plateau up to 500 metres above sea level and so thick with trees that it was considered impassable. For that reason the Ardennes region was weakly defended. On May 10 the impregnable barrier was outflanked and the forest was penetrated as the German armour crashed through.

The French had neglected this region, mainly because they were relying on the massive fortifications of the Maginot Line. The Germans had to contend with little more than a bemused Belgian cavalryman, who peered uncomprehendingly through the trees. While the Panzers raced through the Ardennes, the blitzkrieg also surged through the Netherlands and Belgium and within four days the Dutch had surrendered, followed a fortnight later, on May 28, by Belgium.

The Germans had devised this strategy, not only as a means of entering western Europe in force and by surprise, but as a feint, designed to draw the British and French northwards, away from their entrenched defensive positions in France. Meanwhile the Luftwaffe was in action, unleashing devastating bombing raids on key targets in the Netherlands and German paratroopers landed both north and south of The Hague.

An English newspaper reporter was in The Hague when the attack began:

> Just as dawn was breaking, hundreds of aircraft came over the city and bombs were falling everywhere. The sky seemed to be filled with planes and parachute troops were being dropped in large numbers on several parts of the city. Meanwhile the bombers concentrated their efforts on the important buildings, including the barracks.
>
> When the smoke and dust had subsided, I saw that several buildings, including the prison, had been destroyed. Bombers accompanied by fighters came over in waves of two hundred at a time, some as low as 250 metres above the ground. While I watched, Dutch anti-aircraft guns bagged six large machines. One, a forty-seater troop carrier, burst into flames, struck another and both came down. They destroyed three houses and I saw forty or fifty bodies in the street.
>
> At the same time, seaplanes with detachable rubber pontoons, each containing forty men, sailed on the shallow water near the shore. Five hundred men were landed on the beach in this way, wading ashore from the pontoons.
>
> Each parachute party numbered about forty, in charge of a sergeant. These men took the town hall, museum and library near the square. A civilian defence corps, armed only with butchers' knives, was formed immediately to counteract the parachutists.

By contrast, Georg Lehrmann's unit virtually walked in when they were sent across the Dutch-Belgian border: "We just marched over Belgium, the Albert Canal, to the English Channel. It was no problem. The Albert Canal had been taken by parachute units. They jumped out backwards from gliders. They couldn't do that carrying rifles, so they had small 25-round machine guns strapped to their stomachs."

Driving on into France, the Germans encountered their first considerable obstacle in the River Meuse. The river was reached on the morning of May 13 and the plan was to cross it at three points. To ensure that the crossing was not interrupted, nearby Sedan, sited on the river near the Belgian frontier, was subjected to an intensive bombardment lasting six hours. After this murderous onslaught, Guderian's engineers crossed the Meuse swiftly, followed by the first of the German infantry.

That same evening the Germans smashed their way over the river and were on the opposite bank in strength. The French defenders, shattered by the onslaught, were unable to stop them. Both the other crossings were successfully forced, and the defence was in tatters.

The Low Countries and northern France offered ideal tank country, stretching out flat and even for miles on end. The defenders, badly deployed and with poor communications, were no match for the surge of blitzkrieg power that overwhelmed them. The Luftwaffe's dive-bombers were already at work, smashing lines of communication and inspiring widespread terror. But there was more to come. Behind the spearheads extending back from the River Meuse there were 25 divisions of supporting infantry.

By May 16 the French defences along the Ardennes were gaping wide and it was evident that a catastrophe was in the making. The Luftwaffe had command of the air, easily repulsing Allied attempts to bomb German targets. The bombing of Abbeville was typical of the blanket destruction wrought by blitzkrieg from the air. Alan Stuart Roger of the Red Cross organization saw what happened:

> Abbeville became one vast desolation of smouldering ruins, fires raging and the shattered streets strewn with dead and dying women and children. The Germans bombed it relentlessly, without any thought of military objectives. They dropped high explosive and incendiary bombs, as well as incendiary darts, which shoot about like jumping crackers.
>
> I saw a house where a delayed-action bomb, ricocheting from the ground, flew clean through the bedroom in which a man and his wife were asleep. By a thousand-to-one chance, the missile landed harmlessly outside. But wherever there was a jam on the road, the Luftwaffe

swooped down, bombing and machine-gunning the processions of fugitives.

On May 21 German forces broke through to the Channel coast, capturing Arras and Amiens as well as Abbeville. The French managed to retrieve Arras the next day, but their air force was nowhere to be seen. What was left of the French air force was reorganizing and refitting, and much of it would not be back in action until early June. The badly disorganized French armies in Belgium attempted to make a hasty retreat from the lowlands but found the roads clogged with panic-stricken refugees. Meanwhile the twin German spearheads were thrusting on, driving deeper and deeper into France.

Many Germans involved in this helter-skelter advance were exhilarated by it, but not all. War and its ugly sights were still new to many of the younger soldiers and they were emotionally affected by it. Herbert Böhm saw what happened when a French tank was destroyed:

> A French tank was shot into flames, and the tank commander got out of the burning machine. As he came into view out of the turret, he was shot, killed by one of the bullets flying all around him. No one actually aimed at him, but he was hit just the same. He toppled to the ground, dead. It shocked me, I can tell you. He thought he was going to save himself, but he was killed instead!

Guderian's tanks raced from the Meuse to the sea in an astounding sweep that exemplified blitzkrieg in its purest and most lethally efficient form. Guderian was impatient and the exhilaration of this swift drive to the sea brought out all his impetuosity. At Guderian's urging, the Panzers frequently covered more than 80 kilometres a day, far outstripping the infantry and causing acute alarm among his superiors. Quite often the mere sight of the thundering tanks eating up the distance was enough to make the opposition move out of the way, and fast. For the Germans, it was a joyride.

Guderian and his tanks were the stuff of which legends were made, and legends were rapidly made in France in the summer of 1940. All over the country, even in places far away from the northern battlefield, wild rumours circulated about fifth columnists and saboteurs who had betrayed the forces – and the honour – of France and delivered them up into the power of the merciless invaders. Gossips whispered about German paratroops, strangely disguised, and further terrible disasters soon to occur.

These rumours both sprang from and further encouraged an increasingly defeatist French cast of mind. This attitude had already been evident in the First World War. Twenty years later, the gloom that settled over the French as France was swiftly conquered by the Germans brought it to the surface. It did not seem to matter now that France had more troops than the invaders, and even more tanks, or that the best of them, such as the heavily armed Char and Souma, were formidable weapons of war in their own right. None of this counted where the ability to use this military strength was lacking, as it was in France in 1940. To make matters even worse, the French and British Allies were indulging in petty squabbles and inter-service rivalries, weakening even further their will to resist. Rarely, if ever, in war had defenders found themselves in such a dire state of helplessness and disarray.

The French, nevertheless, resisted desperately, even though they were outclassed. Georg Lehrmann fought against them in the front line:

> The French fought partly from trenches, but it wasn't the trench fighting of 20 years before. In 1940, when soldiers moved forward, they went in waves, not lines. The First War was a war of man against man. There was some of that in the Second, but it was much more a war of machines. We were motorized, we had armoured cars. Well, they weren't really armoured cars, they had just three millimetres of metal. On top we had a 2cm cannon and machine guns, and men fired from those moving vehicles, too. Of course, the attack took place over quite a wide distance but it wasn't disproportionately wide, the front line, not like in the First World War. Mostly we were the ones who attacked. The French fired back, of course, but German superiority was too great. The French apparently hadn't expected it. We also had larger amounts of weaponry than the French.
>
> We had relatively few casualties, and of course, we had marvellous support from the Luftwaffe. Our Ju-87 Stukas terrified the French just

as they had terrified the Poles in 1939. I suppose that when you're already tense and anxious, and thinking you're going to be killed any moment, the screaming of the Stukas is enough to put you over the edge. Many soldiers simply ran away as if banshees were after them.

I've got to admit, though, that I was frightened, too. Not by the Stukas, of course. They were on our side. It was the whole business of fighting and killing and dying that frightened me. I never trembled so much in my entire life as when we went into the fighting. I sometimes felt I was frozen with fear.

We saw terrible things, really terrible. I remember once that we were involved in fighting and were camouflaged under some brushwood when we saw a French plane shot down. The plane spiralled downwards and then suddenly it twisted around and dropped down right on to one of our vehicles. The noise, the flames, the smoke … in a flash, the vehicle and its crew were gone. It was very hard to see that kind of thing, but there's always that selfish gratitude you feel that it didn't happen to you. It might have done, you know. The vehicle that was destroyed was only about 100 metres away.

We couldn't do anything. It was too late for help. In a few moments it was all burned out, just a mass of twisted metal. And the fighting was still going on around us. When that happens, all you can do is keep your head down. First rule in war – when there's a bang, get down fast, lightning fast; the one who got down fastest had the greatest chance of survival.

By May 20, after only 10 days, Guderian's tanks had reached Amiens and the last link between the defenders in the north and the south was severed. The next day, the Germans captured Abbeville, and by May 23 all the ports on the English Channel were in their hands. Three days after that, in Dover, Operation Dynamo, the evacuation of the British Expeditionary Force from France, was set in train.

The task could not have been more monumental. What had to be done was to lift the Allied armies from the beaches, jetties and piers of Dunkirk and sail them to Britain. In the event the figure, which included 112,000 French and Belgian soldiers, reached 338,000, the bulk of the Allied troops trapped in the Dunkirk pocket. At this juncture an extraordinary and still controversial situation had intervened to give the British some hope that they could pull off this extraordinary feat. On May 26 Hitler issued the order for Guderian's tanks to halt at the Dunkirk pocket and allow the Luftwaffe to finish off the British. The Leibstandarte Adolf Hitler, of the Waffen-SS, commanded by Sepp Dietrich, were in position on the Aa Canal, south-east of Dunkirk. Dietrich ordered his men to ignore Hitler's order. They captured the Watten Heights on the opposite side of the canal at Dunkirk and were told to go into the attack. However, even this elite was unable to interfere with the effect of the "halt" order. The pause gave the British two days to complete their escape. Even though some of the heat was off, the Germans did not make it easy for them. Georg Lehrmann, who was there, recalls that Dunkirk was still a place where many soldiers lost their lives and never went home:

We arrived at Dunkirk, where the English were trying to escape. They took everything that was able to float – big naval ships, small yachts, small boats – and took off. We were able to pick up all the chocolate and cigarettes they had left behind. We stayed in Dunkirk for about 36 hours. Our guns were trained on the fleeing soldiers, who couldn't defend themselves any more, and we fired on them like crazy. I've often wondered why we did so. They wanted to get away, so what was it all about? When we'd finished, the Stukas arrived and thundered into the crowds of men on the beaches.

One of the private ship owners who went to Dunkirk to help in the rescue described the German bombardments:

On the afternoon of May 30, when we got there, the German planes were coming over all the time. German troops couldn't have been very far away because they opened fire every now and then, and the shells would fall among our men. The aircraft came over from a northerly direction, eight or nine in a line, and so low that we could distinguish their markings quite plainly. They were using tracer bullets. Our men took cover and fired back with their rifles.

On Saturday June 1 the Germans started bombing attacks on the ships. At first we were fairly lucky. Then another wave of bombers came over one after the other in a line, and they hit us. We soon had a very bad list, so we had to abandon ship and take to the boats. We kept the AA gun going all the time and as the ship was going down, our fellows were firing the pom-poms.

Unfortunately most of our boats had been wrecked in the attack and most of us had to take to the water. I swam away and managed to get on to a raft, where several others joined me. The Germans hadn't done with us yet, for they came back while a tug was taking men off the forecastle. They bombed the tug and all the men had to swim for it and get picked up again. Some climbed on to a wreck, but the Germans saw them and came back and bombed them there, too. There must have been hundreds of planes which kept returning again and again and when they had sunk the ships, they still weren't satisfied, but would bomb us again after we had been rescued.

Vice-Admiral Bertram Ramsey, commander of the naval forces from Dover that went to the relief of Dunkirk, was just as graphic:

The Germans sent over hordes of bombers, literally hundreds. They made Dunkirk docks a shambles. The whole place was on fire, and the heat was so great that no troops could come down to the docks.

We had to make alternative arrangements, or else we could not get any men away. The only part of Dunkirk harbour where a ship could go alongside was a narrow pier or breakwater of wooden piles. Eventually, there came something like 250,000 men off this pier, a place never intended in wildest imagination for a ship to go alongside and perform such a task.

The task was certainly monumental. There were no gangways, and narrow mess tables were put across the planks from the pier to the ships. The soldiers "walked the plank" to safety, mainly in the dark, and most of them were so tired that they could hardly drag their legs. In one day 66,000 men were taken off the pier.

The Germans did everything they could to stop the evacuation. First they mounted heavy batteries commanding the direct route to England passing near Calais. The British diverted to a new route, even though it meant that a 76-mile journey became a voyage of 175 miles. The Germans promptly brought up artillery batteries commanding this second route, and a third had to be found which had never been used before. Not surprisingly, either. The third route was obstructed by sandbanks which had to be swept and marked by buoys before it could be used.

On June 4 Prime Minister Winston Churchill reported to the House of Commons:

> The Germans attacked on all sides with great strength and fierceness, and their main power, the power of their far more numerous air force, was thrown into the battle, or else concentrated upon Dunkirk and the beaches.
>
> For four or five days, an intense struggle reigned. All their armoured divisions, together with great masses of German infantry and artillery, hurled themselves in vain upon the ever-narrowing, ever-contracting appendix within which the British and French armies fought.
>
> Meanwhile, the Royal Navy, with the help of countless merchant seamen, strained every nerve to embark the British and Allied troops. Two hundred and eighty light warships and 650 other vessels were engaged. They had to operate upon the difficult coast, often in adverse weather, under an almost ceaseless hail of bombs, and an increasing concentration of artillery fire.
>
> Meanwhile, the Royal Air Force engaged the main strength of the German Luftwaffe and inflicted upon them losses of at least four to one.

Despite the Luftwaffe, the German E-boats and U-boats out in the Channel, the magnetic mines and the gunfire from the shore-based batteries which had Dunkirk harbour in range, the evacuation was completed in nine days, by June 4. The exploit was greeted as if it were a triumph, even though Churchill warned: "We must be very careful not to assign to this deliverance the attributes of a victory. Wars are not won by evacuation."

The French, left to face the Germans alone, fought on for another two weeks, but they were unable to contain the might of the blitzkrieg. German forces entered Paris, marching past pale, shocked Parisians, some of whom wept openly, on June 14. Six days later the French surrendered. Two days after that, the French signed a truce with Nazi Germany, but in the most humiliating circumstances. The signing took place in the same railway carriage in which the French had received the German surrender in 1918. Twenty-two years later victors and vanquished even used the same table and the same chairs. Now, it was the turn of Britain, the last combatant still free to do so, to stand alone against the might of Nazi Germany.

Once the battle of France, the "six-week war", was over, Germans garrisoned in France began to enjoy some of the more hedonistic privileges of a soldier's life. Hans Lehmann remembers it as "a lovely time":

> It was high summer by the time the fighting in France ended. Afterwards we were stationed in different parts of France. We lived in private houses. When we were stationed by the River Loire, there was another river called the Deloire. Nearby was a very peaceful village. It was beautiful, very beautiful, directly beside the water.

Georg Lehrmann was stationed at Le Mans, though, like Lehmann, he had only a limited time to enjoy himself:

> I was billeted in a beautiful château. It was really lovely, the area around Le Mans. There were lots of pretty girls, lots of wine, lots of fun. The sort of life soldiers dream about. It happened so quickly, too. The war in France had lasted only six weeks and then it was finished. Our troops had been good, damned good! But that fool Hitler soon spoiled it all. He wanted too much, didn't he?

What Hitler wanted was what he had always wanted. He had said so as long before as 1923, in his *Mein Kampf*, the book he had written while he was in prison for subversive activities. *Mein Kampf* was much more than a book. It was a statement of intent and a major theme was Lebensraum in the east, living space for the overcrowded German people. Like Kaiser Wilhelm II before him, Hitler coveted the huge resources of Russia and his hatred of communism added extra fuel to his ambitions.

The process of moving east had already started in Poland, where the Poles were "relocated" and their lands handed over to new German settlers. More often than not, "relocation" was a euphemism for the concentration camp. Beyond Poland lay the vast expanses of Russia and by August 1940 German divisions were being transferred to Poland in preparation for the opening of a new, eastern, front. The German forces were frequently regrouped to conceal their numbers and Georg Lehrmann and Hans Lehmann were among the many thousands of soldiers who were obliged to leave behind the delights of France and march east.

First, though, Hitler had to secure the southern flank of his invasion forces. To this end he made treaties with Bulgaria, Hungary and Romania. That was the easy part. All three had right-wing governments that were in tune with Hitler's own. They were only too pleased to join the Axis, the group of powers first formed with the "Pact of Steel" concluded by Germany and Italy in 1936.

Japan joined the Axis in 1940 and the three Balkan countries, followed by Slovakia and Croatia, subsequently enlarged the grouping.

Yugoslavia was all set to belong, too, and on March 25, 1941 the Yugoslav prime ministers and foreign minister signed an agreement with Germany in Vienna on behalf of the pro-German regent, Prince Paul. Riots followed, and two days later the 17-year-old King of Yugoslavia, Peter II, supported a military coup d'état which removed the Prince from power. The agreement with Germany was immediately rescinded. Churchill commented: "The Yugoslav nation has found its soul." They also invited their fate.

Hitler, infuriated, decreed that Yugoslavia was to be smashed "with merciless brutality, in a lightning operation". It was another opportunity for blitzkrieg. The Yugoslav capital, Belgrade, was heavily bombed on April 6, 1941 and the German forces swept through the Vardar region in the south. The Royal Yugoslav Army was caught in a barely mobilized state, poorly dispersed to contain the onslaught. The result, as gleefully broadcast on German state radio, was inevitable: "Some 50,000 men and eight Yugoslav generals have been captured by a single German division. The roads present a picture of a complete military rout. They are strewn with abandoned and broken-down tanks as well as rifles and machine guns."

Yugoslav resistance had been vigorous, but there was no doubt about the outcome. Within 12 days Zagreb, Sarajevo and Skopje had fallen. On April 13 Belgrade fell and three days later the Yugoslavs surrendered. The Germans claimed to have captured 20,000 prisoners and a large number of guns and other war material. King Peter, a close relative of the British royal family, fled with his government to London.

The rapid defeat and occupation of Yugoslavia left another country still implacably opposed to the Germans and their demands: Greece. Germany's Italian allies were supposed to have taken care of the Greeks after their invasion of October 28, 1940, but fanatical Greek resistance impelled them into a humiliating retreat. As his forces floundered, the Italian Duce, Benito Mussolini, appealed to the Germans for help.

The Greeks knew very well that the forces of Nazi Germany, and their appetite for vengeance, made them a very different prospect from the Italians. They, too, called in aid, from Britain. Piraeus, the port of Athens, became a supply centre for the British forces and Hajo Hermann was ordered to lay mines at the entrance to the port to prevent them using it. His flight did not go according to plan:

> We were stationed in Sicily and apart from the mines, I had loaded two bombs on to my plane. This I was actually not allowed to do. I was told to unload them, but I only pretended to do so and flew off with my squadron with the bombs still on board.
>
> We flew in low over the bay of Patras over Corinth. First I dropped mines into the entrance, the rest of the squadron sprinkled their mines down too, and then I spiralled upwards and made a clean run in, to aim at this large "tub" moored at the quayside. We didn't dive down but flew on a horizontal line, at about 1,000 metres, not very high. The spotlights wove all around us and the flak was shooting quite wildly, but my navigator paid no attention. He looked through his glass and I made corrections according to his instructions until he had released both the "forbidden" bombs.

I took the plane down to make sure we'd been on target, and then a detonation wave rose up, so enormous that I just hung in the air completely unable to steer. I thought my plane was doomed. You can't imagine a more violent detonation. Later I learned that the Royal Navy Admiral Sir Andrew Cunningham reported that the harbour was totally destroyed. "It was an explosion of atomic dimensions," he said.

The British couldn't get into or out of the harbour because this one hit of ours sank 41,000 tonnes of shipping at one blow. How did that happen? It's very difficult to sink so much tonnage even in a whole year, but what we'd done was hit a transport ship full of ammunition.

Everyone in the harbour seemed to be stunned. The flak stopped, the searchlights stopped turning and I just floated calmly above it all and watched. There were explosions all along the quayside, because bombs that had already been unloaded detonated and flew across the harbour.

But there was one British soldier – I'd really like to find out his name – he was the only one who took up his gun, a 4cm, and fired at me. He hit one of my engines. I realized that I was never going to get my aircraft back to Sicily, so decided instead to fly to the island of Rhodes on our remaining engine. We had loaded quite a lot of fuel for the return journey, so the plane was heavy and sank lower and lower until we were flying only 50 metres above the sea. All of a sudden I saw these cliffs sticking up out of the water. I managed to cheat my way past them, and we decided to offload some of the fuel so that we could fly at a more reasonable height.

Unfortunately there was a fault in the system and we couldn't stop the fuel flowing out. By the time we reached the southern tip of Rhodes, our tanks were on their last drop. There was a layer of high-lying fog and I couldn't see anywhere to land. We were managing to fly at about 800 metres by this time. I wanted to make radio contact with the airport, but the Italians who were manning it had decamped because the English had bombarded it. We were able to see one of the wrecked Italian planes, a Savoia, still smouldering.

The Italians had switched off the electricity supply, but luckily there was a German radio operator who had an emergency unit. He wound it up and gave me bearings. I came down through the clouds, not flying, but gliding, and managed to land. The needle was at zero. We didn't have a drop of fuel left.

The German invasion of Greece took place on the same day, April 6, 1941 as the invasion of Yugoslavia. It also proceeded in the same way. Two German corps stormed into northern Greece from Bulgaria, followed on April 8 by the Second Panzer Division. This new blitzkrieg soon proved to be unstoppable. The Germans drove speedily towards the south, driving the British forces before them.

The Greeks, meanwhile, had been overwhelmed. The last of their forces, in the west, capitulated on April 21, leaving the British to confront the Germans alone. There was a last stand at Thermopylae, but the German assaults proved too strong. Australian and New Zealand troops managed to hold the perimeter while the British organized an evacuation to the island of Crete.

Within a day the Germans had come after them. On May 20 the skies over Crete suddenly filled with German aircraft and a relentless bombing raid followed. Eyewitnesses reported that the Luftwaffe came from every direction in successive waves. Often there were more than 60 planes at a time, and they were flying in such close formation that the sky went dark.

The Germans had the sky to themselves. There was no air cover by the Royal Air Force.

The Luftwaffe was carrying men as well as bombs. The Seventh German Fliegerdivision parachuted down, together with an entire field hospital, doctors, orderlies, beds and Red Cross flags. It was the first major airborne assault in military history. The local Cretan population were waiting for the Germans, and killed every parachutist they could found. The slaughter was such that the Fliegerdivision lost around half its strength. Several of the Germans were dead before they reached the ground.

German control of the air greatly hampered the soldiers on the ground, but had no effect on their will to resist. A Maori sergeant with the New Zealand contingent on Crete later told what it was like:

We were unable to move owing to the unremitting bombing and machine-gunning from the German dive-bombers, but when the sun went down, we were able to fight back. We fixed our bayonets and immediately it was dark, we charged, yelling the haka, our war-cry. Our first obstacle was a solid line of German machine guns, but we quickly overran them and after a great fight lasting until dawn, we killed practically every German who was there. But then, when daylight returned, waves of German airborne reinforcements began to arrive. Within a few hours, around 130 Nazi troop-carriers, escorted by clouds of fighters, had landed and throughout the day we were attacked by more than 200 dive-bombers. We sheathed our bayonets and lay hidden in the rocks or in the drains. With the welcome cloak of darkness, we fixed our bayonets and charged and again cut the enemy to pieces. This went on for four days and four nights.

The parachutists were also coming down in the mountains, and so many of them were killed by Greek soldiers that "in the battle area, it was impossible to walk more than three yards without stepping over dead Germans".

The balance of the struggle for Crete nevertheless inexorably set against the British and they had to be evacuated from the island. About 45,000 had left by the time the campaign came to an end on May 27. Some 9,000 became prisoners, according to German estimates, and 6,000 were reported either killed or missing. Hitler could now be satisfied at last that he had cleared the ground for his projected invasion of Russia. He looked forward to another blitzkrieg victory, but in this he was severely mistaken.

The triumph of blitzkrieg, in Poland, western Europe and the Balkans, had been influenced by the confines of the battlegrounds and the brevity of the campaigns. No battlefront so far assaulted by the German lightning war had been wider than 300 miles and no campaign had lasted more than around two months. The great maw of Russia, where the front was to be six times as wide and space to manoeuvre or make strategic withdrawals was virtually infinite, was quite another matter.

Heinz Guderian was appalled at the prospect. He was acutely aware that the main guiding principle of blitzkrieg, the concentration of maximum force against a single objective, was going to be undermined, if not completely dissipated. As the German forces advanced into Russia, they would diverge further and further away from one another instead of drawing closer and becoming more concentrated. This would dissipate the power of their attacks and made the quick, disorientating punch of blitzkrieg redundant. The nature of the ground in Russia removed the vital asset of mobility and the apparently endless reserves at the disposal of the Red Army meant that they could recoup losses rapidly. None of these adverse conditions had obtained during the halcyon days of blitzkrieg success in 1940 and early 1941.

Almost the only blitzkrieg element left for the Russian campaign was surprise, as Ernst Preuss observed on invasion day:

> We advanced at the beginning, on the first day of the war, on June 22, 1941, when we marched into Russia. It was the longest day of my life. It started at 0500 hours. We had been told that the Russians had attacked us, so off we marched to teach them a lesson. We had no enemy contact, we just advanced and advanced, with the tanks, and that continued into the night with hardly a pause and it wasn't until the next day that we met the first light resistance.

Hans Lehmann encountered Russians rather sooner than Preuss but he had no doubt that the invasion was unexpected: "We were stationed on the border, everywhere in the woods and so on. And then it began abruptly, into Russia we went. The Russians were stationed close to the border on the other side, and they were caught totally by surprise."

CHAPTER TWO

The Germans in Russia

T HE THREE AND A HALF MILLION German troops who embarked on Operation Barbarossa on June 22, 1941 crossed from Poland into Russia at three in the morning. They did not expect to be there for long. Within five months at most, Hitler had promised, the communist giant would be laid low and Russia would become Lebensraum, or living space, for the German people.

Hitler's assurances and the confidence of the armed forces was based on a massive misinterpretation of the nature of the battleground on which they were now embarking. Hitler, at least, had been warned, but chose to ignore it, when Colonel-General Eduard Dietl, commander of the land forces in Norway in 1940, gave him a chilling picture of what to expect in Russia. Although Dietl was writing about the most extreme conditions, those found around Murmansk and the White Sea in the north, his description was a metaphor for one of the most demanding, most inclement and most dangerous areas in the world for military operations:

> The landscape in the tundra outside Murmansk is just as it was after the Creation. There's not a tree, not a shrub, not a human settlement. No roads and no paths. Nothing but rock and scree. There are countless torrents, lakes and fast-flowing rivers with rapids and waterfalls. In the summer there's swamp, and in the winter there's ice, snow and it's 40–50 degrees [Celsius] below. Icy gales rage through the eight months of Arctic night. This belt of tundra surrounding Murmansk like a protective armour is one big wilderness. War has never before been waged in this tundra, since the pathless stony desert is virtually impenetrable by formations.

In his post-war assessment of the Russian campaign, General Erhard Rauss, commander of the Third and Fourth Panzer Armies, had a similar opinion: "He who steps for the first time on Russian soil is immediately conscious of the new, strange, the primitive. The German soldier who crossed into Russian territory felt that he entered a different world, where he was opposed not only by the forces of the enemy, but also by the forces of Nature."

The German military, for their part, had always been more interested in central Europe, where, historically, most continental wars had taken place. Although the Germans had fought in western Russia during the First World War, they had never systematically studied the effects of extreme cold on troops, animals, weapons or motor vehicles, nor manufactured the special clothing that would be needed for the men if the campaign went on into the winter. The nature of the Russian fighting man, his stoicism, his acceptance of death, the small value he placed on human life, his tendency to go on fighting whatever the losses and however hopeless his position, the emotional imperviousness that enabled him to climb over piles of dead comrades to get at the enemy – none of this was sufficiently acknowledged in the German plans for the invasion of Russia.

Hitler was well aware of the warnings of history, but was planning to escape the constraints of geography and climate. With the arrogance of ignorance, by conquering Russia blitzkrieg-style in a single campaign before the winter. His grand plan was a three-pronged attack, the first heading for Leningrad in the north, the second towards Moscow and the third towards the Caucasus and Odessa on the Black Sea in the south. It appeared straightforward, and the Germans expected a speedy victory on all fronts. After all, the Poles, the Belgians, the Dutch and the French had quickly collapsed under the weight of the rapid German advances of 1940. The Russians, they believed, would do the same. General Alfred Jodl, Chief of Operations of the Wehrmacht, was contemptuous of the Russians' chances against the might of German arms.

"The Russian colossus," he said, "will be proved to be a pig's bladder: prick it and it will burst."

As the Germans were soon to discover, this was a gross underestimation of the difficulties Russia presented, and just how far the Russians would go to defend their country. They would rather destroy it or, through their "scorched-earth" policy, leave it desolate and unlivable rather than see it under foreign occupation. War in Russia was total war and the Russians were the total enemy.

Russia had been invaded twice in modern times, in 1709 by King Charles XII of Sweden and in 1812 by Napoleon Bonaparte. Both had lived to rue the day. Russia proved to be the graveyard of all their hopes, and the punishment for their temerity could not have been more severe. The Russians knew how to use their country's vastnesses and how to delay an enemy until their cruel winter arrived to destroy him. Unable to defeat either Charles or Bonaparte in battle, they withdrew further and further east, so that the invaders had to pursue them. On the face of it, this sort of unopposed advance or advance against only light resistance made the conquest of Russia appear easy, but the face of it was deceptive.

What the Russians were doing was luring King Charles and Napoleon, in turn, into the great maw of one of the world's most extensive countries. At the same time they destroyed or removed food, supplies, machinery – anything and everything that might give succour to their enemies. Meanwhile the invaders' lines of communication and supply became stretched to the limit as they advanced deeper and deeper into the Russian trap, tortured in turn by the broiling heat of the Russian summer, the rain and mud of autumn and the bone-freezing cold of one of the most punishing winters in the world.

In 1941 Russia would once again resort to this traditional policy, but on the brink of the invasion, in June, morale and expectation in the German ranks could not have been higher. It was an exciting time to be young, fit, well-trained and serving the Fatherland in a war they were convinced was justified and winnable. This was certainly the viewpoint of Henning Kardell, a volunteer who joined the Wehrmacht in 1940. Kardell was already a veteran of the war in western Europe by the time he arrived in Russia, and after his disappointment at the cancellation of Operation Sea Lion, the proposed invasion of Britain, he saw Russia as another chance to strike at the enemies of Germany:

> Yes, we believed the war was justified. We thought that the Soviet Union was going to attack us. The British had already done so. Soon after the campaign in France I was sent to the Channel coast near the Aa canal and saw the south coast of England and the chalk cliffs at Dover and was led to believe that we would soon be going across. I felt very bad when the invasion was called off and a lot of us swore at Hitler for denying us our chance. We didn't have much time for Hitler. We called him the "Land Rat". "The Land Rat is afraid of the sea!" we said. We didn't believe in him all that much. We were serving the Fatherland, that's what mattered.

Seventeen-year-old Wolfgang Reinhardt of Infantry Regiment 630, a Hessian-Thuringian-Bavarian regiment, felt the same way. For him, the war was a great adventure:

> I didn't take it very seriously, really. After all, at 16 or 17, you

don't have war in perspective. We were raring to go. It was the way we were brought up. For "Führer, Volk und Vaterland" – that was our motto. We were youngsters and didn't know any other way. In fact, the oath we took more or less told us that there wasn't any other way. I can remember it word for word even after so many years: "I swear this sacred oath by God: that I will give unconditional obedience to the leader of the German people and the supreme commander of the army and as a brave soldier I am prepared to risk my life." We were proud, we were so proud when we took the oath.

We weren't concerned with politics. In fact, we knew very little about the political scene in Germany and what went on there. Most people said that it was best not to speak of such things at home. It was dangerous. You never knew who might be listening. But we knew we had to win, and when Hitler said we will win the war, we have the weapons to do so, our revenge is coming, then we believed him. It was drilled into us.

Once Reinhardt and his comrades were going into battle, their training switched automatically into action, and when the order came to attack, they did not hesitate:

We attacked – that was the order and we just obeyed it. We weren't afraid at all. It didn't cross our minds that anything would happen to us, not even when we were beaten back on one occasion and had to run through a field of maize while the Russians peppered us with bullets. They came whistling past left and right. There were sunflowers in that field, and only the stems were left standing. The bullets came from every direction and I thought one of them was bound to get me, but none of them did. No, I wasn't afraid at all.

Edmund Bonhoff, 21, saw the war quite differently. He soon learned how to be afraid of the Russians. By the time his unit crossed the border on invasion day, Bonhoff was already a veteran, taking part in the blitzkrieg attack on France in 1940. Bonhoff, who was conscripted from the German labour service into the military, was already in place on the border with Russia in January 1941, but when the invasion came five months later, there was no rapid blitzkrieg advance for him. His was a horse-drawn unit:

> The motorized forces could drive and drive and we with our horses couldn't keep pace with them. Eventually we reached Lake Ilmen and remained there for a time. Before long we thought we'd been forgotten. No supplies came and we didn't have enough food. So we took to living off the land. Fortunately it was summer and the potato crop had been planted. We dug them out because we were hungry. It's like that in war. You have to do whatever you can to survive.

Weather-wise, Russia is a country of extremes – too much heat in summer, too much rain in autumn and too much snow, ice and cold in winter. Summer may have provided much-needed food for Bonhoff and his comrades, but logistically it made enormous difficulties for the German armies and especially for the motorized units. With summer temperatures topping 32 degrees Celsius, the speed of the blitzkrieg advance in the first few weeks after the invasion became a liability. Vehicles disturbed the fine layer of dust lying over the Russian road. It whirled up in clouds, clogging air filters and radiators. Engines became overheated. The sun burned down so fiercely that it stripped the paint off the tanks.

The German troops sweated profusely. Red dust caked their faces and bare arms. Their feet were blistered, red-raw patches caused by excessive sweating appeared on their skins. They suffered such agonizing thirst that they disobeyed orders and drank water from wells the Russians had poisoned with the carcasses of dead animals. If they survived, they were liable to be court-martialled.

By the autumn of 1941 Edmund Bonhoff's unit had moved on to positions along the wide road between Moscow and Leningrad. If Bonhoff thought that Russia in summer had been difficult, he soon found its depredations were more than overtaken by the rigours of autumn:

> The area around the Volga was an area of marshland and we got stuck there. Our guns were normally pulled by six horses, but the marshes meant we needed double that number to keep them moving. The

roads were dreadful. They were made of tree trunks placed side by side. It might have been a quick way to build a road for the Russians, but for us it was like moving over a succession of obstacles.

Autumn comes early in Russia and the autumn of 1941 was even earlier than usual. In early September, while the rest of Europe can still be enjoying the last remnants of summer warmth, the air has already turned cold, the leaves have already begun to fall and there is that sharp, harsh, icy feel in the air that presages the imminent arrival of winter.

First, though, there came the Rasputitza, the season of mud, the result of the heavy autumn rains. Wagons, vehicles and the renowned Panzers became bogged down and forced a complete halt. The German supply carts had wheels that were too narrow for the muddy terrain and sank deep into the soft ground. Pathways, cart trails, country roads and even hard, stone-made roads became impassable. The German advance was not simply stopped, it was crippled: the mud reduced the effectiveness of artillery shells, deadening or preventing explosions. Infantry were unable to move any great distance, and even then, their attacks were often curtailed. The mud penetrated weapons, causing them to malfunction and making them impossible to keep clean.

Six out of every 10 tanks of General Heinz Guderian's Second Panzer Group, part of Army Group Centre, which had been detailed to capture Moscow, were put out of action by mud in the autumn of 1941. Unlike the Russian tanks, their tracks were too narrow and they sat too close to the ground to move easily – or at all – over the mud-clogged surfaces. Although the emphasis in Operation Barbarossa was on blitzkrieg and fast armoured vehicles and tanks, the Germans brought to Russia a form of transport from a much earlier age of warfare: horses. But the mud claimed them, too. They sank neck-deep and, exhausted by their struggles to get free, thousands of horses died.

Georg Lehrmann, serving with AR20, the Horse-Drawn Artillery, in the Demjansk pocket, has never forgotten what it was like to be in Russia during the Rasputitza of 1941, which, according to several other German veterans, was worse than anything known elsewhere in the Second World War, or even in the First:

There were no roads and everything gradually turned into mud. We either moved on the railway lines or along makeshift roads built of logs and timber. You can image what happened to the vehicles. There were no spares that weren't loose, all the suspension units were broken, we put wooden beams beneath them so that we could keep going. Everything was covered in mud. Everything went rotten. Our vehicles became useless. We had to tow them if we could, but many times they were towed away.

As Lehrmann recalls, there was one solution:

We were told by another division, if your vehicles won't work, try to find Russian tanks; and so we went off to find some, there were enough of them lying around. When we found tanks that were not burned out, we stacked up sticks of dynamite to blow out the drive shaft where the gun was mounted and used these to tow the other vehicles. We had 10-ton tractors to tow the artillery guns and we used these as recovery vehicles. There were so many abandoned Russian tanks that other divisions were able to fetch their own. We knew exactly where they were and in this way we managed to drag ourselves out of the mud. But it was a tremendous effort.

Even though fully informed of the problems caused by the Rasputitza, Hitler ordered Guderian and his other commanders to maintain their advance. The Führer, whose eccentric views on strategy, tactics and warfare were the despair of his generals, saw the Rasputitza as a temporary problem. Momentum had to be maintained at all costs. But, moving on, or rather, the effort of trying to do so, hampered the Germans even more. Fuel was used up more quickly – it was scarce enough, in any case – engines became overstrained, pistons wore down and many drivetrains, the power connection between the engine and the wheels or tracks, were irreparably damaged.

It was not until the end of October 1941 that the first hard frosts came and the mud froze, releasing its captives. The damage and delay caused by the Rasputitza was cited by Field Marshal Fedor von Bock, commander of Army Group Centre, as the most important reason the

Germans failed to capture Moscow. While their enemy was embroiled in the mud, the Russians, operating on an intact rail system, were able to reinforce their troops and strengthen their defences. As a result, the Germans were presented with an immovable obstacle when, at long last, they approached the Russian capital in November 1941.

By then the worst Rasputitza for years had been succeeded by the worst winter. Even for Russia, the cold was extreme. As its grip tightened, the temperature plunged to -40 degrees, the landscape turned white with snowdrifts several feet deep, the sky was slate grey and men began to freeze because adequate winter clothing had not yet come up the logistic chain. Some of them took gruesome measures to get hold of warmer clothing, as Edmund Bonhoff remembers: "We used to saw the legs off frozen Russian corpses in order to get their warm felt boots. We stood them up against a stove and when the legs had thawed, we pulled them out and dried off the boots."

None of this had been in Hitler's plan: according to him, the war in Russia should have been over several months earlier, an army of occupation should have been in place, with the best of everything at its disposal, and he should have been basking in the triumph of another brilliant success. Edmund Bonhoff was only one of millions of Germans who had to face the results of Hitler's arrogant miscalculation. His five months became six, became seven, became a year, and still the Russians had not given in.

Hitler's timetable was already in trouble by the middle of August 1941, when the Germans had managed to advance in the area around Leningrad against stiff Russian resistance. By September 6, with autumn already approaching, they had cut the railway line to Moscow and were closing in on the southern approaches to Russia's second city.

From then on, the struggle for Leningrad was a grim war of attrition and on January 7, 1942 the Russians launched two offensives aimed at breaking the German stranglehold. The first of these formed the so-called Volkhov pocket in the north. The second offensive, launched south of Lake Ilmen, went in near the city of Demjansk and it was here, in the resultant Demjansk pocket, that Edmund Bonhoff became one of some 90,000 encircled Germans. The Germans received some supplies, by way of a small, 800-metre wide gap forced through by SS troops, but conditions in the pocket were atrocious. For a start, Bonhoff remembers, they had nothing at all to eat:

Added to that, we were being bombed all the time, with everything the Russians could throw at us. Besides this, we got sick. I developed spotted fever, a very serious illness which I'd first contracted in France. Three others got it, too, and for five weeks I seemed to be living in a sauna, with a fever temperature of 41 degrees. I lay there, as if I was in a sauna, together with three others.

Bonhoff was evacuated from the pocket in a Junkers, but he had barely recovered when he was flown back in again. The flight back was as dangerous as the fighting on the ground, all the more so because the Junkers was carrying armaments: "There were ammunition boxes underneath in the Junkers and on top of that were eight to 10 soldiers and because of the Russian artillery firing at us, we had to fly just above the trees."

The Junkers – and Bonhoff – survived. Eventually both the Russian advances were halted and the trapped Germans managed to clear both the Volkhov and Demjansk pockets. They did so at cost:

I took part in the advance and the retreat in stages, and then en route our guns were stolen. The Russians came after us, with their T-34 tanks, and we were supposed to stop them with our guns. It was hopeless. We had to leave the heavy guns standing there and we were then fired upon with our own weapons. We'd been told that the Russians were morons – too stupid to do anything like that. What a cynical lie that was!

The T-34 tanks were among the many shocks the Germans received in Russia. They had considered the Russians incapable of producing such effective armour. Weighing around 26 tons, the T-34 had armour up to 2.5 inches thick, and carried a 76.2mm gun and two machine guns. In some quarters the T-34 was considered the best tank of the Second World War. Wolfgang Reinhardt concurs:

The T-34 had the advantage over our tanks of being probably more easily produced. We saw many damaged T-34s, so we were able to study them. The tank driver sat inside on a wooden box and had the ammunition in the back. The steel armour-plating wasn't smooth, it was rough. It had probably been rushed into production. Even though everything about the T-34s was simple, they certainly worked. Our Panzer tanks were much more complicated and needed special spares. If we couldn't get hold of spares for the motorized vehicles, then that was it, nothing could be done.

Günther Bünke, who was conscripted into the military when he was 20, also fought in the Demjansk pocket. Bunke, however, did not have the luxury of observing the T-34s or of considering their merits. On the contrary, he was on the business end of their guns, and very nearly became one of their many victims when two of them approached his position:

One of the tanks drove into a marsh hole with its caterpillar track and tipped over, and the other one drove away. Overall, we didn't have much to do with the tanks, just that one time and on one other occasion. The infantry attacks came more often. And there were frequent artillery bombardments, too. We had the 8.8mm and the 15cm howitzers, mortars and rocket launchers. At first we had single rocket launchers and afterwards combined rocket-launchers. The Russians had the Stalin Organ.

The "Stalin Organ", the Germans' name for the Katyusha rocket mortar, was the Russians' answer to the Nebelwerfer, the "smoke thrower", which could fire six rounds every minute and a half and had a range of up to 7,700 yards. The Stalin Organ was not a precision weapon, but its solid-fuel, fine-stabilized rockets could blanket a battle-field with continuous, roaring fire. Launched in batches of between 32 and 48, with a range of 6,500 yards, they contributed an element of terror to the orchestra of weaponry to which the Germans were subjected. Günther Bünke has vivid memories of the experience:

At night you could see the firing and the flares all around and so on and we felt that we were surrounded; only a very narrow path led out of the pocket. It was cleared very quickly soon after the end came at Stalingrad in 1943, because it could not be defended. As usual we were worried about supplies, food and ammunition and so on. It was a very unpleasant situation.

What followed, though, was even more unpleasant. Bunke's unit was moved to the marshland near the River Volkhov. Here Bunke and his comrades were forced to dig in order to survive, though the groundwater saturating the marshes tended to flood in if they dug too deep:

In the Volkhov marshes, we were only able to dig a trench to waist height so that we could lie in it; otherwise, at Leningrad, there were proper trenches, real trench warfare. At Leningrad we were in positions so close to one another that we could talk to the Russians and throw hand grenades. That was a terrible time. While were still at the River Volkhov, we saw Russian tanks – T-34s. Two of them approached us and it was a really uncanny feeling when they drove up and fired at us.

Otto Bense was another soldier who confronted the terror of the T-34s, as well as a particular Russian artillery piece which the Germans called the "ratch-boom" because of its rapid action:

The feeling is difficult – no, impossible – to describe. When a tank fires – a tank has a gun on board which has an unbelievable discharge – and when tanks approach, if you see them coming, what can you do? You feel helpless. You're confronting a mechanical monster. All it knows is how to kill. Either you get down or creep into a hole. You take your chances. Either the tank drives past or you've had it.

For a soldier there is nothing worse than a tank attack. In my opinion. I was an infantryman and I know it, I can judge. The artillery is behind the front line, the ones who were lying in the filth, those were the infantrymen. The infantry had fewer men. It was always said: One in the front with infantry and 10 behind. That was the rule. We used to say that the man in front was the "sand rabbit". He had to spoon out the dirt and behind was the artillery. They were a couple of kilometres behind the front line, so the infantry was very much on its own.

As far as we were concerned, the air around us was full of metal. The Russians only had one artillery piece we called a "ratch-boom" – a 7.5cm gun. You heard the discharge and then it exploded. If you are with the artillery and you hear the gun fire, boom, then you can get under cover. But with this Russian "ratch-boom", that was impossible. Discharge, explosion – that's how it was, before you could even blink. Many soldiers were killed because of that damned "ratch-boom".

Tanks or machine guns were not the only weapons waiting to kill any soldier unwise enough to stick his head up and into view. There were also the snipers, the unseen sharpshooters who were the most insidious of enemies. Otto Bense was an eyewitness of their deadly work:

The Russian snipers, they were the most dangerous people of all. The Russians were placed in the trees and they were camouflaged, so we never knew whether they were there or not. Their weapons had telescopic sights. They seemed to be all over the place, where you wouldn't imagine them to be. Once I said to one of my colleagues, "Be careful", then crack, ping, and he was dead. It happened in a moment.

We knew that snipers aimed primarily at officers, including non-commissioned officers. I suppose the idea was if the officers were killed, the soldiers under their command wouldn't be able to organize an attack. I was a sergeant, so I was on the list. Pretty well our only defence was to remove all our badges so that we couldn't be recognized as officers from a distance. The SS did the same. They had a special braid and they removed it. The SS were extra-special targets. The Russians would take prisoners when it was just the Wehrmacht, but if they got hold of SS men, it was different. They killed them all, shot them all out of hand.

The Russian sniper was an even more dangerous presence because he was unseen. Even when he was spotted and killed, it was a shock:

We were in the woods near Minsk. We saw no one, no one, and we had losses and more losses. Suddenly a man fell out of a tree in front of me, dead. He was in a camouflage outfit with a leaf pattern, and he had been seen by one of our men and shot down. He fell at my feet. The Russian soldier who was sitting in the tree in camouflage. And he had fired from up there and we arrived but there was no one there – always from above, from the top of the tree, they killed us. And he fell dead at my feet. Until that moment I had not known he was there.

The Russians, desperate to relieve beleaguered Leningrad, threw everything they had at the Germans trapped in the Demjansk pocket. Otto Bense recalls being at the receiving end:

We were surrounded mostly by the Russian artillery and the Russians had planes, fighter planes, battle planes, they were armoured underneath and with an MG they could fire downwards. They flew in at low level and bombarded us with shrapnel bombs and dropped little bombs that caused a lot of injuries. This went on by night as well as by day. As soon as it was dark. In the Demjansk pocket, the Russians flew over in planes, old sports planes and so on, which we called "coffee machines". They gurgled, just like coffee machines – blup-blup-blup-blup-blup. They bombed us continuously. They dropped shrapnel bombs, small bombs, bop-bop-bop everywhere.

It was a real war of nerves. The planes that came over at night were the worst. They kept on circling overhead, all night long. The Russians left us Germans soldiers nervous wrecks – for some it was so bad that that they went mad. This rattling, no lights, and boom, here a bomb, there a bomb, and those small shrapnel bombs – it destroyed our nerves, I can tell you.

Meanwhile the trapped soldiers went hungry for most of the time. Bense remembers how meagre their rations were:

There was one loaf of bread a day and three men had to share it. I guess there were about 60–80,000 men, four to six divisions with artillery and tanks in the Demjansk pocket, and they were living on a third of a loaf a day each. That went on until the SS managed to punch through and rescue us. Everyone says the SS were criminals and murderers, but those SS were in the concentration camps. We all know about them. The battle troops of the SS, that was a different SS, they were special units. If the SS hadn't existed I probably wouldn't be here any more, I'd be dead or whatever. The SS commander – Obergruppenführer Eick was his name – he smashed us out of there under cover of night. We'd never have made it without him.

The retreat from the pocket was very costly for the Germans. Moreover, it was a retreat that took place at an inconvenient time for the Nazi propaganda machine, when they were supposed to be winning. It was a case for a bit of judicious censorship and the official story was different. Otto Bense and thousands like him knew differently. Bense is understandably sardonic about the rosy propaganda picture:

It wasn't called a retreat by the army commanders: they called it "straightening out the front line". A German army does not retreat! Oh no, no, no! It had to be "straightening out the front line". It was even said that there were no German casualties. Imagine that, when so many died during the retreat. The tales they told about Demjansk also had it that the Germans lost no tanks either – we had it all firmly in hand, they said.

About 52 tanks – Russian tanks – were supposed to have been destroyed and at least there was some truth in that. Though the T-34 was so dangerous – it was a tank that drove everywhere – many of them were hit by our PAKs, the Panzer Abwehr Kanone. PAKs were the anti-tank guns and the infantry had them with us in our positions: 7.5cm with a long barrel, they were able to penetrate the tanks. But you couldn't do anything against a tank with normal weapons, they had been made so secure.

Otto Bense was lucky, but he knew how easy it was to be killed in places like the Demjansk pocket:

At the moment an attack takes place, you switch off, everything, and either it goes all right or you get hit and you're gone; and it was always like that, especially when the Russians fired at us with their heavy artillery, the normal one with 10 pounds and the heavy 17.5. They had grenades like that; when a Russian grenade exploded, either it hit you and you were dead, you were blown to bits, or it exploded beside you and you just about managed to survive by throwing yourself into a hole in the ground. Many times, in the Demjansk pocket, I thought: "It's over. That's it, the finish!"

Hans Lehmann recalls being under fire with rather less fatalism. The worst thing, he says, was the suspense:

When there was an air raid we looked up to see: there they are, did they release the bomb yet? Not yet? Then, there they were, almost directly above us. That was good. We knew that when they released bombs directly above, the bombs would fly away from us. If they were still in front of us, then you could calculate roughly where the bombs would fall. Believe me, you didn't want to be directly in the area where the bombs fell, because there, everything was smashed to pieces.

Heinz Frauendorf, one of the many conscripts in Hitler's armies, managed to develop a sort of tolerance during his service in Russia:

I was a conscripted soldier for six years, against my will, of course, but there was no chance of getting out of it. The men born in that year, 1920, and also in 1919, 1921 and 1922, we were sent as cannon fodder to the eastern front to die a hero's death for the Nazi officers and generals. Anyone from that age group who survived must have had a dozen guardian angels.

When it comes to actual warfare, it may sound cynical, but you just get used to it. You get into a routine and develop an almost animalistic instinct about it. You know what to expect, so you're not surprised when you get it. For example, you don't hear the mortar until it has made impact, then you do; it hisses in the air a bit, and at the moment when you hear that hissing, you know you've got to throw yourself on to the ground like greased lightning or you've had it.

On the other hand, you can hear the "arri", artillery shells, and you can tell quite accurately just where they're going to fall. If you knew they weren't coming in your direction, you didn't bother about it, but you could always hear them. Once, we heard eight 10.5s, I think they were, coming straight for our position. We thought it was the end, but we were lucky – not one of them exploded – six or eight duds!

Frauendorf's fatalistic attitude did not exclude fear, but it was fear that veterans like him could handle:

Naturally we were afraid when we were preparing for an attack. You got ice-cold shivers down your spine, but by the time we'd been in Russia for three or four years, we had fear under control. It was worse for the youngsters who came from home as replacements and were immediately involved in some dreadful attack or defence or whatever. They didn't have the chance to acclimatize, and we of the "old guard" knew that we could write them off. They just wouldn't get through it. There were only a handful of us who'd been there from the beginning, and we could cope with it.

When the war was over, the heat was off and Heinz Frauendorf, like other veterans, realized he had survived when so many others had died – and the memories came back to haunt him:

After the war I had nightmares even decades afterwards; one experience that I found really terrible followed me as a nightmare. I was with a mortar unit and one day we all had short spades, because we had to dig our mortars in. That was something we'd learned from the Russians: the deeper you were dug in, the greater the chance of survival.

I was looking for a good position for our mortar; there was some loose sand and bushes and scrub and suddenly, without any warning, there's this Russian in front of me in a one-man hole, on his own. He looked at me, I looked at him. Believe me, we both got the shock of our lives. I had a spade in my hand; my ability to react was good, but he must have been a beginner to have dug himself in there in the first place. I knew he was going to shoot me, so I struck first. I killed him with the spade. That followed me for a very long time. It's only in the past 20 years that I am no longer affected by it.

At the time, though, Frauendorf had no time to think about what he had done. As soon as the Russian was dead, the war came crowding back in on him, and the "ratch-boom" and "Stalin Organ" were responsible:

> When I'd killed the man with the spade, we were fired on immediately from the "ratch-boom" gun. Ironically, the Russians had got it from Krupp and it was a lovely German weapon, a precision weapon. We were really afraid of it, because with the "ratch-boom" discharge and impact were almost simultaneous.
>
> Then there was the "Stalin Organ", as we called it. It could fire 36 shots in a relay. I was under fire the first time in 1942. We already knew a lot about the Stalin Organ. The shrapnel went away upwards. Our smoke shell mortars were different: their shrapnel went out flat over the ground. The Russians threatened us with gas if we didn't stop using the smoke shell mortar; but for new arrivals the Stalin Organ was hellfire. Fire one of them at a gun crew and they were all killed instantly, the lot of them.

Leo Mattowitz was a new arrival to war when he went to Russia. He was one of the lucky ones, and beat Frauendorf's gloomy prediction to survive into old age. But in Russia he was very young and real, live war, its killing, its casualties, its horrific sights and experiences, became too much for him. Mattowitz still lives with the trauma, try as he might to forget it:

> I don't want to know about those times any more. I must not be reminded of it, I get high blood pressure at the very mention of it. The trouble is, I remember it all only too well. I can't get it out of my mind. Probably I never will. I lost so many friends. Masses of them! There were 20 boys in my school class when the war began. Only two of us were still alive when it ended.
>
> Masses of them lost, masses of them! It is indescribable.
>
> When it all began there was so much I didn't know. And I learned

in the most terrible way, I can tell you. The worst time for me came right at the start, on the very first day of the invasion, when we drove through the towns and there were dead civilians – men, women, children – lying everywhere. Till then I had never seen a dead body in my life and I couldn't eat a thing for days, it affected me so deeply. Afterwards, of course, I had to get used to it, but it wasn't right. It wasn't right.

Fortunately Mattowitz had the sense not to speak of his doubt where the wrong ears could hear. It was a punishable offence to cast even the slightest aspersion over any aspect of the campaign in Russia:

You only had to say, "It'll never work out" or something similar and you'd be arrested and never seen again. That actually happened to one NCO I knew. But at least I could pray, even though I wasn't very religious. So I did and hoped that God knew what I thought.

I didn't have the time to brood over it, though, because by the second day we were already involved in battle. We were stationed on three high points in Polen Grodnow, and we had to fire on some villages with our heavy guns. Our infantry had already advanced and we were told that our reconnaissance had discovered that the Russians, armed to the teeth, were in those villages. An officer told us that they wanted to attack Germany. The area around us was full of them and they were going to attack us. So we had to attack first.

As Mattowitz later discovered, he had been fed with propaganda. German soldiers heard a great deal of anti-Russian, anti-communist talk and, in their dangerous situation, they had no option but to believe it. But that did little to relieve young Mattowitz's fears:

I hadn't slept at all the night before the attack, I was shaking so much. I'd never taken part in an attack before. Then, just after three in the morning, we got the order to fire. But there was something wrong. By the time the attack was over, there were only dead civilians in the villages, dead women, burning houses, and not one single soldier. We'd been killing civilians. The officers had lied to us. It was unbelievable!

Mattowitz, only 18 years old, encountered Russian soldiers soon enough, and with them, their merciless winter.

In Germany there were large stocks of winter gear but hopes of getting them to the front sank in the face of a much more vital imperative: reinforcements and ammunition had to take precedence on the overstretched lines of communication and the inadequate Russian rail network. This cost the Germans thousands of lives. If the Russians did not kill them, then their winter often did the work instead. Thousands who managed to survive faced unimaginable sufferings. Leo Mattowitz still bears the scars today:

> We went up as far as Moscow and the "great cold" set in. I still suffer from it today – with frozen toes. If I hadn't managed to get hold of a hat from a dead Russian, then my ears would have gone too.
>
> The Russians attacked us with such overwhelming power that anyone who didn't experience it cannot believe it. Cossacks on tanks, Cossack regiments, the majority of them were Mongolians. Stalin fetched 10 whole divisions from Siberia and Kazakhstan and they were brought up towards us. All those thousands of men! It made me feel very small and unimportant. I realized that I was not even a cog in the big wheel. I was just a bit of dust.

Mattowitz was a sensitive lad, too sensitive for his own good, and before long the war and its horrors proved too much for him. He reached the edge of his endurance on the day he found himself in a trench. Around him, or so it seemed, were lengths of wood. Then he discovered that they were corpses:

> Dead men. I'd been lying among dead men. My God! I couldn't take it any more. I collapsed. But it wasn't only that awful experience in the trench. It was also the lice that crawled all over us. They got under our collars, everywhere. We couldn't get rid of them. Then I got a lung infection and the doctors suspected it was spotted fever. There was a lieutenant from East Prussia, he looked at me and said, "My young lad, you don't look too good." "No," I said, "I'm not well." "Off to the main

dressing station," he said. The wounded went there as well as those who were ill like me, falling over with their feet frozen, toes, socks hanging on them. It was -40 degrees [Celsius] by then. The cold was unimaginable. I'd never known anything like it.

Hitler had been so confident that, by the time the winter came, his campaign in Russia would be over, that there had been no move to winterize weapons or equipment. It was the ordinary soldier, like Leo Mattowitz, who paid the price of the Führer's arrogance:

Everything mechanical came to a dead halt. Nothing worked at all. Not like the Russians. They were used to it, they took proper precautions. Their machine guns worked, their motors kept running. We didn't even have anti-freeze. Just imagine it: before we left the vehicles we had to let the water run out because it would freeze overnight. We had absolutely nothing, we were totally unprepared for the winter. Totally.

For Mattowitz, though, his illness was a lifesaver and an escape from the freezing grip of Russia in winter. But he had to suffer for it:

I was put into a hospital train, together with men who had suffered horrific injuries. Some of them had arms missing. Some of them had trodden on mines and had their feet or their legs blown off. They were unloaded in the field hospitals at Smolensk, Vitebsk and Minsk. I was in the first wagon behind the engine, and it was hellishly cold; I could walk, but it was so cold that I blacked out.

When I'd recovered, I learned that the ones who could walk, like me, were taken to large towns like Brest-Litovsk, Warsaw or Trier. I must have got worse on the train journey, because I remember someone saying, "We can't save him, he has a temperature of 40 degrees." I supposed that was why they took me out on to the station at one train stop. The station had a small hut and there were layers of men in there, all of them frozen solid. I was going to be next, it seems. I was taken to the hut because the doctor had said, "We can't save him."

Mattowitz might had died there and then. He would certainly have died had he been left in the station hut. But fortunately another doctor thought to examine him more closely:

> He looked at my eyes and said, "We can't put him in there yet. Maybe he's got a chance." So they put me back on the train. They gave me whatever medicines they had – of course, there was no penicillin at that time – but what they gave me seemed to help.
>
> At another station along the line, some Red Cross nurses brought in food. It wasn't much – half a loaf of army bread, tins of sardines, sausage and pork – but most of the men couldn't eat it. They had bullet wounds in their legs, arms or heads and they were unable to move.

There was no point in letting the food go to waste, especially after Mattowitz learned from the engine driver that food was very short at home in Germany:

> The engine driver said to me, "I have three children at home and there is very little to eat there. Couldn't you give me a bit of bread or get some of the tins of pork for me." "Yes, I will," I said. I got a backpack, went from section to section and asked, "Are you going to eat that?" "No, you can eat it." When my backpack was full, I took it to the engine driver. He fell around my neck and kissed me and said, "When the trains gets to a big town, come to the engine, I'll hide you and take you all the way to Trier, my home town."
>
> So, every time the train stopped and those men who looked as if they might improve were sorted out by a staff doctor, they were offloaded at places like Brest-Litovsk, which was a delousing station, but I got to Trier, a much better place.

It was at Trier that Mattowitz discovered he was not suffering from spotted fever after all. So much the better. Spotted fever was a very serious illness and a killer. However, Mattowitz still had lice – lice proliferated in winter – and his uniform had to be burned: "I was so full of lice that I had lice bites in my body that could still be seen up to a few years ago, it was that bad."

Like Mattowitz, Henning Kardell got his first taste of the war in Russia on the very first day of the invasion. The circumstances, though, were rather different. After the brilliantly successful German blitzkrieg in western Europe in 1940, Kardell stayed on in France until 1941. It was in February of that year that the focus of Kardell's war changed. He was ordered south-east into Romania, where the Germans were determined to protect the vital oil wells, ostensibly against the British. In reality, the threat, as perceived by the German High Command, came from Russia, even though the Russians were not yet combatants in the war. They were, in fact, allies of Germany under the Non-Aggression Pact signed in 1939 by Hitler and the Soviet leader, Josef Stalin. It was a marriage of convenience between two leaders who distrusted each other, one of them, Hitler, simply biding time until he was free to attack his ally. Today Kardell calls this alliance a "fairy story we were told" and events soon proved how right he was to think so:

> In February 1941 we travelled by train through Europe to Romania. We were stationed on the border with Bessarabia in the area of the Pot. We were to travel with Russian trains through the Caucasus to Persia in order to get the oil away from the British. Then, suddenly, overnight the whole picture went into reverse. It was June 22, 1941 and we were told we were at war with Russia!

Signs of this new war soon appeared. Russian bombers came over and dropped bombs on a house where Kardell and his comrades relaxed in the evenings with a bottle or two of red wine. They were none too happy about that, he recalls. In company with Italian and Romanian troops, Kardell soon saw action:

> At the end of June we began the assault over the Pot in the Soviet Union and over the Dniester in Bessarabia into the Ukraine. There was a bridge across over the River Pruth which led into Russia proper. We rode up on our bicycles, threw them into the ditches at the side of the road and waited for Lieutenant Jordan to blow his whistle – our signal to jump up over the bridge. As the whistle sounded we felt liberated. We had no time to be afraid, we felt liberated. I don't remember

feeling joy that the war was finally under way, but it was a relief. The order had come, and we were going into action.

The Germans ran straight into murderous fire:

> We went across the bridge and firing broke out immediately, with machine guns from this side and machine guns from the other side. There were only 45 men in the platoon, it was carried out with just the one platoon under this Lieutenant Jordan. Next morning we were counted and then we were only 22 of us. But there was no fear. This was war and that's the way war was.

After the battle at the bridge the Germans marched on to the Crimea, where intense fighting took place around Kerch and Sevastopol, but first, Kardell's faith in the justice of the German cause was jolted, if only for a while, by an encounter with a Russian prisoner. The prisoner was very young – 18 or 19 – about Kardell's own age. He had been shot through the arm, and the Germans had bandaged it. The Russian said only one word, but that word spoke volumes: "He said 'putschook' – 'why?' Why does it have to be like this? Why? That's when we began to think. Why should young men be killing each other, be ordered to kill each other?"

It was a rhetorical question. Obeying orders was the only response available to men in battle, and like millions of others, Kardell obeyed:

> For soldiers only orders count, all that matters. The war continued, the killing went on and I played my part. I threw hand grenades into trenches. There were many killed on the other side, but there was no time to think about it, there was no time to be afraid, there was no time. You went out, you did your job, you killed. You knew it would be your turn one day. You didn't reckon to get to the end of the war alive.

Karl Meding, too, remembers what it was like to face the fact that every day, every hour could be his last. Meding was 19 when he first went to Russia and he managed to escape death twice: once, when he had no helmet and was shot in the head after peering over the edge of a parapet, the other occasion soon afterwards, when he was being taken to the command post and trod on a mine. Fortunately Meding had only a grazed head and a shrapnel wound in the arm to show for his close brushes with death, but the fear of it was always there. His injuries took him away for the battlefield for a few months but after he recovered he was sent back to Russia, and arrived there on December 20, 1942. Midwinter.

We were near Vitebsk in central Russia and it was -30 degrees [Celsius]. I had to live in a hole for several weeks, from Christmas Day 1942 until the end of January 1943. I shared it with a comrade who was older than myself. There wasn't much room for two in a hole roughly two and a half metres by one metre. There were wooden poles over it and on that lay hay and on top of that, snow. The temperature had dropped even lower by that time. It was -40 degrees.

The snow blew towards us; and one of us always had to stand outside this hole and see if the enemy was coming. We were always looking towards the east and the wind came from the east. Even the fear of death, which was always with us, wasn't as terrible as this. It was undoubtedly my very worst experience in Russia.

At night, when the moon wasn't shining or it wasn't stormy, one of us used to go to fetch food. We used to put the food in our pockets in the hope of keeping it warm, but it didn't work. Butter and bread froze solid. We froze. Everything froze. We used to huddle there with our feet wrapped in straw, stamping them on the frozen ground to get some extra warmth. You couldn't make a fire and all we had to warm up our coffee was some little candles. We didn't have any special clothing to deal with the cold – just a shirt, vest, jacket and ordinary military over-coat.

In February 1943 Meding at last managed to escape from the icy hole he had been forced to call home when he was billeted on a Russian family in a village near Vitebsk. The Russians were hardly better off, but at least they had a stove and a hut sealed from the worst of the winter weather. As Meding discovered, survival Russian style was primitive. For one thing the family had no food. Meding and three others billeted with him had to feed them from their own rations:

It was as if we were all living back in the Dark Age. The family's goat, hens and ducks were all in the hut with us. It was made of wooden beams with a gully down the middle filled with clumps of moss placed one on top of the other so that the whole building was sealed tight.The hut was partitioned with a board and stacks of straw, There were tents folded together and we slept on those.

There were five people in this family – a grandfather, grandmother and three children – and they slept, as is usual in Russia, on top of the stove. It was fired from below and they slept on top of it. We slept on the ground.

German propaganda had seen to it that soldiers' heads were filled with stories of Russians as uncivilized savages and stupid, inferior Slavs. According to Hitler, they had to be expunged to make room for the German Master Race. The reality did not always match the publicity. Wolfgang Reinhardt found that the Russians he encountered were remarkably friendly and compassionate. In 1941 he was with the German forces who marched southwards, towards the Caucasus:

Our final destination was a wood with ravines, which I think was called the Malakova ravine. We were stationed there from the autumn of 1941. We had a very friendly relationship with the Russians. The position was fairly quiet; we'd built it up with bunkers. The Russians were 200 metres away across the ravine and they had done the same. So we were positioned very close, close enough to hear the balalaika music they played for us in the evenings.

There was a sawmill below and it produced wooden posts. We had an unwritten law that in the mornings we would go down and fetch posts to build our bunkers with, and in the afternoon the Russians would fetch posts in their turn. Nothing bad happened, we were in total agreement with one another.

The exigencies of war were such that this mutually agreeable situation was bound to change. The catalyst was Stalingrad. Though they were sited far away from the battle, the consequences for Wolfgang Reinhardt and his comrades in the Caucasus were brought home with the fall of Stalingrad at the end of January 1943. This brutal, bitter and horrifically costly struggle, fought in the snow and ice of the terrible eastern winter, signalled the end of all Hitler's hopes that he could succeed where Napoleon had failed and conquer Russia. Stalingrad was also the signal that abruptly altered the amenable situation Reinhardt and his fellow soldiers had so far enjoyed at the Malakova ravine: "The whole thing was fairly peaceful until Stalingrad fell, and then the Russians came over like a shot and surrounded us. Then the single attacks began; we attacked areas where the Russians had set themselves up and we were ordered to destroy an advance gun position."

The Germans managed to destroy the post, but during the attack Reinhardt was wounded. He lay on the ground, unable to walk and return to his own lines. Then an extraordinary thing happened:

> Two Russian women came out of a house and carried me in. I remember there was this religious icon in the corner with the eternal flame. They put me on to a couch; you can't really call it a couch, it was a sofa, a worn-out sofa; the Russians didn't have many comforts. The two women wanted to keep me there, they lay me down and wanted to look after me, but I became frightened and thought, "What if this doesn't work out? I've got to get back. Somehow, I must get back." The women seemed to guess how nervous and upset I was, so they took hold of me and took me some way back until one of our tanks drove by and brought me to the command post. From that moment on, I liked the Russians. They have a wonderful mentality.

This was not the majority view, of course. For many more Germans there was something terrible about the Russians. It was not for nothing that so many Germans made such efforts to avoid being captured by them at the end of the war. They already knew what to expect, for the eastern front had been a nightmare scenario, a place of unimaginable suffering in the face of a savage enemy fighting in a savage climate.

The Russians were all the more dangerous because they were capable of irregular as well as regular warfare. When the fighting had passed them by, but they had not been captured, they became partisans, operating against German supply lines. They infiltrated behind German positions and attacked, as it were, from within. German troops found themselves ambushed. Or, as Otto Cranz recalls, they were suddenly attacked by Russians who managed to enter their bunkers:

> A Russian shock troop cleared out our bunker one night in a surprise attack. I had returned from the night watch and had just lain down on the plank bed made from thick wooden beams which kept us off the damp ground, when I heard Russian voices shouting. They had surrounded the bunker. They fired through the rear window and the door with sub-machine guns. They threw in hand grenades, which luckily rolled beneath the thick wooden beams and exploded there. Fortunately the beams were 3cm thick, so that I was unharmed apart from the shock.
>
> We had an NCO called Fuchs. When we went to his hut next morning, all we found of him was bits of flesh that looked like goulash. I suppose that he heard a noise, went out of the door and the Russians threw a live grenade at his feet and blew him to pieces. We found one of his hands on the bunker roof.
>
> Fuchs had recently come back from occupied Norway because nothing was happening there and he was bored. And look what happened to him!

This was only one of the many fearful sights of carnage Cranz remembers:

> One soldier fell beside me, his thigh had been ripped away and I tried to tie off the wound with a rope from an ammunition box. But the blood just shot out. I don't think he survived. He was taken away by medics and we never saw him again. There was also a man named Hanson. He came from Hamburg. He, too, fell beside me and at first it looked as if he wasn't badly injured, just a small cut on his neck. But his jugular vein was severed and the blood shot out like a fountain all over the place, and he was dead.

Benedikt Sieb was laying mines to prevent the Russians breaking through when he came under frenetic Russian fire. He was injured and the sequel was gruesome as well as terrifying:

The Russians were everywhere there with tanks; they could drive because the ground was frozen hard. They attacked left, right and centre. We had to lay mines quickly so that the tanks couldn't break through. I went to fetch the mines with an NCO, the Russians were firing their shells, we jumped from ditch to ditch, the grenades exploded all around us. I thought, "Damn, you won't be getting out of here again." Because if I got hit I was sure there would be only ash left over.

The NCO was more frightened than I was, he grabbed hold of me tightly from behind, and a shell exploded behind us, and he sort of saved my life. Because the shell exploded behind, ripped his fingers open and I had these shrapnel pieces all over me, the shrapnel about 10cm in size, you can't imagine it, the size of them. Had he not had his hands in between, they would have gone right through me. Now I had all these pieces of shrapnel inside me, I could not walk. I felt as if I had been hypnotized. No one was going to come and rescue me with all this shooting going on.

So I crept on all fours towards the bunker and they pulled me in there. They said, "You have to be carted off straight away", because I was full of blood and I had the bones – pieces of his fingers – stuck in my back-side. They took me to this "death bunker", but there was heavy shooting all around. The Russians shot at everything, at the dressing stations as well.

When I was packed in that bunker, I noticed this groaning, thought: "What's groaning here? – there are others in here." And it was the dying. They died, you could tell, because their last cries was always for their mothers. I thought: "Damn, how will you get out of here? If you keep on bleeding you'll meet the same fate." Then a medic arrived and shouted into the bunker, "Are there any living in here? If there are, you'll have to come out by yourselves – with this shooting going on we won't get you out." I said, "OK, I'll try" and I crept out on all fours towards the operating bunker. When I arrived I saw all these bones lying around and eyes and all that.

I was taken to Staiarussa, where the doctor gave me an anaesthetic straight away and dug out all the splinters. Later I felt my backside and noticed huge holes, wounds. They had cut out a lot so it wouldn't rot. Now I was lucky that they tried to get me out of the bunker, and that was difficult. On the way to Staiarussa, a number of times they left me standing in the middle of the road and ran to seek cover. I thought, "If you get a direct hit now, that'll be the end of you." But thankfully I made it.

From Staiarussa, Sieb made a nightmare journey to Riga, the capital of Latvia:

I was loaded on to a transport together with Austrians who were sick, and was sent to Riga. But the Austrians didn't treat us well, said, "If we give you food and drink and look after you, then you'll only shit and piss here." They didn't give us anything. I starved for three days. That's the way it is. When you are at the front, it's really about survival, everyone wants to survive, no one bothers about comradeship or whatever and the officers didn't bother about us. They were in a dilemma, they wanted to survive too. We ordinary soldiers were just cannon fodder.

It was hardly surprising that, when asked what their worst experience in Russia was, many Germans named the remorseless style of Russian warfare. Henning Kardell was one of them:

We were on the eastern side of the River Neva near Leningrad and the Soviet army had made a bridgehead across the ice. The trench fighting was intense. We had so many corpses – both Russian and German – that we couldn't bury them, so we just piled them on top of each other. The nearest thing to a proper grave was the earth we put between them. Then it snowed and everything froze solid. Our trenches consisted of corpses. We had rats. They chewed their way through the corpses and were as big as cats. I was only 19 and it was very hard for me.

But there were more horrors to come:

Our situation was so bad I tried to find a way out of the noose – we were encircled. I had risen in rank by then, from non-commissioned officer to lieutenant. The soldiers trusted me and crept after me. Then the Russian tanks arrived and rolled over about 100 of them, so that their legs and arms flew off.

That's what the fighting was like and when I heard this terrible screaming, I was lucky enough to be able to jump into a ditch. I jumped and was up to my neck in snow. I heard voices from above telling me to give myself up. Suddenly the Russians were throwing hand grenades. They exploded beside me, but I suppose the snow deadened their effect. As the tanks had no more ammunition they drove away. I was taken prisoner by the Russians on the same evening.

That experience with the tanks was the worst thing I ever lived through. So many of my comrades were crushed to death by tanks and I saw it all. Besides myself, only a sergeant and another non-commissioned officer survived.

In Russia, Leningrad was a disaster for the Germans second only to Stalingrad. They besieged and blockaded Leningrad, but the struggle resolved itself into a battle of attrition punctuated by attempts on both sides to break the deadlock. Ultimately the Russians triumphed, but it took 868 intense days of some of the most gruelling fighting in the Second World War.

Henning Kardell was posted to Leningrad from the Crimea as a result of the German success in overcoming Sevastopol and Kerch, where the land and sea fortifications were the strongest in the world. They had fallen in July 1941, and Kardell remembers being told that whoever could take these mighty fortresses could also take Leningrad, which was surrounded by six major fortification areas.

The battle for Leningrad began on August 19, 1941, when the Russians opened up with artillery fire aimed at the German forces moving in from the south. Before long it was clear that the Germans were getting nowhere, even though their presence was strong enough to prevent a breakthrough by a Russian relief force moving in from the Volkhov area. The stalemate persisted. The Russians were unable to get through. The Germans were unable to take Leningrad or, as Kardell puts it, both sides were "second in winning".

Kardell also recalls that the German forces lacked a very important advantage: "The Luftwaffe were all flying to Stalingrad, so we had no Luftwaffe and we couldn't do much without the Luftwaffe."

The monumental struggle for Stalingrad had begun only four days after the battle at Leningrad, and resolved itself into the bloodiest kind of close-quarter combat, with the Germans fighting their way through building by building, sometimes room by room, against defenders who fought for every pile of rubble down to the last brick.

Herr Senneberg received a taste of the fanatically savage Russian resistance which prevented him from reaching the battle area itself:

> On November 22, 1942 we arrived in Kalatsh. Kalatsh is a town on the Don which has a bend there, it was only a few kilometres to the bend in the River Volga. Kalatsh was the last station on the rail line before Stalingrad and we were supposed to be getting off there. But the Russians were already firing at the station. We had to leave the train, and try to find cover while mortar shells exploded around us. We were told that we could no longer get to our troop inside Stalingrad, because a few hours before, the Russians had closed the ring around the city.

There was nothing to do now but retreat, but the Italian and Romanian troops fighting with the Germans were already withdrawing – and fast:

> Italian and Romanian troops streamed past us en masse – the Russians had broken through in their sections and closed the pocket. I don't mean to suggest that the Italians and Romanians were inferior fighters: they were badly trained and badly equipped, and the Russians knew that.
>
> Then we retreated ourselves, and encountered more and more survivors who had managed to get out of Stalingrad. We were formed into a so-called Marschkompanie, a "trained replacement company", which was supposed to put up resistance. We fought against the Russians continuously and we went through villages where the people said to us, "How is that possible? Yesterday troops from the Red

Army were here, today you're here!" They couldn't understand it, there was total confusion.

In my opinion, theoretically, if the Russians had had enough troops at that time, they could have marched on through to the Ukraine. But instead they tried to stabilize the German front lines. We arrived at the River Donitz. It was partially frozen and we were positioned to prevent a Russian landing on the opposite bank. It became very quiet then, there was hardly any fighting. But we saw our planes flying over, the Ju-52, a transport plane and the He-111, the Heinkel 111, a bomber, which always flew in the direction of Stalingrad. And as we observed them, sometimes only half of them came back.

Afterwards Senneberg was involved in a second attempt to get into Stalingrad, this time by air:

One day we were told, "You are going to be flown in, you have to be flown into Stalingrad" and we were put on standby and taken to an air base to be loaded into transport planes. There had been two airports in Stalingrad where the German planes could still land, but one of them was overwhelmed by the Russians, so that there was only one available and they could no longer fly us in. The fighting went on and we were to be pulled out, the remainder of the troops from Stalingrad.

We were formed up and marched off to Germany, to Spremberg, where the remnants of the former tank-infantry battalion 125, which had fallen at Stalingrad, were gathered together. They were injured men or men who had just been flown out. Some were on leave, and we who had been due to go to Stalingrad, and all the leftovers, were going to be formed into a new battalion. The veterans who had marched on Stalingrad said to us, "Hopefully we'll get better tanks now", because they had marched on Stalingrad with tanks that had been looted, 3.5 or even weaker, though sometimes there would be a 7.5 there too. They didn't think much of them – they called them "equipment for knocking on tanks". We were inferior to the Russians as far as tanks were concerned.

Once we had been withdrawn, we were told that we would be getting the 8.8-calibre, a long-barrelled gun which was mounted on a tank. Although we were protected by armour, the tank was open at the top. A normal tank could swing its turret, but we couldn't do that. We had an action radius of only 45 degrees, the rest was up to the driver, who had to direct the tank to the left or right. When the Russians shells came over a distance, we heard the driver say, "There's one coming" and then we took cover quickly, in the deepest hole we could find.

Leningrad was a different kind of battle from Stalingrad. It was a stranglehold affair, as the Germans tried to starve the Russians out while shelling them continuously from a distance. It was a slow and, for the Germans, ultimately unsuccessful business. The battle for Leningrad lasted a year longer than Stalingrad and cost 100,000 German lives. Henning Kardell remembers seeing one German die at Leningrad in the name of comradeship:

The comradeship in Russia was always a great experience, even when it had its tragic side. When we were in the trenches at Leningrad, the Russians were only about 200 metres away, close enough for us to hear them talking, and certainly close enough for them to throw hand grenades into our trenches. I remember one German soldier fell in the minefields in front of the barbed wire and yelling for help. There were mines round about and because we didn't know where they were, I forbade everyone to leave the trenches, so that no one else would get killed. But the soldier was the close comrade of one of my men. He went out to bring his friend back and was killed when he trod on a mine. We mourned that man, for his courage and his self-sacrifice. What he had done was the most one man could do for another.

CHAPTER THREE

The U-Boat War:
Days of Success 1939–42

U-BOAT WARFARE has all the hallmarks of guerrilla fighting. It is furtive and clandestine. It relies on the silent, stealthy approach, the ambush and the fast escape before the enemy can respond. Surprise is its natural currency. Between 1939 and 1945 it took exceptional men with exceptional nerve to fight this kind of war, and do it in an enclosed, claustrophobic atmosphere from the unnatural confines of the world beneath the sea.

The German surface raiders – Bismarck, Scharnhorst, Gneisenau,

Admiral Hipper and the pocket battleship Admiral Graf Spee – received most of the publicity in the Second World War at sea. They acquired a glamorous reputation for daring, even in Britain. The Royal Navy's pursuit of the Graf Spee, which was scuttled by her captain, Hans Langsdorff, outside Montevideo harbour on December 17, 1939 as the British task force waited for her, had all the makings of a Greek tragedy in which a noble adversary was driven to death by an unkind fate. Despite their headline-making successes, the activities of the German surface ships were curtailed by the overwhelming strength of the Royal Navy and they had only a minor influence on the conduct, and outcome, of the war in the Atlantic. The U-boats, in fact, did the great majority of the work.

At the start of the war the U-boats were relatively few – only 57 in all, a fraction of the huge fleet Hitler had promised Rear Admiral Karl Dönitz, commander of the Kriegsmarine's submarine arm. Even so, their importance was fully realized and so was the special nature of submarine warfare. Great care was taken to ensure that crews were an elite. Health requirements for men serving on the U-boats were much more stringent than they were for other combatants. Ernst Günther Röhde was one of the few who passed the test:

> If you were physically healthy, then you could join the Navy, but for the U-boats, they were a special breed who underwent a special medical examination to ensure that they were what was called "fit for U-boats". When I volunteered at the end of 1940, they first of all put me through the mangle, as we called it, in every aspect of my health and I was pronounced "fit for U-boats".

Even then, the numbers who actually served on the U-boats could be whittled down, as Herbert Lange remembers: "There were 20 of us who were selected as being fit to serve in the U-boats and we had to go straight to Wilhelmshaven for a medical inspection. After that only eight men were left, eight men who satisfied the health and fitness regulations. I was one of them. We were all proud of that, I have to say."

U-boat crews went through intensive training before putting to sea. Ernst Günther Röhde recalls the daily routine, which was hard going:

I was with the training commando in Memel. We went out every day with four torpedoes in the tubes and four in reserve which we used as replacements. There was a target ship, the Daressalam, which sailed around in a square and sometimes a boat would suddenly appear. You have to fire at this angle or at that angle, and the torpedoes ran 10 or 11 metres below the surface and ran underneath the ship. We had acoustic equipment on board and in the head of the torpedo, where the dynamite is normally packed, there was a large searchlight and when it ran below the ship we could see exactly if it had run towards the bow, amidships or astern. They went for three or four kilometres to where there were torpedo recovery ships.

Once the pressurized air had escaped from the torpedoes, then, because the head had such a large volume, it stood upright in the water. At the front there was carbide, which gave off smoke and smelled horrible when it came in contact with the water. The torpedo recovery ship was able to see clearly where the torpedo was, bobbing around in the water, because it was only 55cm in diameter and just about six metres long and moved with the currents. They were recovered, and prepared for reuse on the recovery ships.

At the base in Memel they were handed over to a tender, where they were refilled with pressurized air. That happened each day over the whole week and two or three times during the night when we had to practise night firing, which had to be practised at night. We could only fire if the wind was no stronger than force five – the boats could have withstood more, but a torpedo weighed perhaps 2,000 kilos, 2,000–3,000 kilos – and we couldn't cope with a wind stronger than force five. We did that every day and for the crew it was unpleasant. Normally on the sea, you sailed for half a day underwater, but we had to surface each time we had fired and then on alarm we had to dive again.

Then came the day when all this practice was going to be put to use in real battle. Herbert Lange was already on board the U-28, out in the Atlantic, west of Ireland, when war was declared on September 3, 1939:

I remember the radio message coming through: "Hostilities against England have been opened." We didn't shout, "Hooray"; we said, "Hm!" If that's the way it has to be, we told ourselves, then roll up your sleeves and get on with it. We weren't actually pleased about it. We knew that our adversary, England, was a hard adversary. No, we weren't that enthusiastic. We had all volunteered, the U-boats were somehow something special. But we knew it wasn't going to be easy.

The German U-boat campaign was limited warfare at the start but over the first 12 months restrictions were gradually removed. The early strategy was to prowl British waters making daylight attacks from periscope depth. The submarines would concentrate on the slowest and therefore the easiest quarry, and found easy prey attacking lone merchant ships. Most of the destruction of Allied ships took place on the surface at this time. Almost before the crew of a ship knew what was happening, a U-boat would suddenly appear from the depths and let loose with its deck gun or torpedoes.

An attack on the surface was potentially a dangerous manoeuvre. Surfacing meant a U-boat was at risk from destroyers or aircraft that were prowling the area. It was necessary frequently, because the electric motors needed regular recharging. Even so, there were benefits, and Herbert Lange enjoyed them: "After some time submerged, we needed air. And during the first year of the war we sailed on the surface a lot, so that as far as our health was concerned, it was lovely, breathing in the fresh Atlantic air."

Surfacing and diving underwater became a regular routine. The U-boats surfaced at night to recharge their batteries and remained there for about four hours, from 2000 hours to midnight. When the batteries were full, the U-boat dived below the surface, resurfaced shortly before daybreak to air the boat and then remained submerged for the rest of the day. The routine did not always go smoothly, but Kurt Wehling remembers a trick the crew on his U-boat played to get out of trouble:

If there were planes around chasing us when we surfaced at night, we would release air balloons with strips of silver foil attached. They floated just above the water with their strips of silver. It was like flypaper. The planes homed in on the silver strips and dropped their bombs on them instead of on us! There were lots of tricks we played!

Spreading oil on the surface was a ploy the Germans used to make their pursuers think a U-boat had been sunk, since when submarines were hit by depth charges, oil came up to the surface automatically. Another trick was designed to fool the sonar (named ASDIC) the British used early on in the war to detect submarines. The early ASDIC, which was less effective than the later 147 HOLDIKS ASDIC, was a simple listening device designed to pick up propeller noise. It was very unreliable, losing contact when depth-charging a U-boat. The Germans particularly found it easy to defeat ASDIC in shallow waters: they just shut down their engines and lay silent on the seabed until the searchers went away.

The first German "kill" of the war was controversial. On September 4, 1939 U-30 sank the Athenia, a British passenger liner, with the loss of 118 lives. Contrary to the London Naval Agreement of 1935, the passengers were not taken off before the vessel was attacked. Britain regarded this as an atrocity, but the Germans claimed the British had themselves destroyed the Athenia in order to provide an excuse to get round another clause in the Naval Agreement: the ban on arming merchant vessels.

According to Werner Ziemer, a vessel carrying armaments, a merchant ship or any other, was easy to identify: "You could tell if there was war material on board by the amount of weaponry carried on the decks. In the early part of the war a boarding party would be sent on board and the ship was searched for contraband. If contraband were found, the crew was taken off in boats and the ship was sunk."

At this early stage the Germans would supply an enemy crew with provisions and tow them to a safe distance before sinking their ship. If they saw enemy sailors in the water, they would fish them out, take them prisoner and then deposit them on a nearby coast. All this gave the submariners a reputation for chivalry. On the Murmansk run to Russia, for example, the U-boat that torpedoed the American freighter Fairfield City after its crew had abandoned ship surfaced afterwards to give the sailors directions towards the nearest land. This, though, became an isolated incident late in the war. As Heinz Reiners explains, the honourable, humanitarian way of fighting did not last: "In the later years of the war it was no longer possible. I experienced this myself: survivors, men swimming in the water would be machine-gunned."

Werner Ziemer had similar experiences:

> Boarding parties were fired at and the hatches on the sides of the ship flew open and U-boat itself was fired upon. This was how the war became more and more merciless, more ruthless on both sides.
>
> Of course, we didn't search a tanker before we sank it. We knew what it was carrying and we weren't going to let the enemy get hold of it. There were also empty ships sailing back to England across the Atlantic. Tonnage was important. If a ship went to the bottom, it couldn't be loaded up again. So we sank the empty ships whenever we got the chance.

Warships were automatic targets for the U-boats. On September 17, 1939 the U-29 sank the aircraft carrier HMS Courageous. This was followed in October by an exploit which greatly raised the profile of German submariners. U-47, commanded by Gunther Prien, managed to penetrate Scapa Flow by night on October 13–14, 1939, and in the confined waters fired two torpedo salvos which sank the battleship HMS Royal Oak. Although U-47 was operating on the surface, she remained undetected and escaped unscathed. At home in Germany, Prien and his crew were hailed as the great buccaneering heroes of the hour, but the bravado ascribed to them was not the most important quality they required.

Clausdieter Oelschlagel considers that, first and foremost, a successful attack required discipline and team work:

> Everyone had to work together on a U-boat. We all depended on each other. One wrong move and it could be disaster for all of us. It was not possible for someone to have a different opinion or to be stubborn or argue. You couldn't work like that. We all had our assigned tasks and we had to interact if we were going to be successful.
>
> We were a very young crew on our U-boat. None of the officers was

more than 24 years old, and the rest of us were aged 18 to 22. The commander was only 25. He was an excellent captain, very disciplined and keen to go into action, but not headstrong or overly daring. We all had a lot of respect for him and when you have a captain like that, discipline comes easily and routine goes smoothly.

On board a U-boat out at sea there was very little leisure for the crew, even during their off-duty hours. Werner Karsties remembers how the engine crews were particularly busy:

The engine crews were on duty in six-hour shifts, six hours on watch, six hours off. During off-duty time they had to try and wash themselves, eat something or get some rest. The junior ratings, from ordinary rating up to to able rating, had to provide the officers with food. So there wasn't much time left over.

If we had been hit or suffered small-scale damage when a depth charge exploded close by, it sometimes happened that the water-level gauges for the tanks burst and had to be renewed or ball bearings had to be exchanged or repairs had to be carried out. That all had to be done during the off-duty hours. If the others couldn't carry out a watch for any reason, then the off-duty men had to fill in there as well. It was the same if there was a leak or we had been hit or whatever. We didn't get much time to ourselves and before we knew it, we were on duty again, looking for ships to attack!

Clausdieter Oelschlagel describes the method U-boats used when making an attack:

When a convoy was seen approaching, we used to dive. From then on, we used our ears. You can hear five times better underwater than you can on the surface. We would listen to the ship's propellers humming above us and making a noise, and then we got the order to man battle stations. The commander sat up in the tower at the targeting periscope, which is in a cylinder. He could move it automatically with his feet, left and right, up and down. The first duty officer was beside him operating the equipment that made calculations for firing the torpedo. We could discharge salvos of two or four torpedoes – the boat had four tubes at the front and one at the rear in the stern. The attack rudder man was also up in the tower.

Down in the control room, the chief engineer was waiting by the hatch to receive the commander's instructions – dive to 12 or 15 metres or whatever. The order came to prepare tubes one and four, and when the commander was in the firing position he said, "Fire!" and then tube one discharged.

Once the torpedo was out and moving, the stopwatch was started to check if the distance was approximately right. Sometimes the torpedoes missed their targets, but if they exploded, then the U-boat crew knew they had another success. Herbert Lange recalls that, even so, there was no joy in it: "In my boat, no one shouted, "Hooray!" It was more like, "Oh, God, the poor devils!"

Karl Ohrt remembers the tactics employed on his own U-boat:

Mostly we used to see the ships on the horizon when we were sailing on the surface. Along the line of the horizon we saw a ship's mast or bridge or whatever. Then the type of ship was identified from a book, so that Germans didn't sink a German ship . We would try to get up close and sink the ship while we were on the surface if it was possible, but if that wasn't possible, then we would get in front of it and try to make out its direction of travel – because they mostly sailed in a zigzag – in order to determine where we could strike at it. Working out the direction of Allied ships wasn't easy: they used to zigzag across the ocean in order to frustrate us!

A vital prerequisite to scoring a success was that everything should be done very quietly. If the crewmen talked, it was in a whisper. There were no loud commands, no sounds at all that could be heard by the enemy.

Werner Ziemer remembers the efforts that had to be made on board a U-boat to remain undetected: "Air and electricity had to be used sparingly. There was hardly any movement in the boat, you didn't even eat, just drank a little. We had to take great care that we didn't rattle anything."

Clausdieter Oelschlagel was first duty officer, manning the torpedo calculator during an attack:

> I used to stand beside the commander in the tower and enter his instructions into the torpedo calculator. These calculators became more and more complicated during the course of the war. Torpedoes didn't always run in a straight line, they ran out on a 90-degree path to the right and then out to the left. They were the LUT or Lageunhabhängieger torpedoes, which could be discharged from any position. Then there were torpedoes that turned in circles within the convoy.

Once a hit had been made, the sounds made by a torpedoed ship breaking apart and sinking were fearful. They could be heard quite clearly through the water and the message from above was unmistakable. Werner Ritter von Voigtländer heard doomed ships in their death throes many times: "Absolutely horrible, to tell the truth, were what the experts so nicely described as 'breaking bulkheads and sinking noises'. When a steamer sank, the remaining air whistled through the gaps and it howled and cracked."

A U-boat attack was made that much easier when the target was silhouetted against the sky at night and it was even clearer if another vessel in the convoy was already in flames and lit up the surrounding area. The submarine crew had no time to hang around to watch their handiwork once a hit had been scored. The first order of business was to escape and survive. Werner Ziemer recalls that in the U-boat war, the will to survive was the only emotion: "It was us or them. We had no other choice. We couldn't stick ourselves in the sand to hide or crawl back to some safe position, like they could on land. Once you'd fired your torpedoes, the enemy knew you were there and had a pretty good idea of where you were, too."

The torpedoes were at one and the same time a U-boat's deadly weapon and its Achilles heel. As the torpedoes sped towards their intended victim, the telltale pattern in the water gave the submarine's position away. From then on it was a battle for survival, with the U-boat trying to outwit the enemy in a tense and deadly game of hide and seek.

A pattern of depth charges laid in a spread could either destroy the U-boat or cause enough damage to force it to the surface. And there the guns of the enemy would be waiting for it. The hunter had become the hunted. Kurt Wehling knew exactly how it felt when positions were reversed and the U-boat became the prey:

> We had surface torpedoes and you could see them, so the ships were warned. Also, torpedoes which didn't hit their targets gave us away because they were self-detonating. So if there was an explosion, nearby ships in the area knew there was a U-boat about. Then it started, the sirens sounded, we didn't hear them, but we knew they were giving the alarm. The destroyers were started searching because the torpedoes had given us away. We dived straight away and they searched for our U-boat with their equipment. The first depth charges dropped down and they exploded, you can hear that. If they are too close, the lights go out and the emergency lighting is switched on and depending on how the depth charges were falling, we would go down deeper still.

The radio operator on board a U-boat was particularly vulnerable when the depth charges started falling. He would give a verbal warning to the rest of the crew. "Wasserbomben!" he said, "Depth charges", but he would have to take off his earphones immediately, otherwise the noise that came through them would have burst his eardrums.

If a U-boat managed to elude pursuit after the first depth charges were dropped, then a crew was not too badly off. Rudolf Guttmann records a lucky escape:

> We went down as fast as possible and all we noticed were the depth charges, there were no direct hits. And we had a terrific helmsman; the engines aren't used underwater, nothing, everything is quiet, and the helmsman was on the ball. There are naval maps on which the sea currents are drawn and he managed to turn the boat into deeper water with the currents, without any engine noise. And the deeper you are, the less effective the depth charges are, and because of that we got out unscathed.

The real attrition in U-boat warfare came in a depth-charge chase. Then the going really got tough. The U-boat would be constantly battered by shock waves, causing objects to fly around and the lights to go out. For Herbert Lange, being depth-charged was a thoroughly nerve-racking experience:

> When we were being hunted with depth charges, it tore at your nerves and spirit. It was terrible all right. And if anyone says that he wasn't afraid, he's lying. Depth charges were truly nerve-racking. There were some comrades who were on the edge of cracking up; but we managed to control them each time.
>
> Twice while I was on the U-952 I experienced really heavy depth-charge attacks, once off the coast of Greenland, which lasted for about eight hours. Afterwards our boat was so damaged that we could only just manage to creep home. During the hunt off Greenland, the torpedo tube became twisted, the attack periscope was faulty and various other things went wrong – there were cracks in the battery, gas formed because of the acid. We were in a terrible state. We were no longer fit for battle. That happened on our first voyage in the U-952, but in a way it had a good effect. It welded the crew together, made us a team, we wanted to look after each other after that.
>
> On the other occasion, in the Mediterranean, there was another hunt with depth charges which went on from early morning into the afternoon. We escaped from the field of the location soundings by means of a zigzag trick. The Mediterranean is a very salty sea and there were layers of salt in which the soundings didn't work. We were lucky enough to sail into one of these salt layers and the enemy lost us.

Herbert Lange remembers how important comradeship and discipline were when the boat was under attack:

> Everyone is at his station so that if a valve blows out or water breaks in, someone is always there to attempt to repair the damage. There are always men with strong nerves who lead those with weak nerves by the hand, so to speak, and say, "Keep calm! We'll get

through it." You have to be an optimist, especially if you're an officer, or a helmsman, because the crew look to you to see how you are behaving, whether you are trembling or not. You have to show yourself to be strong, be an example and say, "Come on, lads, it's not that bad."

Not all crewmen under the intense pressure of the depth charges were able to view the situation with such equanimity. One sailor on Werner Ritter von Voigtländer's U-boat lost his nerve completely:

This man – he was one of our deep-sea helmsmen – leapt up during a depth-charge chase. We'd already been chased for more than a day, with a few interruptions, but the depth charges always resumed. It was just too much for this fellow. He leapt up and turned on the main pressurized air distributor, on the "Christmas tree" we called it, where all the distributors for the individual flooding chambers were – where there's a large wheel for the pressure adjustment. He wanted to get the boat up to the surface. We'd all have been goners if that had happened, but this man was so far out of his mind that he didn't care.

Fortunately our control-room mate, Willy Difflüh, calmly tapped his skull with a spanner and he tipped over and collapsed, Willy turned the "Christmas tree" off again, and we rolled this fellow head down in a hammock, tied it up and lay him down in a corner so that he couldn't do anything else stupid.

The incident had caused problems inside the U-boat:

After that we had the problem of air in the diving chambers. There's water in them if you are underwater, but when the boat moved this way or that way, then the air rumbled from the rear to the front and the noise of the water was horrible – you could hear it all over the place. Meanwhile the enemy was up above, so we couldn't expel it through the main air duct because a huge bubble would rise to the surface and give our position away.

All the same, we managed to survive and the fellow who'd lost his nerve was later given a desk job at Brest with the flotilla there. Our commander hadn't reported him or anything, but officially the man could have been court-martialled. He wasn't any use, really, he was a bit weak. During the rest of the trip he wasn't put on watch, but was given other jobs.

Werner Ritter von Voigtländer's own personal bugbear was the ASDIC:

We heard it go, "Ping ping … ping ping"! Then gravel would rattle across our deck, and we knew they'd got us again. We listened and heard "Bloop!" and it gurgled a bit and the depth charges were on their way. As soon as the first charge exploded, we set our engines to half or full speed ahead. We brought the boat to the surface and the main bilge pumps were switched on. That expelled the water which had forced its way into the boat.

We used to count the depth charges. They came in series of five … one, two, down came the third and the fourth. Once the fifth had exploded – "Whoomph!" – then everything was switched off and we stood there in our socks going at 1.5mph. Often we thought: "We're not going to get away! We've had it!" One hour, not even that, three quarters of an hour at full speed would take us seven and a half miles, and then the battery was empty. We crept along and it was a real game of cat and mouse.

They were up there, we were down below. We turned a little left here and little right, then left again and so on. Of course, we tried to deceive the enemy, pretend we'd sunk. We had a very small torpedo tube and we ejected a cartridge from it. This formed a spread of gas bubbles in the water and the ASDIC could pick it up. We waited to see if the ruse had succeeded. It was a very tense moment, but if the gas bubbles had worked, we noticed, because the depth charges began to fall a few hundred metres astern. Then we relaxed, we were happy.

Karl Ohrt remembers another trick played by the U-boats with a weapon called a "pill thrower":

If we were travelling underwater and had been located – location was mostly carried out through soundings – a diesel engine makes a certain sound. The "pill-thrower" used to imitate this sound. It was fired by the men in the engine room. The people on the ship hunting us would hear it and follow it, perhaps sailing in the direction of the "pill" for 20 minutes or half an hour. By the time they realized they were on a wild goose chase, we'd sailed some distance ourselves and it was much more difficult for our pursuers to find us again.

Escape from pursuing hunters was a tense experience for Clausdieter Oelschlagel:

We sat totally still, almost on top of one another, mostly in the bow in order to keep the boat down. All you could do was to count the depth charges.

When a depth charge went off, there was an enormous bang. The whole boat would leap up in one piece, dust flew everywhere, all the dust from behind the tubes flew out, the whole boat went "Whoomph!" and then everything fell down again. There was just an unbelievable noise. Dreadful.

The lights were turned out so as not to use additional electricity and we kept quiet so as not to use up too much oxygen. That was important too, not to use up too much oxygen in the longer diving periods and later when we were lying on the seabed.

The carbon dioxide that began to build up after a while had some alarming effects. At first the boat was full of fresh air, but as the dive proceeded, that began to change:

When the boat travelled on the surface, masses of fresh, cool air came into the chamber at the very front, in the bow. The diesel engines running in the stern sucked the air through the entire boat. At the moment when there was an alarm dive the boat was full of fresh air; that was a great advantage: the air wasn't stale in the chambers but exactly as it was on deck.

After a while, though, we used to start breathing very quickly because the build-up of carbon dioxide was affecting us. We began to feel very light-headed, but we couldn't do anything about it. The

Rudolf Guttmann, a U-boat crewman. Gutmann was a galley cook, preparing meals alone for 48 men.

U-boat volunteer Kurt Wehling, who made six trips on U-73.

Putting out to sea in a U-boat. Mortality rates soon grew to catastrophic proportions.

Werner Ritter von Voigtländer today, reunited with U-boat comrades.

Von Voigtländer as a Second Duty Officer in the German navy.

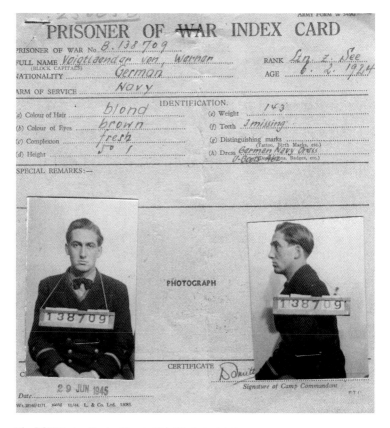

The POW Index Card with von Voigtländer's details.

Werner Karsties, who joined the German navy as a 19-year-old volunteer in 1940, rising to the rank of first mate by the end of the war.

Ernst Günther Röhde as an 18-year-old U-boat volunteer. The crews of these vessels were "a special breed" and had to be passed as "fit for U-boats".

Rohde and his comrades take the oath in Breda, in the Netherlands.

A U-boat in dock. Helmut Benzing would spend five years in a prisoner of war camp as a result of his time as a crew member.

Hamburg-born Helmut Benzing, pictured in 1943. "I built the U-boats – 1 didn't want to sail in them."

Benzing in 1950, on his release as a prisoner of war. "We worked day and night and could launch one U-boat every 10 days."

The unusual toilet arrangements aboard U-293. The year is 1943.

Helmut Benzing's pay book and identity card.

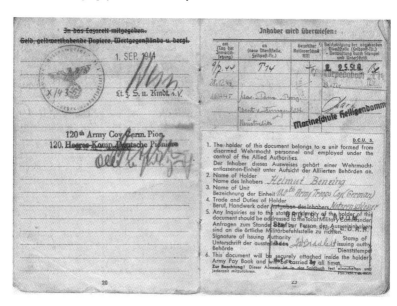

Heinrich Schmidt receiving the Italian Award for bravery in 1942. "The third 'eel', as we called our torpedoes, penetrated the Barham's ammunition chamber and the ship sank within a few minutes. It was sad. We heard later that 846 people on board had been drowned."

Heavily bearded after weeks at sea, these men receive long-awaited mail from home. Heinrich Schmidt is second from the left.

June 6, 1942; Schmidt receives the German Cross.

Clausdieter Oelschlagel in 1939, before his conscription to the German navy. "It was depth charges here, depth charges there, depth charges everywhere. It ruined our nerves considerably."

Oelschlagel with fellow cadets at the beginning of the war. "Everyone had to work together on a U-boat. We all depended on each other. One wrong move and it could be disaster for all of us."

Heinz Reiners (left), photographed with a comrade in 1940. Reiners was sunk three times during a mission to Narvik. "Three times into the ice-cold water up there in Norway!"

Reiners's Narvik badge. "I experienced this myself: survivors, men swimming in the water, would be machine-gunned."

DIE EHRE DES SOLDATEN LIEGT IM BEDINGUNGSLOSEN EINSATZ SEINER PERSON FÜR DAS VOLK UND VATERLAND BIS ZUR OPFERUNG SEINES LEBENS.

This propaganda poster reads, "A soldier's honour is found in his unconditional commitment to his people and his fatherland even at the sacrifice of his own life."

Herbert Lange, who served as an NCO in the German navy throughout the war.

Ernst Preuss, an NCO in the 20th Armoured Infantry Division. "In 1945, you would have had to be an incorrigible optimist to believe that the war could still be won. The war could not be won. Everybody with any sense knew that."

Eckhart Strasosky. "Either we defended ourselves to the last, or we would be crushed, but it was very hard, fighting the Russians."

Strasosky, pictured with his mother and sister in 1940. "I was wounded three times, the third time in the knees through artillery shrapnel in an artillery attack on our position."

Ernst Preuss poses for the camera on an armoured car. "When we heard that Hitler had been killed on the front line in the service of the Fatherland, we thought, 'Thank God, the war is over.'"

Huh! wie ist es kalt geworden.

"Brrr! It's so cold." By a freak coincidence, the winter of 1941, when the Germans were struggling in the Russian campaign, was one of the coldest on record.

Wrapped up for the Russian winter. Leo Mattowitz recalls:"It was minus 40 degrees by then. The cold was unimaginable. I'd never known anything like it."

A German column in the snow. Karl Meding remembers: "I had to live in a fox-hole for several weeks, from Christmas Day 1942 until the end of January 1943. There were wooden poles over it and on that lay hay and on top of that, snow. The temperature had dropped even lower by that time. It was minus 40 degrees."

Operation Barbarossa – the Germans advance into Russia in June 1941.

ventilation couldn't be regulated so well below the surface. Normally it was passed through some sort of a calcium filter and pumped out with a fan, but when you dived down to the seabed with the enemy above you couldn't switch the equipment on.

Once a U-boat had managed to elude its pursuers, any damage caused by the depth charges or the result of wear and tear had to be repaired out at sea. Werner Ziemer was literally in the middle of the Atlantic Ocean when his boat developed rudder trouble:

> I volunteered for the job. The side rudder had started to make a noise and had to be greased. That could only be done on the surface. So I did it, and was awarded the Iron Cross, First Class for it. What I'd done, you see, was save the boat and the crew. But it was crazy, really. What would have happened if an air raid had taken place or a destroyer had appeared in front of the bow while I was doing the job? You don't think of that at the time, but afterwards, when you've got time to reflect, you realize that the boat would have had to dive and I would have been left floundering in the ocean.
>
> That actually happened once, when we'd been attacked by gunfire. Two members of the crew lay dead on deck. Heaven knows if they were really dead or not. Considering what happened soon after, I hope they were. They collapsed up there, one of them had been shot in the head and the other one fell over. We never saw them again because they were still on the upper deck when we had to dive. The others came storming over because the alarm had been given. They jumped down the hatch, the hatch was closed and the boat dived. But when you were out on deck, you tried not to think about that sort of thing happening. You did your duty and that was the first consideration.

Despite their vulnerable, essentially isolated position when at war, U-boat crews enjoyed, or rather assumed, privileges not open to their compatriots in other services. Soldiers, for example, were very carefully monitored for correct behaviour. Any sign of deviation from the strict Nazi line, the slightest hint of criticism or dissent, was heavily punished.

U-boat crews, on the other hand, were much freer to express themselves and on Werner Ritter von Voigtländer's boat, they felt a sort of comrade-ship with their British opponents:

> Just imagine: we used to sing our English shanties on duty! "Rolling Home" or "Blow the Man Down"! Even Adolf Hitler couldn't stop us doing it. Before the war I had served time in a juvenile prison because we had copied English jazz records and so on, when we were at school. Jazz was forbidden, of course. But we had some of these same records, and we played them on board, with great enthusiasm.
>
> The Nazis could interfere with us only when we were in harbour. I remember that we were once berthed in Wilhelmshaven when a Nazi Party official, a political guidance officer, came on board. The Nazis must have known what we did at sea, because they didn't trust the U-boat men past the end of their noses. Anyway, this official got short shrift from our captain. He said, "You know what, you're in the way. You have no life jacket, you have no respirator kit, you have no idea – go back home, we can't use you!" I was amazed. It was a very brave thing to do, but our captain just bundled that official off the ship, sent him unceremoniously home.

Even when in port, U-boat crews had a tendency to break the rules. Karl Ohrt once helped smuggle a small dog on board:

> We had a dog when were sailing out on commander training even though it was verboten to have dogs on board. We had sailed back from Gotenhaven, it was night time, evening and a small dog, a puppy, crossed our path. He kept following us, whimpering. We couldn't just leave him, so my mate held the dog when we passed the guards and gave in our cards. They didn't notice, and we brought him on board the boat. We managed to keep him for six weeks. No one knew he was there, not an officer nor an NCO. No one knew we had a little dog up front in the crew room. It couldn't go on, of course, and one day the dog was discovered. But we decided to have a souvenir and took him up on deck, where everyone who had had anything to do with the dog sat down and we had our photograph taken. The next day we had

to give him in. But by then he was getting too big for us anyway.

When a U-boat sailed into harbour after completing its mission, there would be a pennant flying saying how many tons of shipping its crew had sunk.

If the tonnage exceeded 100,000, the commander was awarded the Knight's Cross. There was a band playing. The girls from the Bund Deutscher Mädel – the female version of the Hitler Youth – were there to greet the returning heroes. Heinz Reiners felt proud when his boat sailed in: "We were given extra pay for being on board, working machinery, a danger allowance, a diving allowance, a basic allowance and our regular pay. We were heroes, no doubt of that. So when we sailed in, we lifted the roof in the harbour. We went a bit wild."

It was understandable. U-boat crews were young men, often very young men, operating at sea in a state of extreme tension. Life on board was hard and often uncomfortable. Werner Ziemer experienced some very cramped conditions:

We were rarely able to take off our clothes, there was one bunk for two men. We also had to take several tons of stores with us and they were stowed away all over the place. When we sailed out of the harbour there were torpedoes between the bunks and on the flooring. The table was laid on top of them and that was how we ate our meals.

The food on board the submarines was good, better than it was in wartime Germany. One man who was well placed to know was Rudolf Guttmann, a butcher in peacetime, who was a cook on the U-boats. Later he went on to become a cook on the famous battle cruiser Gneisenau:

No one complained about the food on the U-boats. There was certainly enough of it. We were spoiled, I suppose – we received "Status 1" food rations. Unfortunately it all tasted of gasoline, but still, no one complained. I didn't have much space for my kitchen. It was the size of a small corner, and there I had to cook meals for 48 men. It's amazing what you can do when you have to!

I did most of the work on my own. The crew used to peel potatoes,

I didn't have to do that. The potatoes, wash the vegetables a bit, they did that. But mostly it was tinned food. We had fresh food only during the first two weeks of an operation. After that it was just tins. The tin opener was my most important tool! If it was broken, I used to use an axe. Chop, chop, chop! But it worked! We had fresh water tanks, there was more than enough drinking water.

During attacks I used to stay in the galley – it was my battle station, so to speak, and everyone remained at their battle stations. If we were submerged and I wanted to fetch 20 or 30 cans for meals from the rear, then I had to inform the control room and they balanced the weight of the boat, pressed water from the front to the back or whatever, because if three or four men went to the rear without telling anyone, the boat would tip over. That didn't happen. The boat floated exactly right, because the weight was adjusted back and forth according to where the men were.

Food was stored everywhere. In the galley, in the toilets at the front, they were crammed full of provisions too. Things hung here and there, shoved between the metal girders and, as I said, in the end it all absorbed the smell and tasted like gasoline.

Clausdieter Oelschlagel found the food was good, gasoline or no gasoline: "It was terrific! We always ate at the table with a knife and fork and so on. No spooning things out of tins like some of our comrades elsewhere. In any case the hardships endured by soldiers in Russia were much worse than those we had to undergo, by and large."

Crews regarded their U-boats as home, and Herbert Lange was very upset when his own craft was destroyed in a bombing raid at Toulon:

Our boat lay in the shipyard, high up in the dock at Toulon, and the crew was on leave. British bombers came over and it was badly damaged. We received a telegram telling us to return to Toulon immediately. We went down to the harbour and saw our boat damaged and lying on its side; then, I have to say, we had tears in our eyes. The boat was our home. It had brought us safely through five operational trips against the enemy and seeing it in that state hurt a lot.

The German submarines were basically very wet, and crews had to live with constant damp:

> We used to call our boat a "stalagmite cave". It was particularly damp at the front section, in the bow, where we kept all the chains and other equipment for transport and bringing the torpedoes into position. Yes, it was wet all right. You got soaking wet on the bridge, if there was a light storm.
>
> We found it very difficult to get clothes and such things dry. All we could do was keep on wearing our wet clothes and wait until they dried out on us. Fortunately we were all young and just shrugged it off. That was the way it was and there was nothing much we could do about it.

Crews washed themselves in sea water desalinated in the engine room, if they washed at all. Washing was something of a luxury on board a U-boat. So was shaving. Many of the German submariners grew beards, which gave them a rather jaunty appearance when they were on leave, but was actually a matter of necessity. While on board, they were like troglodytes, sometimes living for months without seeing daylight. Their world beneath the sea was a malodorous world of sweat, noise, oil and heat. Werner Ziemer put it bluntly: "The air stinks down there. It stinks!"

Diving could be another unsettling experience. The tower hatch on the U-boat was closed and in a very short time water was already splashing over it and the craft was on its way down. Clausdieter Oelschlagel still remembers what it was like:

> When the U-boat was going to dive, you heard the alarm. A switch was thrown, men scrambled through all the rooms and the lights flashed off and on. Until then we'd been using the diesel engines, but now the diesels were stopped and the connection shaft to the e-engine [electric engine] was disengaged. The e-engine was switched on and we went over immediately to full speed.
>
> That was especially important when enemy planes were around. When they attacked or were visible on our tail, we managed to dive down to 50 or 100 metres within 45 seconds from the time the alarm

was given. But if someone was too late in recognizing the plane or the plane swept out of the clouds on an attack course, then it was hair-raising. In some instances it was better to stay on the surface and try to outmanoeuvre the bombs.

When the boat dived, then we normally went down at an angle of 25 to 30 degrees. Sometimes it was more, and then everything that was lying around loose tumbled down around us, including food. There were two deep-sea helmsmen, a chief engineer, and there were deep-sea rudders at the front and the rear. One was turned upwards, the other downwards, and we manoeuvred partly with the engine. We could dive only when we were at full speed.

With all these pressures and discomforts to contend with, it was hardly surprising that, once in harbour, U-boat crews often went to extremes. The authorities ashore were well aware of it: "Onshore we used to be pursued by 'watch dogs', as we called them: the field soldiers or the gendarmerie. Their job was to make sure that we didn't give them the slip. If you travelled to Brest on the train, there were always controls in Metz because everyone knew we were going to play the fool."

Heinz Reiners believes this wild behaviour was justified:

It was like this. We never really knew whether we were going to get home or not. We were a bit superstitious, I suppose. Once a trip was over or almost over, we never said, "We'll be home in three days." We might not get home, we knew that. We heard that this boat was overdue, that boat was overdue. No one knew what had happened to them. It could have been us. So we let loose once we'd reached safe harbour. We went with girls of easy virtue because we had plenty of money and wanted to forget what we'd been through. It seemed the best way, the most obvious way. We often got drunk, too. That's the way it was.

But at heart, it wasn't what we wanted. We wanted some lovely girl to fall in love with, a nice, respectable girl who'd love us in return. But all we had were girls you had to pay and in the end it just made you sick. It's all right for a while, but eventually that way of life just made you sick.

In 1939, 1940 and on into 1941 the German U-boats enjoyed great success. The conquests of Norway and France by June 1940 had increased their range by opening up harbours beyond Germany as new bases of operation. The U-boats took full advantage and between June and October 1940 they sank 274 merchant ships, for the loss of only six submarines. The new bases on the French coast enabled them to patrol much further into the Atlantic, where they posed an even greater threat than before to the vital supplies coming across the ocean from America. This was an indispensable lifeline. If it were cut or crippled, it was perfectly possible that Britain could have been starved into submission.

Rudolf Guttmann recalls the tactics that were used when hunting convoys:

> Our job was to sail up and down through a grid square. Up and down, up and down and so on and continually watch, watch, watch. If we saw any ships we reported them to Admiral Dönitz at U-boat headquarters. There was a large map there and on it they recorded our sightings. Convoys were reported by more than one U-boat. This way it was possible to determine in which direction the convoy was sailing. U-boats from other areas were directed towards the convoy.

The British convoy system nevertheless afforded some protection for the ships it comprised, and together with other anti-submarine tactics, obliged the U-boats to alter their own strategy. They concentrated instead on lone ships or stragglers and if they attacked convoys, they attacked at night.

This put the lookouts on the convoy ships at a great disadvantage. In the early stages of the war convoys still relied mainly on visual observation to detect surfaced submarines. That could be difficult enough by daylight, but at night it was almost impossible. In the dark, the low profile of a U-boat could easily be missed. Consequently the tactic of attacking by night was extremely successful. Enormous tonnages were sunk in this way.

One U-boat commander, Otto Kretschmer of the U-23 and U-99, became a submarine ace, sinking around 238,327 tons in all. During one voyage alone he accounted for seven ships. It was once thought that Kretschmer, who was awarded the Knight's Cross with Oak Leaves and Swords for his exploits, was the first German submarine commander to exceed the quarter-million-ton mark and had achieved it within a fairly short time: before March 27, 1941, when the U-99 was sunk by two British destroyers and he became a prisoner for the rest of the war.

Some two months before the death of Günther Prien, a Welsh collier, the 2,473-ton Sarastone, which was en route from Lisbon to England, caused serious damage to a U-boat and sailed on without completing the kill only because the captain, John Herbert, was under orders not to risk his cargo:

> The chief engineer came to me and explained that our boilers had blown. "We shall have to leave the convoy and take a chance on our own," he said.
>
> Our engines would not carry us faster than two knots. So while the rest of the ships steamed on, we altered course and headed for Lisbon. Two days later the second officer on the bridge shouted down the voice pipe to my cabin: "There's something on the horizon that I don't like, sir." When I got to the bridge I saw what appeared to be a mast about three miles distant. Then I saw it rise higher, until the streaming conning tower of a U-boat emerged.
>
> I put Actions Stations on, and swung the ship round to bring the U-boat astern. But while she was still lying on our quarter, she fired, the shot falling off our starboard side. It was a warning to stop. We kept on. The U-boat's speed was about 15 knots and she overhauled us rapidly for 10 minutes, but without firing. Then, when she was about 4,000 yards away, she loosed five shots. We held our fire. We had only a 12-pounder, but I'd already talked over with my naval gunner, James O'Neill, what we'd do in such a predicament and our plans were made.
>
> The U-boat was getting closer and closer. I held my breath waiting for the moment when we could open fire with hope of damaging her. Her shells fell uncomfortably close to our ship. The submarine was about 2,000 yards off when O'Neill opened fire. His first shot fell short, but in perfect line. He fired again and scored a direct hit.

We all cheered. I shouted, "Go on, O'Neill, give it to him!" His second shot fell at the base of the aft gun, putting it out of action and causing yellow smoke to rise in a cloud. Our third and fourth shots were near misses, but the fifth burst 20 feet abaft the first hit, and the yellow smoke now turned black. After that we sailed on. The U-boat was still firing at us, but the Germans had only one gun left now, and we got away.

The U-boats were chased by British submarines as well as by surface vessels and the duels did not always go the Germans' way. The Royal Navy's HM Submarine Salmon, which damaged the light cruisers Leipzig and Nürnberg during the German invasion of Norway, was somewhere in the North Sea on December 4, 1939 when it came across U-36 on the surface. A member of the Salmon's crew described the action in a letter home:

It was a bright sunny day, two o'clock in the afternoon. This U-boat was chugging along on the surface about two miles ahead of us. We got into position and let go our "tin fish" in quick succession. One of them got her right amidships and cut her clean in half. She went straight to the bottom.

We surfaced and had a quick look round for survivors, but there were none. All we saw was the top half of a man's body with a life jacket holding it up. Pretty grim, but who knows how many innocent women and children might have been killed by that U-boat had we missed her.

Later the same month the Salmon sighted the German steamer Bremen and prepared to attack. Then the steamer's air escort was sighted:

We sighted the steamer during the afternoon and prepared to stop her by firing a shell across her bows. Now, according to international law, a merchant must not be sunk by a man-of-war unless that man-of-war can rescue her entire crew. So the position was that we must tell her to stop and force her to alter her course towards England, but under no circumstances must we attempt to sink her.

We came to the surface, manned the gun, loaded it and were about to fire when we noticed that the Bremen was escorted by half a dozen aircraft. As we are fair game for anyone when we're on the surface, we dived in about 30 seconds and left the gun loaded, the gun crew flying down the hatch as if the devil was after them. If we had fired that gun, I should certainly be dead by now. Those Luftwaffe aircraft would certainly have found and bombed us. This area is full of enemy craft, as we are just outside their base, and it was by the grace of God that we have not been sighted and sunk.

Luckily, neither the Bremen nor the aircraft saw us, so we stayed down until she was well past, then came to the surface again and wirelessed her position, course and speed to the Admiralty.

The Admiralty never caught up with the Bremen. She sank in 1941 after a disgruntled German seaman set her on fire.

Between 1939 and 1941 the United States was not yet a combatant, but the American policy of "all aid short of war" increasingly laid her ships open to U-boat attack. One of them was the destroyer USS Kearney, which was damaged by a torpedo on October 17, 1941, but survived. The USS Reuben James was not so lucky. On October 31, with four other destroyers, she was escorting a North Atlantic convoy 600 miles west of Ireland when she was torpedoed and sunk by the U-552.

The U-boat on which Werner Ziemer served typified the wide range the Germans submarines were able to enjoy at this time:

We sailed from Trondheim on our first operation against the enemy, sailing between the Shetland and Faroe Islands. We weren't chased with depth charges, we got through without a problem; we got hold of a convoy off the coast of England. Our boat sailed on the surface through the escort and we then chose the individual "pots", following the convoy together with other boats up as far as Newfoundland. By the time we got there the convoy had ceased to exist, it was destroyed.

After that we sailed back to the front-line docks in Brest and the First U-Flotilla. We had a short home leave, we were newly equipped and the boat was overhauled before we undertook our second operation, down to the south Atlantic through the Bay of Biscay. We didn't get far before we sank a frigate and a corvette off the coast of Portugal.

By this time, though, British anti-submarine tactics had caught up with Ziemer's U-boat:

> We were still off the Portuguese coast when we got it in the neck, and how! We were attacked by Sunderlands, the RAF flying boats, and when they attacked, all we could see was a wall of flame from left to right, from one end of the wing to the other. The Sunderland shot one of our deep-sea bunkers to pieces. A deep-sea bunker was an oil bunker that was used later as a water bunker, a deep-sea bunker, when the oil had been used up.
>
> Because of that, we left a telltale trail of oil which was clearly seen by the aircraft above, and we were chased with depth charges for a whole day. Our commander was getting tired of all this and turned our boat round, through 360 degrees. "This is ridiculous," he said. So he mixed the old trail of oil with a new one and then they lost us. After the attack by the planes we had two dead and 16 men injured and had to sail back into the front-line docks at Brest.

Germany's legendary Type VII class submarines did most of the fighting in the U-boat war. They were ideally suited for it. The Type VIIs, the convoy-combat boats, had a low conning tower, only 5.2 metres above the surface, and were hard to see even in daylight. At night they were practically invisible, especially when viewed bow-on. These submarines could dive in less than 30 seconds and it was no effort for them to reach depths of 100 metres. They could make double that depth if necessary. The depth and endurance of the Type VIIs were twice that of their Allied counterparts. These U-boats had a range of 7,000 miles, doing 12 knots on the surface, and could travel 90 miles at four knots when submerged. This was steady, but Herbert Lange found it very slow:

> The electric engine could travel at a top speed of only 8mph when we were submerged. At full speed, that meant the battery only had enough power for 90 minutes. We had to be careful, but by going at a slow or at least minimal speed, we could hold out for 24 hours or

more. Of course, we had to surface some time, and that was when the enemy had his chance to chase and destroy us.

Despite the disadvantages, Lange believes the Type VIIs were much better suited to submarine warfare than the Italian or British submarines, even though these were outwardly superior:

> Basically, the German U-boats were not comparable with the Italian, which lay heavily in the water, or even the English ones. Our boats were battleships, so to speak. Later there were bigger boats of approximately 1,000 tonnes, which made longer trips to the Far East. They were also more cumbersome and practically unusable in a convoy battle because they were that much larger. Their losses were correspondingly higher. They were more awkward when diving and if they were hit, then that was the end of them. Mostly there was nothing left. Our Class VII boats were substantially more stable and more robust. The British were afraid of them. They regarded our U-boats with fear and loathing. To them, I suppose, submarine warfare appeared ruthless, cunning and impersonal.

The Class VIIs certainly had remarkable endurance, as was demonstrated by the U-331 after it had torpedoed the battleship HMS Barham off Bardia, Libya, on November 25, 1941 and was forced by British depth charges to go deeper than any U-boat was safely designed to go. Heinrich Schmidt was on board the submarine:

> We received a message one afternoon. It read: "Three English battleships are sailing out of Malta, the Queen Elizabeth, the Barham and the Valiant."
>
> They were protected by eight destroyers and RAF aircraft and sailed across our tubes in the area near Tobruk. We didn't notice them. The ships didn't notice either that we were so close to them, just around 700 metres away.
>
> We knew why these battleships were there: they wanted to put an end to Rommel's African campaign. Our commander was at the periscope and saw the English fleet. Their signal flags were hoisted and that

meant "Attack". Then the Barham turned away and all we saw was a white-grey wall. The commander ordered all four tubes to be made ready, which we did and then we fired a salvo of four.

We hit the Barham from a distance of 500 to 700 metres with a salvo of four torpedoes. The third "eel", as we called our torpedoes, penetrated the Barham's ammunition chamber and the ship sank within a few minutes. It was sad. We heard later that 846 people on board had been drowned. After the Barham was hit, the Valiant approached, intending to ram us, but at that moment the Barham exploded and she had to turn away.

The attack, though successful, had caused the U-331 problems even though the explosion on board the Barham saved the submarine:

Because we now had four empty torpedo tubes, we weren't heavy enough. We didn't flood them immediately, as we should have done, and that's why we went up to a periscope depth of 13.5 metres. But when the Valiant had to turn away, we escaped being rammed. The Valiant fired at us, but way over our heads because the angle was too steep.

Finally, we escaped by going down to extreme depths, but it was risky. Everyone was ordered to the bow to add their weight and we dived. The depth pressure gauge hadn't been switched on and the commander didn't know how deep we were. It read 60 metres, and when we switched on the depth pressure gauge, we discovered that it was more than 200 metres. That's why we were lucky enough to get out of it.

After that we didn't hear the depth charges the British fired at us. We were too deep for that. But we'd done our bit to help Rommel's African campaign and we'd got away with it. Afterwards we received a confirmation from Grand Admiral Dönitz that we had been down deeper than any other 7C boat. Late that evening we started to surface. We went up a metre at a time and surfaced at 11 o'clock at night. We saw an empty Mediterranean: the battleships were no longer to be seen. The sinking of the Barham was kept secret by the English Admiralty until two months later, when they reported it to be lying at a depth of

31,300 metres in the Mediterranean. The other two battleships, the Queen Elizabeth and the Valiant, were holed by Italian one-man U-boats off the coast of Alexandria and were out of action for one year.

The U-331 survived, but it had been a very dangerous manoeuvre. U-boats going down that far risked a massive build-up of pressure that could cause the hull to implode. Even worse was the nightmare of being trapped alive on the floor of the ocean. The only prospect then was slow death by asphyxiation.

Heinrich Schmidt lived to tell the tale because the U-331 managed to get back to the surface late the same evening.

The challenges of the Atlantic and the water around Britain were daunting enough, but they had nothing on the conditions the U-boats found when they opened a campaign in Arctic waters in July 1941. Extending operations as far north as this was occasioned by the Allied convoys that were carrying aid and supplies to the Russian ports of Murmansk and Archangel.

The Arctic waters were the most dangerous and inhospitable in the world. There was the unending, numbing nightmare of fog, ice, blizzard, heaving seas and the freezing, howling winds of Arctic storms. New fears were added to the already fraught lives of those on board the U-boats: frostbite, or drowning in seas so cold that simply falling in was a guarantee of death.

The ports of departure for Allied ships on the Murmansk run were Loch Ewe in north-west Scotland, 1,600 miles distant, or Reykjavik in Iceland, 1,500 miles away. Most of the distance was under U-boat surveillance or attack and not all the Allied merchantmen sailing it were given protective escorts. In these circumstances the chances of a convoy reaching its destination intact were poor. Or, as Prime Minister Winston Churchill put it: "The operation is justified if half gets through."

Ultimately the Murmansk convoys carried more than 22,000 aircraft, 375,000 trucks, 8,700 tractors, 51,500 jeeps, 1,900 locomotives, 343,700 tons of explosives, a million miles of field-telephone cable, together with millions of shoes, rifles, machine guns, tyres, radio sets and other equipment – and as a result assisted in keeping Russia in the war. This achievement was enabled only by gargantuan effort and at tremendous risk. Most of the convoy ships were carrying some form of armament, so that a torpedo from a submarine or a stick of bombs from Luftwaffe aircraft could mean instant, total destruction for both the vessel and its crew. Most merchant ships were too slow to outrun the German U-boats and the early convoys were too lightly armed to put up an adequate defence.

This did not mean that they were sitting ducks for the prowling submarines. During the voyage of convoy PQ-16 in May 1942, a submarine had its conning tower blown clean away by one of the ships, the Expositor. In September, during attacks on convoy PQ-18, the U-88, U-589 and U-457 were sunk by convoy escorts. However, the Murmansk run was not the sort of battlefield in which either side had the advantage for long. Both Heinz Reiners and Werner Karsties were on U-boats seconded to hunt Allied ships in the fearful Arctic environment. Both had their successes. Reiners's U-boat claimed a destroyer and a merchant ship and Karsties took part in a torpedo attack against a large refrigerator vessel.

Karsties's U-boat had been searching for prey for three or four weeks without any result, and the refrigerator ship looked promising. Its captain, however, had other ideas:

> We set off towards the ship at full speed on the surface and once it got dark we dived, and from a short distance away, discharged a torpedo. But the captain of the ship was so crafty that when he saw the wake of torpedo – the torpedo runs through the water and the propeller creates a wake, a ripple – he stopped immediately. The torpedo ran past, and as soon as the torpedo had gone past he gave full speed ahead and sailed on. He escaped and we lost our torpedo.

The U-boats were nonetheless capable of doing extraordinary damage. One convoy ship, the Penelope Barker, struck by two torpedoes from a German submarine, had its 20mm guns blown out of their mountings, its stack knocked down, its bridge partially destroyed and 11 of its crew killed. The Penelope Barker sank in 10 minutes, together with her cargo of tanks, locomotives and cars.

At home in Germany exploits like these made Reiners, Karsties and other U-boat men into national celebrities on a par with the famous Luftwaffe aces, but Clausdieter Oelschlagel knew that there were shortfalls in the conduct of the struggle that resulted in heavy losses of German submarines and aircraft:

> We made several trips in northern waters, mostly in the Kola inlet in the estuary to the Barents Sea near Murmansk. Initially we didn't have much success in hitting the convoys at sea because our greatest failure was the lack of reconnaissance aeroplanes. We didn't have enough planes at sea to report sightings of convoys in time. The men who were in action in the planes up there, you couldn't envy them. They flew the BV 138, a tri-engine seaplane, which was relatively slow. If they came across a convoy, mostly with just an auxiliary aircraft carrier as an escort, they were shot down in seconds. That was all badly managed.

To cut down on losses and improve prospects of success, the Germans devised a new tactic. Its success was limited:

> We knew in advance when an Allied convoy left harbour, in northern Scotland or Iceland. Rather than harry the ships on the way, all our available U-boats were stationed close to Murmansk on the premise that we'd have a better chance if we attacked the convoy as it neared the port. The first time it worked very well, but the Allies soon cottoned on to what we were doing. The second time, they knew where our U-boats were going to be up to eight days before a convoy set sail. So they lay in wait for us and let us have it. It was depth charges here, depth charges there, depth charges everywhere. It ruined our nerves considerably.
>
> We had to dive for our own safety and wait for the convoy underwater. What we did was this: we lay on the sand 200 metres down until the convoy sailed by. Then we surfaced and attacked. I was on the U-968 and even in those difficult times we managed to bag a few kills – we sank four or five merchant ships on one occasion.

Despite the difficulties and the shortfalls, the U-boats and the

Luftwaffe managed to make the Murmansk run a veritable gauntlet for the Allied convoys. After August 1941 the Germans sank more than one-fifth of all the supplies sent to Murmansk by convoy. These losses were so severe that the British decided to reduce the Germans' chances by restricting the convoys to the long nights in winter. In July 1942, however, the rule was broken, with dramatic results.

Early that month convoy PQ-17, comprising 35 ships with a close escort of six destroyers, four corvettes and two anti-aircraft ships, sailed from Iceland bound for Murmansk. Distant cover was provided by the British Home Fleet and seven ships of the US Navy. The U-boats were waiting and on July 3–4, when PQ-17 had already passed north of Bear Island, they fell on the convoy, accompanied by strong Luftwaffe air cover. Their efforts scored minimal success, but then the scenario was abruptly altered. It was reported by Allied signals intelligence that the battleship Tirpitz, the heavy cruiser Admiral Hipper and the pocket battleships Admiral Scheer and Lützow were heading towards the vicinity of the convoy and would reach the area on the night of July 4–5. Aerial reconnaissance confirmed this a day later.

The German reason for the presence of these ships in northern waters was the defence of occupied Norway against Allied attack. This was something neither the British nor the Americans fully realized: to them, the Tirpitz and the rest were commerce raiders out to add more kills to their already daunting record. From this point of view, their presence close to PQ-17 made for a first-class emergency and the British and Americans reacted accordingly. PQ-17 was ordered to scatter on the premise that siting the ships over a wider area would give them some protection. The covering force of corvettes and the six destroyers of the close escort was then ordered to depart and confront the big German surface ships.

It was a disastrous decision. Far from protecting the convoy, it made the task easier for U-boat and Luftwaffe attack and facilitated its destruction. The Germans homed in and only 11 ships of PQ-17 managed to reach their destination. The other 24 were all sunk by U-boats and torpedo bombers.

The tragedy of convoy PQ-17 did not end there. It happened that the reconnaissance report was wrong. The big German ships were still at anchor in Norway, at Altjenfjord, until July 5 and though they left port, they returned a few hours later when it transpired from German intelligence that the Allies knew they were at sea. The U-boats and the Luftwaffe proved quite capable of destroying the ill-fated convoy on its own.

All the same, this spectacular German success in the Arctic was not an accurate guide to the overall situation in which the U-boats found themselves in mid-1942. By then the U-boats were becoming seriously overstretched in their efforts to patrol three operational zones: the Arctic, the Atlantic and the Mediterranean.

Werner Karsties had already discovered the problem of operating in the Mediterranean, where the Royal Navy and the Royal Air Force were rampant. At stake was the survival of the small but vital island of Malta, which provided bases for the British to patrol the Mediterranean sea routes and protect their forces in Egypt. The Germans also had an important interest: to prevent the British from disrupting the supply lines to the Afrika Korps in North Africa.

A number of German U-boats, Karsties's own craft among them, had been redirected to the Mediterranean after only three months in the Arctic, in September 1941. Others were dispatched from French ports. Karsties recalls:

> When we were up in the Polar Sea, we were ordered to Gibraltar because a large convoy had been reported, sailing from England to Gibraltar. We lay submerged for two days, surfacing at night to get air, observing the traffic around Gibraltar and waiting for the most suitable moment to get through. Afterwards, getting past Gibraltar proved amazingly difficult. The water currents are completely different whichever way you're going – in, out or out, in.
>
> We managed to sail through the Straits of Gibraltar eventually, though we had to do it on the surface. Then we took the boat down to a certain – let's call it "swimming depth" – because the searchlights from Ceuta, which was on the Moroccan shore, and from Gibraltar on the opposite side, shone just above the tower of the U-boat. The crew on deck had to duck their heads so that they didn't get caught in the searchlights from both sides. Once we had got through the narrowest

part of the Straits, we were lucky enough to be able to dive underneath a fishing fleet and we travelled through most of the Mediterranean underwater and landed at Messina. I thought that was my worst experience of the entire war, but I didn't know what was going to happen.

In the Mediterranean, I was the closest I ever came to death. We were attacked in broad daylight by a plane which came out of the sun so that we couldn't see it. If you look towards the sun you can't see anything else but this brilliant glare. It makes your eyes ache. So, out of the blue, or so it seemed, the bombs began to fall. Another aircraft joined in, and we managed to shoot down one of them even though our gun jammed.

Then the second plane fired flares into the air and that lit up the whole area like fireworks night. It was a signal and a destroyer answered it. Fortunately we managed to dive before we were hit, but we had to stay down at a depth of 200 metres for a full 24 hours. We didn't dare surface and while we were submerged we were attacked with more than 100 depth charges. There was a sound like someone was repeatedly striking a small hammer against the metal boat and that told us that the enemy was searching for us by sonar. If there are two destroyers or warships or whatever, and the sonar sounds cross one another, their target is supposed to be at the point where they cross. Now they knew where we were, they kept on raking us with more and more depth charges.

The depth charges were mostly thrown over the stern. We knew that because we could actually hear them being rolled over the deck. There was a pause and then "Smack!", you could hear them hitting the water. There was a hissing noise and we waited for the bang. Depending on how big the explosion was, you could calculate the sort of damage it was going to do. Fortunately the depth we were at saved us. The explosive power of depth charges was reduced because of the increased water pressure. So we managed to escape, but I've no doubt that death came very close that day.

The sea war in the Mediterranean in 1942 was just as ferocious as the action on the Murmansk run. Sixty-five major British surface vessels were sunk and the U-boats accounted for 37 of them. One of their kills was the prestigious aircraft carrier HMS Ark Royal, which was sunk by the U-81 on November 13, 1941. The Barham was torpedoed by the U-331 12 days later.

Despite their successes, the overall cost to the Germans of the war in the Mediterranean was very high. Sixty-two U-boats were destroyed in the course of the war, 13 of them by September 1942. All of them went down with all hands and the number of submarines lost was on the rise. This was no temporary setback. The U-boat crews had given the name "the happy time" to the halcyon days they had enjoyed in the first years of the war, but now it was coming to an end.

CHAPTER FOUR

The Luftwaffe:
Eagles Ascending 1939–42

THE CREATION OF THE LUFTWAFFE, which, like the Greek goddess Athena from the forehead of Zeus, sprang fully armed into view in 1936, had been part of Hitler's policy of rearming Germany in secret. One of the many punitive provisions of the Treaty of Versailles of 1919, which ended the First World War, had been a ban on a German air force as well as substantial reductions in the size of the German army and navy. Clandestine rearmament took place nevertheless, and Hitler announced it to a shocked world in 1935.

Karl Born remembers how the existence of the new air force was revealed: "There was an air show in London, and Hitler disguised his men, the National Socialist flying corps, so that they could take part. He wanted to see if the English would object, but when they made no objections, then they were told, 'This is the German Luftwaffe!'"

The build-up of the Luftwaffe had been concealed behind an apparently innocent interest in gliding and flying clubs. The manufacture of warplanes had been masked by Lufthansa, the German civil airline, which flew passengers in Junkers, Fokkers, Messerschmitts and other aircraft that were designed for easy conversion to military use.

The Hitlerjugend, the Hitler Youth, had been at the core of the policy of rearming Germany while at the same deceiving her erstwhile enemies. Outwardly the Hitler Youth catered for boyish enthusiasms and a sense of adventure. What was really happening was the creation of the most highly trained, highly motivated and most militarized teenagers in the world. The future pilots of the Second World War joined the Flieger-Hitlerjugend and began their training building and flying model gliders in order to learn the principles of flight. After this they graduated to a gliding test which involved being shot into the air attached to a simple glider wing. They used this to fly a short distance and then come safely in to land. Eventually the Flieger-Hitlerjugend graduated to flying gliders and piston-engined aircraft, all ostensibly in the name of boyish fun.

The degree of enthusiasm invoked in the "flying" Hitler Youth was exemplified by Alfred Wagner, who was so keen to fly for the Fatherland that, during the Second World War, he volunteered for duty on every possible occasion: "When you're young, enthusiasm takes you over. It's like a driving force you can't control. I volunteered for the Luftwaffe when I was 17. To me, it was a marvellous adventure. Flying was enormous fun, and I was full of enthusiasm for it. If we were asked to volunteer to fly somewhere, I was always first in the queue!"

The heroes young men like Alfred Wagner longed to emulate were the intrepid aces of the First World War, whose daring in dogfights with the enemy had made them into legends – Baron Manfred von Richthofen, the "Red Baron", Werner Voss, Max von Müller, Ernst Udet and Hermann Goering, who later became head of the Luftwaffe.

Goering, who first met Hitler in 1922 and became a keen disciple, was the son of a diplomat. He made a distinguished name for himself in the First World War and became famous as one of Germany's top air aces, with 20 "kills" to his credit. After the "Red Baron" died in action in 1918, Goering, aged 25, succeeded him as commander of the renowned Richthofen Squadron. Goering was commander for only four months before Germany's defeat and surrender and his great personal vanity as well as his strong sense of nationalism were mightily offended by the terms of the Versailles treaty. Like many Germans, Goering felt the armed forces had been dishonoured and, after falling under the extraordinary spell Hitler exerted over his followers, he joined the Nazi Party determined to right this wrong.

From Hitler's point of view, Goering's personal devotion and his exploits in the First World War fitted him perfectly to head the new Luftwaffe he intended to forge. With Ernst Röhm, another veteran of the war and chief of the Sturmabteilung, or SA, the Nazi stormtroopers, Goering became a principal lieutenant of the future Führer.

Although Goering was awed by Hitler's personality and often acted like his minion, he had a charisma of his own which could fuel enthusiasm in others. One of those he personally inspired was Hajo Hermann, who later flew 370 missions with the Luftwaffe and downed 10 Allied aircraft:

> Goering actually determined my career as a flyer. I was an infantryman and scrabbling around with a steel helmet and machine gun on the army training ground near Berlin. He rode up, wearing the uniform of an infantry general, and called down to me, "Well, what's it like down there, then? Isn't it a bit tough? Wouldn't you rather come up here to me?" and he pointed upwards towards the sky.
>
> At the time I had no idea who he was. We didn't have television, so we weren't familiar with the high-ups in the armed forces. But he pointed to the sky and said, "Up there, become an airman." And I said, "Yes indeed, Herr General!" Shortly afterwards I was ordered to go to Berlin for an air force medical examination and then it began.

Later, during the war, Hajo Hermann received special favour from Goering after the pilot had developed the night-fighter technique known as the "Wild Boar". This was an attempt to put a stop to the night bombing of Berlin by the Royal Air Force in 1943 and 1944, and involved the use of Messerschmitt 109s as night-fighters. Guided only by ground radio, the Me-109s successfully hunted down the RAF bombers. Hajo Hermann refined his "Wild Boar" with camouflage: the undersides of the aircraft were painted black and an additional flame dampener was added over the exhaust stubs. Some of the Me-109s were equipped with a whistle device that helped the ground crews identify the Luftwaffe aircraft as they returned from their missions.

The "Wild Boar" and its successes came to Goering's attention and Hermann found himself shooting up the ranks: "Goering promoted me immediately, that happened quite rapidly. At the beginning of 1944 I was a captain and at the end of the year I was a colonel. He put me up for a higher decoration, which I was then awarded by Hitler."

Hitler followed Goering's recommendation even though, at that stage in the war, he was out of favour with the Führer. Hitler's disillusionment dated from 1940, when, despite Goering's swaggering and boasting about "his" Luftwaffe, it had lost the Battle of Britain and therefore undermined the chances for another successful German invasion.

Hermann acknowledges that Goering made mistakes but this had no effect on his loyalty: "I cannot with the best will in the world make a disparaging judgment about this man because he did too many good things for me. He gave me his trust and raised me to higher positions. I don't bear an absolute admiration for him, but as Shakespeare wrote, 'Taken all in all, he was a man.'"

In 1936 Hermann flew with the Luftwaffe's Condor Legion in Spain, where it supported the Nationalist forces of General Francisco Franco and gave an awesome demonstration of what Europe could expect from a future war. The seeds of the Spanish Civil War, which began on July 18, 1936, had been sown five years earlier, when the rise to power of Republican liberals had forced the King, Alfonso XIII, into exile. Franco, who proved to be a dictator in the Hitler-Mussolini mould, rebelled against the anti-militarist policies of the Republican government and invaded Spain from Spanish Morocco. In Germany, Hitler's sympathies were naturally with Franco and the Condor Legion was detailed for "special duty" in Spain.

The Legion consisted of four bomber squadrons, 48 aircraft in all, and four fighter squadrons, backed by anti-aircraft and anti-tank units. With this, the curtain went up on a new and terrifying form of air warfare: the blitzkrieg, with its heavy bombing raids and dive-bombing tactics, as demonstrated by the Junkers-87 "Stuka". The First World War in the air had at times been a relatively gentlemanly business, with some pilots jousting in dogfights like medieval knights in the lists and adopting a chivalrous approach to their opponents. By 1936 all that had disappeared. The Condor Legion in Spain was out to terrorize, annihilate and paralyse the Republican forces and on April 27, 1937 was accused of atrocity over the bombing of Guernica, the cultural and spiritual home of the Basques.

It was market day and Guernica was crowded with visitors from the surrounding area. Suddenly, it was later reported, the sky filled with Heinkel 111s and Junkers-52s, escorted by fighters, and the crowds in the town square were pounded with high explosives and strafed with machine-gun fire. Incendiary bombs rained down, setting fire to buildings. The Mayor of Guernica later told newspaper reporters: "They bombed and bombed and bombed."

One reporter arrived in Guernica soon after the aircraft departed: "On both sides of the road, men, women and children were sitting, dazed. I saw a priest and stopped the car and went up to him. His face was blackened, his clothes in tatters. He couldn't talk and pointed to the flames about four miles away, then whispered: '*Aviones ... bombas ... mucho, mucho...*'"

Smoke, flames, the nauseating smell of burning human flesh and the dust and grit from collapsed buildings filled the air.

"It was impossible to go down many of the streets, because they were walls of flame. Debris was piled high. The shocked survivors all had the same story to tell: aeroplanes, bullets, bombs, fire."

Despite such dramatic reports, the bombing of Guernica became controversial when the Condor Legion denied involvement, even though the town contained military installations – a communications centre and a munitions factory – that could have counted as legitimate targets. Blame was ascribed instead to the Republicans, who, it was said, had destroyed Guernica themselves. However, the style and power of the attack on Guernica bore a chilling resemblance to the way the Luftwaffe later fought in the blitzkrieg campaigns against Poland and in western Europe. It became clear that the destruction of Guernica had been only a rehearsal.

Hajo Hermann found that the Condor Legion did not always have things their own way. The Republicans, too, were receiving aid from the outside. On receiving suitable payment in gold, the Russians sent them their best fighter, the Polikarpov 1-16 Rata. The Rata was the first fighter in the world to combine cantilever monoplane wings with retractable landing gear at a time when almost all fighters were biplanes.

Hajo Hermann remembers what happened when the Luftwaffe aircraft had to confront the Rata, an aircraft the German pilots came to respect, with good reason:

The Polikarpov 1-16 Rata was the best plane that turned up in Spain. On one occasion I was shot at by a Rata. It flew in an arc from in front of me, flying past, and the rear gun was fired directly into the cockpit. Afterwards there were quite a lot of bullet holes in my plane. Some of my comrades in the Condor Legion got as many as 250 bullets in battles with the Rata.

They were really hard planes to fight against. You couldn't see them against the horizon. They used to come from Alcalá de Henares, Getafe, the areas around Madrid, and climbed up rapidly and you couldn't really see them over that area. Then suddenly there they were!

You couldn't hear the Rata, either. That was the peculiar thing.

In the air, everything takes place absolutely silently, secretively, and then suddenly, from out of the silence, comes death. That's what it was like. You thought you were watching the Ratas from a distance, then a tiny spot suddenly becomes enormous, with a huge engine in front of your nose, and they're firing at you.

The Ratas often approached our planes head on. That was danger-ous for us. We could defend ourselves very well from the rear. We had a rear gunner and down below in the bowl, in the "pot" as we called it, we had an observer who could fire to the rear. We also had machine guns pointing out of the side windows, but we were vulnerable in the front. That was why an officer on the General Staff, Kraft von Delmensingen, ordered machine guns to be fitted to our wings.

The deadly nature of the Rata was made clear when Hajo Hermann was flying a Ju-52 to attack a Republican position at Bilbao, in northern Spain:

> Another of the Condor pilots flew in front of me to the left. Suddenly the Rata flew between us and our man was a goner. His aircraft began to burn and immediately turned into a fiery, red ball. The plane just disintegrated and fell to earth flaking into pieces.
>
> It was a tremendous shock, but only for a tenth of a second or so, and it taught me a lesson for the future. When you're flying in war, you have to keep on towards the target. That's your duty and you must do it.
>
> Of course, you know you can suffer the same fate – that's the way war is. But it's no good dwelling on it, even when you've just seen a comrade blown out of the sky. It always seemed to me to be so futile to expend a lot of emotion on the victim. Later I went to war having made the decision once and for all: to engage in war, do it well, do it with determination. You have to reach your targets and you have to win.

Hermann had had other plans for his Luftwaffe career when he was sent to Spain. An unfriendly commander, he believes, was responsible:

> I went to Spain, I think, because my commander in Thüringen wanted to get rid of me. I had done something undisciplined for an airman, and when this commander was told to send one man from our group to Spain, he chose me. At first I regarded it as a punishment and I was dismayed because I had other aims. I was just about to go on a "blind-flying" course in order to train as a "blind-flying" tutor but he said, "Listen you can do that later, go to Spain first. Sign this paper stating that you will keep everything we talk about a secret, because officially, the government isn't supposed to know anything about sending German airmen to Spain. Off you go, then, you will be there

for three weeks and are to fly Nationalist troops from Morocco over the Straits of Gibraltar to Spain. General Franco is waiting there for them."

After a while in Spain I changed my mind and, instead of a punishment, it began to look like an adventure. I travelled to Cadiz on a steam boat together with several others from another garrison and in Cadiz we had our first experience of war. A very simple double-decker plane approached, a French plane, and dropped a few small bombs. It didn't look like much of an attack, but the bombs exploded smack against the hull of our ship. A little later a Spanish battleship sailed up and fired shells across the harbour so that fountains of water spouted up all round us. I used to like the pictures of the sea battles in the First World War, Skagerrak and so on, where water fountains spouted up, but I had never experienced it and here I saw it for the first time. That's how the Spanish episode began.

When I arrived in Toledo, it was in October 1936, there had been a lot of fighting and it looked pretty grim. I saw the corpses and awful scenes where the Republicans had killed priests and nuns. They lay everywhere on the ground, blood everywhere, in the villages too.

Later we flew from Salamanca to attack Madrid, where the Republicans had ensconced themselves in the university district. Madrid was a very heavily defended town. But we didn't spread terror there, like some people say, or drop bombs down into the middle of the city. Our task was to bomb the front-line positions.

We also attacked the northern front line. But it was all very primitive down there in Spain. The Spaniards were totally unprepared for fighting on their own territory, as I discovered after we were ordered to fly from Burgos to attack the front line in the north. Most of the harbours in the north, like Bilbao or Oviedo, had been occupied by the Republicans. It was an important industrial area, with iron ore and coal deposits. I was given the task of flying in advance to Burgos to prepare the airfield for missions and it turned out to be very, very difficult. There was nothing there. I had hardly any materials and so I spoke to the Archbishop of Bilbao and said that I needed the floodlights he had at his cathedral to use on the airfield. He didn't like that at all. He refused at first, but then I told him, "We are fighting against atheists,

you must surely agree with that." Well, that changed his mind and I got
my floodlights.

Service with the Condor Legion in the Spanish Civil War afforded
Hermann a great deal of varied experience in air warfare:

> I flew transport missions, carried over 2,000 troops across the sea,
> and was then re-equipped for bombing. I carried six 250-kilogram
> bombs in the Ju-52 and flew different missions, mostly against ships,
> mainly against Mexican and Soviet supply ships that sailed into the
> harbour at Cartagena with supplies for the Republicans.
>
> When we flew on missions we were escorted by the Italian Savoia
> Marchetti 81, I think it was called, and the C32. They were quite
> ingenious machines, equally good as our Heinkel-51 fighters.
>
> There were substantial air battles during attacks on the suburbs of
> Madrid which the Republicans defended bitterly, the university quar-
> ter. We were busy dropping our bombs and our Heinkels suffered
> considerable losses.

Hermann used his opportunities in Spain to experiment with new
ways of fighting from the air. He flew out one day and dropped stones
and iron bars into the Straits of Gibraltar:

> That was an invention of mine. It was considered quite mad, of
> course, but it wasn't a bad idea at all. When we flew over the Straits
> – we were heavily loaded with armed men – the Russian destroyers
> used to fire up at us. We were hit too, in the front and the rear. Many
> of our passengers were badly injured. They made a terrible fuss.
> You'd think the world was coming to an end.
>
> So I told them, "Now we'll send our greetings to the people down
> below" and got together some bars and old junk which I'd loaded up
> into the rear of the plane close by the door, where the commander of
> this unit sat. I said to him that when he got the signal he should open
> the door a little and push all the junk out with his foot, that would make
> some lovely noises down below, and it did too. The noise caused by
> non-dynamic objects like that is enormous. I know because I once

experienced it myself. A toolbox fell out of a plane by accident and landed on the ground with a tremendous crash, it was indescribable. So I did it on purpose this time, and though we didn't hit much, there was plenty of noise and people on the ground were terrified.

If Hermann had been sent to Spain in the first place because of indiscipline, his behaviour did not improve much once he was there:

General Mola was Nationalist Commander in Chief of the northern front line in Spain and I had to report to him to apologize for being rude about the Spaniards. I had complained that they worked too slowly, and I was to apologize, but before I even had time to open my mouth to excuse myself, General Mola said, in French, which I myself spoke, "Listen, why have you given me so few flak guns?" At the time I was involved in training the Spanish soldiers to use flak, so I assured General Mola that more of the guns would be coming and he seemed satisfied with that. He seemed to forget all about my rude remarks. I was supposed to be sent home in disgrace, but instead I was allowed to stay in Spain.

After that I was on a mission, flying from Melilla in Morocco to attack Cartagena, but there was a problem. Italy, Germany, Britain and France had agreed to patrol the coasts of Spain so that neither the Nationalists nor the Republicans could bring in new forces. At least that's what we, the Germans, said we were there for and the others, I suppose, would have done their best to turn back my aircraft. Fortunately Admiral Fischl was with his fleet, anchored outside the three-mile limit by the Costa del Sol, near Almeria and Cartagena. He ordered a floodlight to be switched on so that I could see my way to Cartagena. That was his idea of non-intervention!

The Spanish Civil War ended with a Nationalist victory on March 28, 1939, when General Franco marched into Madrid. The Condor Legion departed for home just as events were prefiguring the outbreak of the Second World War less than six months later. Two weeks before the civil war in Spain came to an end, the forces of Nazi Germany had occupied Czechoslovakia, contrary to the agreement made with Hitler by the

British and French Prime Ministers, Neville Chamberlain and Édouard Daladier, at the time of the Munich Crisis late in 1938. This latest aggression on the part of the Third Reich was followed by another, the invasion of Poland on September 1, 1939, and this time Britain and France did not stand by and watch, but declared war.

The campaign in Poland, which barely outlasted September, was the first illustration of what the Luftwaffe could do in a full-scale, all-out war. At the time of Munich the Luftwaffe had already been a considerable force, with 1,669 aircraft, including 453 fighters, 582 bombers and 159 dive-bombers. By the eve of the war, only nine months later, it had more than doubled its size, with 3,750 aircraft, of which 1,170 were bombers, 335 were dive-bombers and 1,125 were fighters, mainly Me-109s, and 195 twin-engined fighters, mostly Me-110s. Despite major problems with aircraft production, these numbers grew as the war progressed, particularly after the brilliant Albert Speer assumed responsibility. No other European power had an air force as large or as impressive as this in September 1939, nor did any have experience comparable to the "rehearsal" by the Condor Legion in Spain.

The value of that experience was clear during the opening stages of the invasion of Poland, when the Luftwaffe bombed, strafed and destroyed virtually at will, and, while not destroying the Polish air force as had been planned, rendered it more or less useless. The Poles had only around 300 modern aircraft, compared with 1,323 first-line Luftwaffe planes, but it was not simply a question of numbers. The Polish planes were primitive compared with their opponents and the shock of the attack caught the Polish armed forces critically off balance.

Hajo Hermann was there in the opening moments of the Polish campaign:

> Surveying the army advancing from the air, it looked just overwhelming. Wherever we were advancing, over an area of around 200 kilometres, you could see where the guns were firing or the houses were burning and the fighting was taking place. The whole landscape seemed to be consumed by war. But I thought about the way the Poles had betrayed us after the First World War and I said to myself: "Well, now you are taking part, this is your chance to erase the great

injustice the Poles have done us."

By 1940, other landscapes "consumed by war" enabled the German armed forces to conquer Norway, Denmark, the Low Countries and France, all in quick, unstoppable succession. Norway, together with Denmark, was invaded on April 9. Oslo was heavily bombed by the Luftwaffe and a British newspaper correspondent was there to record the result:

> With German bombers wheeling overhead like birds of prey, the rattle of machine gun fire on the outskirts of Oslo and the heavy thud of bombs echoing down the fjord, the bewildered crowds in the city's streets were sheltering in doorways and flattening themselves against the walls. With a piercing crescendo of noise, a great four-engined machine dived right over the house tops and streaked skyward again, its tail gun covering the length of the street.
>
> The Germans had landed at Moss, twenty miles from Oslo on the east side of the fjord. Their ships were in the fjord and their aircraft had bombed the airport. German bombers were wheeling over a ridge at Fetsund, also 20 miles from Oslo. Black puffs of anti-aircraft fire pitted the sky for the whole length of the ridge. The thud of bombs, the rattle of machine guns echoed in the air. The Luftwaffe's target was Kjeller, the Norwegian military air base.

Norway was conquered and occupied. So was Denmark, but the one flaw in the run of German success in western Europe in the early summer of 1940 was the escape of the British Expeditionary Force, together with large numbers of French and a few Belgian soldiers, from the port of Dunkirk in northern France. Hermann Goering believed that these men, vulnerable and exposed as they waited for rescue from England, could easily be finished off by the Luftwaffe. He was wrong. In a foretaste of what it would encounter in the Battle of Britain, the Luftwaffe was fended off by the Royal Air Force in a series of punishing, hard-fought battles. Hajo Hermann was flying over the Dunkirk area while the Royal Navy and the fleet of private "little ships" were lifting the soldiers off the beaches and piers and the RAF was on guard:

We found ourselves on our own over the harbour at Dunkirk. It was teeming with British soldiers down below and I attempted to unload my bombs on to two of the ships. I missed, and the Hurricanes came after us, blazing gunfire. Our plane was hit and smoke began pouring out of one of the engines. The other engine packed up. The plane slid down into the water about 100 metres from the beach. The entire cockpit was smashed up.

Suddenly we were under the water. But, thank goodness, we all got out. I had a hand injury, but I had to ignore that. What was more important was that the escaping English weren't too far away. So we crawled cautiously on to the beach, through the surf, always crawling, always to the east, away from the English. So we were saved. But for us, the operation at Dunkirk was over.

The Luftwaffe destroyed the town and the harbour at Dunkirk, setting them alight with incendiary bombs. But it was unable to make good Goering's boast that it could annihilate the men on the beaches. A total of 370,000 escaped, to fight another day. It was a day that would soon arrive.

By June 22, 1940, when France capitulated and Britain became the only combatant still free to oppose the Nazis, it seemed only a matter of time before the island country was invaded and added to Hitler's new European empire. Despite the failure at Dunkirk, Goering, in his flamboyant buccaneering fashion, was certain that his Luftwaffe was on the brink of another spectacular victory.

There were several reasons why he was mistaken. Firstly, the Royal Air Force was the first up-to-date air force the Luftwaffe had encountered. On the brink of the Battle of Britain in mid-1940, statistics appeared to prove that the RAF had scant chances, with only 1,911 first-line aircraft, to the Germans' 4,161. Three Luftflotten, or Air Fleets, numbers 2, 3 and 5, were deployed on airfields stretching from Brittany to Norway, including 898 bombers, 708 single-engined and 202 twin-engined fighters. Luftflotte 2, based in north-eastern France, Belgium, the Netherlands and northern Germany, was to attack the south-east of England. The western half of England was the responsibility of Luftflotte 3, which used airfields sited from the French Atlantic coast to west of the River Seine. Luftflotte 5, based in Norway and Denmark, was to make diversionary attacks on targets in northern Britain.

These forces, though formidable, suffered from several disadvantages. The first was that they were being required to act out of character. The Luftwaffe had been designed as "flying artillery" acting in support of ground forces, not for a strategic bombing campaign or for a prolonged air war.

Until the Battle of Britain began, in mid-August 1940, Germany's pilots had not yet faced a well-armed, well-equipped, up-to-date air force. They had enjoyed a comparatively easy run, operating in attack areas close to Germany against inferior enemies, and operating over land. Britain, too, was not that far from the Germans' reach after the conquests of 1940, a minimum of only 21 miles across the English Channel. The Channel, however, was an important deciding factor, as it had always been when the defence of Britain was at stake. So was the presence there of the Royal Navy. That made it potentially hostile territory for Luftwaffe aircraft flying over it, whether to tangle with the RAF or to "blitz" British cities.

Although they appeared well placed, on the coasts of Europe nearest to Britain, the range of the Luftwaffe aircraft was limited by this narrow but deceptive waterway. The Me-109, for example, had a radius of action, out and home, of little more than 100 miles, with only around 80 minutes of tactical flying time. This was barely enough to reach London and do damage before having to fly home and, hopefully, avoid ditching in the Channel.

The rapid conquest of western Europe had been exhilarating for the Germans, but the very speed of it presented new and taxing problems. There was no time before the attack on Britain to prepare new air bases and set up adequate supply lines. There were no local facilities for the repair of damaged aircraft, which had to be taken back to Germany instead. There was also a critical lack of reserves, no reliable method of plotting the positions of RAF aircraft and no ground-to-air facilities for guiding the Luftwaffe planes.

The new difficulties the Luftwaffe encountered in the Battle of Britain were largely due to Goering's lack of foresight, his poor planning and his overweening confidence in the might of the Luftwaffe. These faults at the top were compounded by the fact that many Luftwaffe aircraft were too poorly armed to be certain of a safe flight across the Channel without a fighter escort. Hajo Hermann remembers how hamstrung he felt when he flew over London:

I bombed London, because the English were already at work bombing Berlin and very heavily. And we only did it by way of retaliation. We hit back, and Adolf Hitler, the evil man, always used to say, if the British stop, then we will stop too. But the British didn't stop. So, God help me, I flew to London 23 times and dropped my bombs down on to it. There was no precise targeting, no strategic purpose in what I did. I felt bad about that. In the City and I don't know what other parts of the town, it was very regrettable.

Unteroffizier Peter Stahl, pilot of a Ju-88, had similar misgivings when engaged in bombing London in October 1940:

During our approach flight to London, it becomes almost spooky in our glazed housing. The searchlights have lit up the clouds, so we are flying blind and feel as if we are hanging in our fuzzy surroundings, sitting inside a white cotton-wool ball with no idea what is happening above and below us. I had to concentrate really hard to "pull together my whole brain" as we used to say, to avoid making errors. That takes nerve! My only wish was to be out of here and quick.

The blitz on London began on September 7, 1940, with a raid on the capital during the evening and the East End suffering most of the damage.

The description of the raid by a 16-year-old eyewitness living in London's docklands was typical of the capital's first experience of being under German fire:

The air-raid siren went at quarter to five in the afternoon. We heard gunfire and the sound of aircraft, so we all went into our Anderson shelter. The planes came over in three batches, we could hear them very clearly, and the guns sent up a terrific barrage. We could hear bombs whistling down all round as we cowered in the back of the shelter, expecting to be hit at any moment.

Bombs were dropping in a field behind us, and we thought that if they didn't hit us, they would surely hit our house. Our shelter shook and so did we. We ate sweets and tried not to mind. All the time, fire engines were rushing past clanging their bells.

When the All Clear sounded and we started to come out of the shelter, my brother said, "Hasn't it got dark?" It was a great smoke cloud all over the sky, thick, black smoke which made our faces dirty just standing there. We thought for a moment that our house was on fire, but it was red from the reflection of burning buildings round about. We could see at least half a dozen fires blazing and great flames shooting up into the sky.

Another eyewitness saw the cloud of smoke rising over the East End from far out in the countryside:

I was driving back from Oxford with friends early in the evening and we were still miles out in the country when we saw a huge column of smoke hanging far away over the house tops. At first we didn't know whether it was merely a cloud. But we guessed what it was when we came on the dramatic spectacle of street after street lined with people, every head turned upwards and eastwards. I reached home in London to find a bomb had dropped in the next street. I was trying to investigate this when I got a call to go to the scene of the fire. A general's daughter, a girl of 19, an ambulance driver, begged to come with me.

We were waiting for the bus when the air-raid warning sounded again. We knew at once where the fire was, because this line of buses immediately came to a halt. They were held up at the other end. We walked some distance. There were heavy bursts of gunfire and we put on our tin hats. A taxi drew up in the middle of the road. "Will you take me to the fire?" I asked. "I'll get you as near to it as I possibly can," said the driver. Then began a mad ride through London.

In one street about a dozen firemen, with hoses and fire pumps, had just managed to extinguish one fire. They told us factories had been hit. It wasn't too easy to breathe. Above the glare we could see the curtain of smoke and above that two balloons.

Suddenly we heard a whirring, rushing sound. "That's a bomb," someone shouted. "Fall flat!" We flung ourselves in the gutter, in a sort of human chain. A few moments passed. Afterwards we took shelter in a garage. When the activity overhead died down, we came out again. What we had seen before was nothing to what we saw now.

The whole air was a bright blaze of gold, with those two balloons still floating above. We shouted for our taxi man. When he arrived, he said he had been blown to the ground by a bomb. Just as we started off again in the taxi, we heard first a rushing, then a heavy explosion and a brilliant firework display in the road directly in our path. A bomb had blocked the road.

Later I talked with a woman who drove in a car over London Bridge and back over Tower Bridge during the evening. She said that nothing moved her so much as the sight of the Tower of London. "It stood there squat and solid and contemptuous, with the whole sky on fire behind it," she said. "It symbolized the whole of our history. It will take a good deal more than Hitler to shake us."

Defiant attitudes like this were bad news for Goering. He had assumed that the British could be terrorized into submission by bombing and strafing. Gripped by this delusion, he had made a serious blunder in sending the Luftwaffe to attack Britain's cities while neglecting to press home the offensive against the British Fighter Command.

Goering's blunders multiplied when he dispatched bombers to assault cities as far apart as Swansea, Aberdeen and Belfast. On one raid, attempting to safeguard the dispersed bomber streams, the Luftwaffe lost 24 fighters to the RAF's 14. The effect of the Luftwaffe's offensive was also blunted by poor intelligence gathering. The wrong airfields and factories were targeted.

As the Battle of Britain progressed, the loss of RAF fighters was heavy, but the loss to the Luftwaffe was heavier. On July 15, 50 German aircraft were destroyed in one day. Between August 13 and 18, the Germans lost 350 aircraft. The RAF lost 170.

In Britain, the summer of 1940 was bright, sunny and warm, perfect flying weather, and thousands of people in the south-east and along the south coast had perfect visibility as they watched Spitfires, Hurricanes and Me-109s jousting high above in the bright blue summer sky. Luftwaffe bombers could be clearly seen as they flew over in packed formations. One eyewitness watched Spitfires attacking a fleet of Luftwaffe bombers over Surrey:

The whole panorama of the beautiful Surrey countryside was laid out before us, but soon the German bombers could be heard high up above. Our anti-aircraft batteries opened fire immediately and the sky seemed full of fighter aircraft going up in pursuit. A German bomber suddenly hurtled out of the sky like a falling leaf. The pilot managed to regain some control as he neared the earth and it seemed as if a safe landing might have been possible, but he made a sudden dive, hitting the ground. The machine immediately burst into an inferno of flame and smoke. It was a terrible scene, taking place just down below us in the valley in brilliant sunshine.

Meanwhile the RAF fighters were zooming in all directions and we could hear the rattle of machine-gun fire above us. A big, black German bomber planed right across our vision about 300 feet from the ground, with engines off, obviously trying to land. Then came a burst of machine-gun fire as he scraped over the roof of a farmhouse nearby. It was astonishing to us that the occupants of the bomber in such a perilous position could still think of machine-gunning the farmhouse as they passed over the roof and pancaked into a field half a mile further on, apparently undamaged.

While this was going on, anti-aircraft batteries were sending up shells at a terrific rate. Shells were bursting in the wood behind us and we felt that any moment some splinters might descend upon us. After a short interval we saw a formation of Spitfires bring down two more bombers on the distant hills.

The next thing we saw, a group of German bombers, hotly pursued by Spitfires, were seen making for the coast. The action had lasted 35 minutes. When it was over, the Surrey countryside was peaceful once again and the only evidence of the battle were the smoking ruins of the German bombers in the fields below us.

The rate of loss suffered by the Luftwaffe in engagements like this was a particular nightmare for Ernst Udet, whose friend Goering had appointed him chief of Luftwaffe supply and procurement and head of its technical office. Udet may have been an ace pilot in the First World War, but he was no organizer. He made a complete mess of the flow of new aircraft required to replace the Luftwaffe's losses. When Goering found out, his first thought was to hide the truth in order to protect his friend, but Udet had another solution. Ostensibly he was killed in an aircraft crash, but in fact he committed suicide by shooting himself on November 17, 1941.

The shortcomings of the German aircraft, especially the Messerschmitt 110, were also exposed during the Battle of Britain. Later in the war, after 1942, Anton Heinemann was a less-than-satisfied Me-110 pilot: "The Me-110 had six guns facing forwards, but because the plane couldn't fly for too long, they were retired. We were given the Junkers-88, which a large additional tank, so that we had a larger margin of safety if we encountered fog or had to be diverted to another airfield."

The Me-109, whose dogfights with the Spitfire gave it a gladiatorial image, had a different Achilles Heel, but a no less serious one. It consumed fuel at a great rate, so much so that by the time it had reached the war zone over southern England, it had only about half an hour of combat time left.

Luftwaffe pilots were at a disadvantage here. If they were shot down or had to parachute to safety, they found themselves in enemy territory, full of people who were only too glad to turn them over to the authorities. The classic image was of a German pilot bailing out and landing in a field, to be confronted by a farmworker with a pitchfork. It was not entirely fiction. It happened more than once.

On July 8, 1940, for example, Mrs Nora Cardwell disarmed and captured a Luftwaffe pilot whose plane had been shot down over the north-east coast of England. She described the incident:

> One of my farm men came to the door and said some German parachutists were coming down. I went to the telephone, but fond it was out of order. I told a boy to go on his bicycle for the police. But in the meantime, I had to do something myself. We had been told that

we had to deal with these parachutists very quickly before they had a chance to do any damage.

I went out into the garden and saw an airman limping across the paddock near the house. There were two or three people about, but they didn't do anything, so I walked up to this young man and told him to put his hands up. He didn't understand until I made signs and then he raised his hands in the air. I pointed to the automatic pistol he had in his belt and he gave it to me.

He was about six foot three inches tall and about 25 years of age. I walked with him in front of me to the road. We waited for about half an hour before the police and soldiers arrived and took him away.

One of the most unfortunate of the Luftwaffe pilots was Gefreiter Niessel, who was Flight Engineer on a Ju-88 bomber when the engines began to fail. The pilot ordered the crew to jump out, but only Niessel did so. He landed safely, but the pilot changed his mind. Realizing that, despite the failing engines, he had a chance to get back to Germany, he flew on and managed to reach base. The stranded Niessel was later captured near Tangmere, in Sussex. It had been his first and last flight.

The Luftwaffe's opponents, by contrast, had the luxury of operating over home territory, with a much shorter run home to their airfields and friendly faces all round if they were forced to bail out. Many of them returned immediately to base and were flying again the same day, or the next.

Despite the ferocity of combat in the Battle of Britain, it did not always occur to pilots on either side that they, not the other fellow, might be shot down and killed. The first time he went into battle the famous pilot Richard Hillary "felt an empty sensation of suspense in the pit of my stomach". It was not fear for himself, but fear at the thought that he was about to kill.

Hillary found himself tangling with a Messerschmitt:

He came right through my sights and I saw the tracer from all eight guns thud home. For a second, he seemed to hang motionless; then a jet of red flame shot upward and he spun out of sight. For the next few minutes, I was too busy looking after myself to think of anything but the rest of the enemy aircraft turned and made off over the Channel and we were ordered to our base. My mind began working again. It had happened.

Like Hillary, the Me-109 pilot Ulrich Steinhilper, who took part in a raid on RAF Manston in Kent on August 19, 1940, was chilled by the thought that destroying an opponent's aircraft also meant killing him:

We roared over the coast just east of Margate and within seconds we were approaching Manston. I spotted a tanker that was refuelling a Spitfire quite close to the airfield boundary. Dropping height to about three to four metres, I saw the tanker rapidly filling my illuminated red firing ring. Increasing the pressure on the trigger and the button, I felt all four machine guns begin to fire. I saw the strikes and flashes as the bullets began to hit home and the tanker began to burn.

Next Steinhilper turned his attention to two Spitfires waiting nearby to be refuelled in their turn. His machine-gun fire tore up the ground and then the Spitfires were hit. The tanker blew up in a ball of fire and the Spitfires began to burn. Despite the elation of success, Steinhilper knew there were men as well as machines down there:

I was assailed by a conflict of feelings. First, I had done what I had been trained to do and done it well. It was a victory for me, and a victory for Germany. I had set fire to thousands of litres of precious fuel and left three Spitfires in ruins. But I had also seen that my attack had cost the life of at least one man and that was, and still is, hard to take.

Ten weeks later Steinhilper was shot down near Canterbury, in Kent. He bailed out safely and was imprisoned for the rest of the war.

The difficulties the Luftwaffe was encountering in the Battle of Britain tried Goering's patience to extremes. He had very little patience in any case, for he was easily dissatisfied with anything less than quick success. As the Battle wore on into September and the RAF showed no signs of cracking, Goering took to criticizing the Luftwaffe fighter pilots for failing him and for lacking aggression. He also drove them hard, refusing to allow rest days or to rotate the front-line units so that they could refresh themselves. The pilots became tired out and disillusioned and for the first time began to doubt their own effectiveness.

It was also a matter of shame for the Luftwaffe when the much-vaunted Ju-87 Stukas had to be withdrawn from the Battle because they proved too vulnerable to RAF attack. The Stukas' undoing was the very feature that had once been considered its advantage: the moment when the Ju-87 positioned itself for its 80-degree dive-bombing run and was about to shriek down on its target below was also the moment when it was most open to attack. The Stukas suffered very heavy losses, most of which occurred as they stooped to make their dive.

The Stukas were so vulnerable that they had to be escorted by Me-109Es. The Ju-87s were very slow-flying aircraft and their escorts, which were superior aircraft, had to cut down on their own speed capability because of it. The Spitfires and Hurricanes were frequently waiting for them and their losses were severe. One Luftwaffe squadron lost its group commander, its adjutant and all three of its commanders within two weeks. This made a young lieutenant, Günther Rall, the new squadron commander and he was only 22 years old.

The Luftwaffe pilots were frustrated, too, by the serendipity of the RAF squadrons, which invariably managed to be in the right place at the right time to intercept them. The explanation was the RAF's radio detection and ranging equipment, or radar, which had already been in operational use before 1939 and was now playing its first vital defensive role in the war. Adolf Galland, the famous German fighter ace, wrote: "We realized that the RAF fighter squadrons must be controlled from the ground by some new procedure, because we heard commands skilfully and accurately directing Spitfires and Hurricanes on to the German formations... For us, this radar and fighter control was a surprise and a very bitter one."

The Germans had radar themselves, and used it very effectively during the war. Horst Ramstetter was convinced the British has stolen it from them and then prevented the Germans from using it themselves:

They blew us out of the sky after our radar system had been stolen by the English. Our radar was able to register approaching formations, to register the numbers and say what was up there. Our control room could say there are fighters in the air, they come from such and such a place. English advance troops picked up this sophisticated technology, the whole thing, from the Channel or wherever, and took it to England. The Battle of Britain was won by the English because of that. They were able to switch off our radar system, all the frequencies, so we couldn't use it. They were very sneaky lads, those English.

Combined with their other disadvantages, German losses in the Battle of Britain – 1,733 aircraft overall, to the RAF's 915 – were so high that it became impossible for the Luftwaffe to carry on. It had become evident that they were not going to seize command of the air and without command of the air, there could be no invasion. On October 12, Operation Sea Lion, the invasion of Britain, was postponed "indefinitely" by Hitler. This postponement was meant to last until the following year, but the campaign was never resumed. Britain, which had not been successfully invaded for almost nine centuries, remained the only opponent still able to confront the Nazis for a year to the day, until Russia was forced into the war by the German invasion of June 22, 1941.

Hitler never forgave Goering for the failure of the Luftwaffe in the Battle of Britain. The shine had gone from its dazzling, invincible image and its reputation was never quite the same again. After the cancellation of Operation Sea Lion, Hitler and Goering met only when it was unavoidable and Goering contrived to keep out of the Führer's way at every possible opportunity. Some Luftwaffe pilots, just as disillusioned as their Führer, came to realize what lay behind Goering's outward bluster. One of them was Anton Heinemann:

Yes, Goering was a great bragger. He boasted he could be called Meyer – a Jewish name – if any enemy plane flew over German territory. What nonsense! How could he have forgotten that the RAF raided the Kiel Canal and the German naval bases at Wilhelmshaven and Brunsbüttel on the second day of the war, in 1939? Besides, against the British we never had command of the air, certainly not during the day, though the night-fighters managed to function until the end of the war.

On June 10, 1940, a few weeks before the Battle of Britain began, Benito Mussolini, the fascist dictator of Italy, had entered the war on the German side. Italian operations were at first concentrated in Africa, where "Il Duce" was intent on building an empire which, he boasted, would one day rival that of the Romans. The Mediterranean, he bragged, was "Mare Nostrum", "Our Sea".

The Italians were not entirely willing combatants. When Mussolini announced his declaration of war to a large crowd in Rome, voices were heard telling him, among other insults, to "Drop dead!" His ambitions in Africa prevailed, just the same, and on July 4 the Italian forces invaded the British protectorate of Somaliland. By September 13 the Italians were moving towards Egypt, where there was a large concentration of British forces and the vital Suez Canal. The British hit back, damaging the Italian fleet at Taranto in November 1940, and invading Italian Eritrea in January 1941. Before long the Italians were in difficulty and Mussolini was appealing to Hitler for help. It was the first, though not the last time, that the Italians' incompetence made them a liability to their German allies.

Hitler's response was to send General Erwin Rommel and several German divisions to help the Italians. At the same time the Luftwaffe's Air Corps X, with 500 aircraft, was sent from Norway to Sicily. Their principal task was to harass enemy shipping and maintain the supply lines to North Africa. The Luftwaffe also went into action in direct support of the German and Italian ground forces on February 16, 1941, when it raided the port of Benghazi, which had fallen into British hands a week earlier. By the time the Luftwaffe had finished, Benghazi was unusable as a base for the British forces in Libya.

Two months later, when the Germans rescued the Italians again by invading Greece, Luftwaffe power proved so strong that the small RAF fighter force on Crete was forced to withdraw from the fray. The Luftwaffe, for once, had command of the air and used it in intensive air raids designed to smash the British forces on Crete.

This was only the preliminary to the first major airborne assault in military history, which was carried out by the XI Airborne Corps in May

1940. Despite very heavy losses, the mass parachute drops continued. The losses so shocked Hitler that he never again attempted a large-scale airborne assault, but within less than two weeks, by May 31, the British had been forced to evacuate Crete and the island was in German hands.

An important target for the Germans in the Mediterranean was the island of Malta, a British possession strategically sited where RAF aircraft operating from its airfields could endanger the supply lines of the Afrika Korps. The Luftwaffe had already raided Malta 114 times by the first week of March 1941. Between September 1941 and June 1942 nearly 14,000 tons of bombs were dropped on the island, the maximum in a day being 500 tons and on one occasion the anti-aircraft guns were manned continuously for 66 hours.

Sir Archibald Sinclair, Secretary of State for Air in the wartime coalition government, delivered a graphic report of one of these raids to the House of Commons:

> The first time the Luftwaffe raided, they came over in the afternoon in two waves. There was quite a good number of planes, too, and they kept diving over the Grand Harbour for half an hour. Then came an interval of about fifteen minutes, and they started all over again… Although the Germans had guts to come down that low, they were terribly shaken. Plane after plane zoomed over very low indeed with engines sparking and smoke coming out from wings and tail. Every imaginable anti-aircraft shell was used against them. The sky was ablaze and I was nearly deafened by bomb and shell explosions. During that engagement, the Germans lost eleven aircraft. When they returned a couple of days later, they lost another nine and next day another nineteen.

For the Luftwaffe, Malta and in particular its capital and chief port, Valletta, was not an easy target. Hajo Hermann was familiar with some of the difficulties:

> When we flew in to attack Valletta, where warships were moored, we had to fly very exactly, maintain height, course and speed with mathematical correctness so that the bomb aimer's measurements could be

correct. For us, that was the critical and very dangerous moment. Down below, the flak could also measure exactly, and when they begin to drive up their barrages, then that is quite something, and you can hear it. You can see when a shell explodes in front of you, it seems quite close, which it is, close to the side. You can tell from the fact that if a plane is hit, then it explodes beside you in the air. Those are very, very tricky situations – the clean, correct approach to definite targets where the ground fire is aimed exactly.

The battle over Malta was to continue in the same punishing vein into 1942 and 1943 and the Luftwaffe also acted to bomb and strafe in best blitzkrieg style during advances by the Afrika Korps, for example, during the battle of Kasserine Pass, in Tunisia, in February 1943. Hitler had been unenthusiastic about diverting German troops to North Africa. To him, it was a sideshow that absorbed men and materiel better used elsewhere. His hand was forced, however, by the dashing, charismatic Rommel. Under Rommel's leadership, the daring exploits of the Afrika Korps made them popular heroes in Germany and the publicity and morale value of their successes were too great for even the Führer to ignore. Nevertheless, Hitler's real interest, a very long-standing one, was the invasion and conquest of Russia.

Russia posed significant geographical problems for an invader. It was the first really extensive area the Germans had attempted to bring under their control and its vast size made it a completely different battlefield from Poland or France. Their much smaller land areas and the good "tank country" provided by their terrain had been well suited to the swift blitzkrieg advance, while allowing the defenders little room for safe strategic withdrawal and no time to regroup.

The Luftwaffe's style of warfare was an integral part of blitzkrieg, but Russia offered few opportunities for winning quickly by lightning war. Not only was there too much territory to cover, but the Russians were able to hide away their reserves in places beyond reach. They were able, too, to disperse their weapons-manufacturing facilities over a very wide area. In November 1941, for example, as the Germans neared Moscow, the city's important SKF ball-bearing factory was evacuated and set up on a new site hundreds of miles to the east.

The Germans lacked the long-range bombers needed to deal with these widely dispersed industrial centres. They were still relying on the twin-engined Heinkel 111 medium bomber, which had first been used by the Condor Legion in Spain in 1938. During the Second World War the 111 comprised the major part of the Luftwaffe's bomber arm. It could fly 1,212 miles at 205 miles per hour with a full bomb load of some 5,500lb, but this was a very modest range and capacity for the task of destroying the Russian arms industry.

Although the Luftwaffe never managed that, its presence in Russia was considerable. Luftflotten 1, 2 and 4 were deployed, comprising a total of 2,770 aircraft, more than half Germany's total front-line strength. This included 775 bombers, 310 Ju-87 Stukas and 920 single- and twin-engined fighters.

Within a week of the invasion, on June 29, 1941, Hitler was already issuing so-called "victory communiqués" detailing, *inter alia*, a dazzling series of Luftwaffe successes: "The German air force delivered a crushing blow at the Russian air force. In air battles and by anti-aircraft fire on land, 4,107 Russian planes have been destroyed. In contrast to these losses are the comparatively moderate German losses of 150 planes."

The Russian High Command countered these claims with a communiqué of their own on June 30, putting Luftwaffe losses at 1,500 aircraft to the Russian air force's 850. Despite the propaganda put out by both sides, the Luftwaffe certainly dealt the Russian air force some very heavy punishment. Early on in the campaign it seized command of the air and by the end of September 1941 it had destroyed around 4,500 Russian aircraft for the loss of around 2,000 of their planes. The Polikarpov 1-16 Rata, which gave Hajo Hermann such problems in Spain, was still the best and most numerous Russian fighter in 1941 and hundreds were destroyed on the ground when the Luftwaffe raided their airfields. In the air, the Ratas were outclassed by the Me-109s and many were shot down.

Karl Born had a very poor opinion of the Russian air force:

> It was very bad. The Russian pilots were cowards. They used to turn away when we came on the scene. They never attacked us, except once when we were in a Fieseler Storch. But we were able to run out the

landing flaps and reduce speed, so the Russian shot past us before he could pull the trigger. The closer we were to the ground, the worse it was for him, because he had a large turning circle and couldn't follow us any more.

There was one Russian aircraft we came to know very well. We called it the "sewing machine". It was an ancient double-decker which always arrived at night and hurled all sorts of stuff down, stones, bits of iron. It was all very primitive.

Command of the air enabled the Ju-87 Stukas to fulfil their traditional role as tactical support for the German ground forces. Horst Ramstetter spent three years in Russia piloting dive-bombers:

At the beginning of the Russian campaign I was immediately sent into action in the last open-cockpit biplane, the Henschel-123, the forerunner of the Ju-87 Stuka. The HS-123 had an engine power of about 900hp and it was so manoeuvrable that in the pilot's jargon "you could turn it around a lamp post". It was a robust plane. They shot at me from below through the lower wing into the upper wing, there was a hole that I could almost crawl through, and the thing still kept flying. I think you'd have to take the wings off, then it would stop flying, and not before. It was that robust.

Ramstetter flew missions that seemed to take him back to a form of warfare from the past:

We flew missions against mounted units at the beginning of the war in Russia. Just imagine that, the Cossacks. Horse-drawn. I was up in the HS-123 when I saw some galloping horses and riders. One of them looked around and I saw his eyes, full of fear. I couldn't fire. I couldn't fire. I couldn't fire at the enemy. He suddenly became a human being for me. Why? In war, it's either you or me, that's the rule for every soldier the world over, either you or me, and whoever is faster, he survives longer. But I couldn't fire, not that time.

I flew 300 missions in the HS-123, in the southern sector in Russia. Early on I never got further north than Kiev in the Ukraine, but later

I flew over Stalingrad, supporting the ground troops. Afterwards I was sent on missions all over Russia as a fighter-bomber. But the HS-123 was very ancient. So I was retrained on the FW 190.

Alfred Wagner was very enthusiastic about the FW 190, which was introduced into the Luftwaffe after 1941 as a replacement for the Me-109:

The FW 190 was much more manoeuvrable in the air than many other aircraft. It had good loading capacity and weaponry and the technical standard was very high. It was also faster and had the advantage of being able to evade other planes quite easily. It swerved away beautifully, and was marvellously manoeuvrable – not as much as the Spitfire, of course, but a great improvement on what we'd had before.

In 1942 an FW 190 on patrol along the Norwegian coast sighted a large convoy heading through the Arctic seas towards Murmansk. The convoy was carrying vital supplies for the Russians: armour plate, steel, nickel, oil, aluminium, cordite, TNT, aircraft parts, guns, planes and food cargoes. For six days the Luftwaffe strove to prevent the ships reaching port and the battle was of mammoth proportions.

One Heinkel bomber flew through a hail of fire from one of the corvette escorts and dropped a torpedo that blasted a huge hole in the engine room of one ship, which had to be abandoned. Soon afterwards 24 twin-engined Luftwaffe bombers came in at no more than 30 feet above sea level. Nineteen failed to get through the defensive fire, but the other five torpedoed three vessels.

Hajo Hermann describes the so-called "turnip" technique, the *Schtekrübe*, which the Luftwaffe used to sink ships:

If you attack a steamer in order to sink it, then mostly you drop the bomb down either horizontally or so that it descends almost vertically and strikes amidships, or in the funnel if possible, or by diving or gliding towards the ship and then releasing it. But there was another technique contrived by people who believed it was not possible to sink a ship by striking it from above because there is so much junk lying around on deck. Sometimes there are armoured tanks and the bomb explodes in the tank, but the ship doesn't sink. With the "turnip" technique, you flew in very low, diagonally towards the ship's side, and released the bomb when you're very close. The bomb goes tearing into the side of the ship and rips open a huge hole. The water floods in and the ship sinks. Of course, the "turnip" technique involved enormous risk because the men on deck could see an attacker coming slowly in straight at the target, so they fire at him with precision and can hit him very easily.

An eyewitness on board one of the ships in the convoy later described the experience of being attacked from the air by the Luftwaffe:

We had six days of almost constant bombing raids. Our escort ships put up a magnificent barrage, but the German pilots came right through it and gave us all they had. A catapult plane on our ship was shot off to meet the attackers. The pilot, a young South African, took off to break up the Luftwaffe formation. We saw him bring down a large bomber and then go off to chase another. But a signal reached our ship that the pilot was wounded and had been forced to bail out. He jumped clear of the machine and made a perfect parachute drop into the sea. A destroyer went to his rescue and got him safely on board.

On the following day a direct hit was made on our vessel. She immediately began to sink. Two boats were launched. One was only an oar's length from the ship when a bomb blew it to pieces, killing five men. In the other boat we had to lie down on our faces during a machine-gun attack by a German plane. Luckily none of us was injured, but our boat was shattered. We found ourselves in the freezing water, clinging to driftwood. We were not left long in the water. The rescue ship did magnificent work, ignoring risks to save our lives.

There was never any darkness to give protection from attacks. We were too far north for that and it was summer, when daylight was perpetual. Every man in the convoy had to be on duty throughout the six days and so-called nights without thought of rest or sleep.

Attacking the convoys was not as easy as it might have appeared, as

Hajo Hermann realized when he targeted an aircraft carrier in the Arctic waters:

It was up in the polar sea, and the prevailing weather was heavy snow showers with very clear intervals. The British had an aircraft carrier cruising around, covering a convoy that was sailing there. I flew beneath the clouds towards the aircraft carrier – you could see for a great distance from beneath the clouds if there wasn't a snow shower. I pulled up high, staying very close to the clouds, because I always had to reckon with the fighters from the aircraft carrier climbing up and shooting me down.

I thought, if the carrier sails into an area of blue, completely clear weather and sunshine, then you are in a dreadful situation. For this reason I thought, when this aircraft carrier comes out from beneath the next shower, that will be the right moment for me to dive down the cloud wall, when the carrier's snout is just emerging, and then I'll drop the bombs in the middle. That, at least, was my plan.

At the moment I began to dive there was clear visibility and I was fired at heavily from the bow of the carrier. As I dived it came further and further out and then the English let loose such a violent barrage in front of us that they hit my right-hand engine. It wasn't disabled but they'd shot through the rods. I had both engines idling during the dive so that I wouldn't be too fast, and this engine with the damaged rods was now running at full speed.

The plane spun away and I couldn't stop it, couldn't keep on target, and my bomb, an armour-piercing bomb weighing 1,400 kilograms, fell about five metres from the ship. It was so terribly difficult to get close to those aircraft carriers.

In Russia the conditions under which the Luftwaffe had to operate were appalling. When the fearsome Russian winter closed in, pilots found their radios refused to work. The weather hampered accurate intelligence gathering. Aircraft coming in to land skidded off the runways, with the result that the Luftwaffe was able to operate at only a quarter of its strength. There were just as many planes lost through accidents as were lost in combat. The antiquated Russian air force, which had been so easily destroyed at the start of the campaign, had been replaced by modern aircraft which, even before the start of winter, made the Russians twice as strong in the air as the Luftwaffe.

At the beginning of 1942 an extra strain was put on the Luftwaffe after the first major Russian offensive of the war attempted to push the Germans back along the entire 2,000-mile front. Despite the seas of mud of the notorious *Rasputitza*, caused by the autumn rains of 1941 followed by the freezing cold and snow of winter, the Germans had managed to advance into the suburbs of Moscow by the end of the year. The Russian winter offensive of 1942 ensured that they got no further. The pressure was taken off Moscow as the north-south battle line in the vicinity of the capital was forced back and the German salients came under threat. For the Luftwaffe, Moscow was a dangerous area. The capital was ringed with mighty – and accurate – anti-aircraft batteries and the toll of German planes was such that the Luftwaffe's last raid, on the night of October 24, 1941, was carried out by only eight aircraft.

The Luftwaffe was called in to airlift supplies to the beleaguered German units on the ground, but there were too few available personnel. To fill the gaps, flying instructors and students from the air training schools were drafted in as pilots for the Ju-52s, the capacious tri-motor freighter aircraft. The Russians did not achieve all their objectives. Sevastopol was besieged and Kharkov remained in German hands, but the invaders were kicked out of Rostov, near the Sea of Azov, and thrown back 120 miles.

Long before this, according to Hitler, the forces of the Third Reich should have been home, dry and victorious. Instead they found themselves still battling the mammoth of Russian resistance, which as yet showed no signs of weakening, let alone collapsing. German prospects brightened, however, after June 1942, when the Caucasus proved to be a weak link in the Russian defences. The Germans managed to capture Sevastopol and organized Russian resistance in the Crimea came to an end.

Horst Ramstetter had flown in support of the German ground forces and personally experienced the ferocity of the Russian resistance:

> The fighter-bombers had to fly low, we had to support the attacking

troops, our troops, destroy supply positions, destroy tanks, bomb troop positions – those were our tasks. We flew down at house height immediately in the range of the Russian guns, which, of course, then raked us with fire. I was shot down, as I pulled up the plane it began to burn, I couldn't bail out with the parachute, so I set my HS-123 down on the ground at an angle.

The undercarriage sheered off, so I couldn't land properly. But I managed to get down and leapt out of the plane before it burst into flames. I was wearing flying overalls, so the heat only burnt me a little. I leapt into a shell hole. Everything boomed and whistled, I felt so miserable, completely alone. Then a tank rolled up, a German tank. "Hey, pilot," I heard someone say. "Come here." I said, "I can't, they're shooting." The tank drove up, I jumped up on to it and went through the whole tank attack. I was never so afraid as I was in that tank.

Ramstetter went on other dangerous missions and once came down to land in the no man's land between the Russian and German lines. A fierce battle was taking place at the time:

There were certain mission targets that were, shall I say, dangerous, heavy concentration of flak, of troops, there were flak tanks sent against us, and I fell between Russian and German troops in the front line and sat in a shell hole. I put my head up and thought: "They were all firing at me! They couldn't be firing at anyone else." "Hallo, hallo," I heard. "Come here, come here." It was an infantryman, a sniper from the German lines, who came leaping over to me because I was stuck there and must have made an impression of helplessness. We called these men the "Frozen Meat Award Warriors", the corporals, they were the hard-bitten men, nothing touched them, they were unshakeable. He said, "Come here." I said, "I can't, they're shooting." He said, "I'll come to you. Look, we'll jump from here to there to there." I said, "Where?" "Over to our lines." I said, "Through that firing?" "Look," he said, "I'll go first and you follow." Then he called, "Where are you?" and I said, "The firing is so heavy, I can't just run through it." I finally got over with the corporal and was glad that I was in the German position and had some cover.

The prime purpose of the Germans' 1942 campaign in the Caucasus became the capture of Stalingrad, which was strategically sited on the River Volga. In German hands, Stalingrad, one of the foremost Russian industrial centres, would open the way into Astrakhan, an important terminus of rail and river communication for the south. The Russians' supply of petroleum would be drastically reduced and they would be unable to use Stalingrad as a jumping-off point for a new offensive in the winter of 1942–43. The Germans now expected to consolidate their conquest of the Caucasus as a prelude to winning the war in Russia.

The Russians were well aware of what the fall of Stalingrad would mean to them, and in late August 1942, when the German Sixth Army attacked from the north-west and the Fourth Panzer Army from the south-west, the Russian 62nd Army, under General Vasili Chuikov, was ordered to stop them, no matter what the cost. Chuikov had every intention of doing so. "Every German soldier," he remarked, "must be made to feel that he is living under the muzzle of a Russian gun." In the event the cost to the Russians was enormous, but to the Germans it was infinitely greater.

CHAPTER FIVE

The U-Boat War:
Days of Failure 1943–45

I N WAR, NEW DEFENCES have always been countered by even newer weapons, and vice versa. This was certainly the case in the Second World War at sea and was one of the main reasons why advantage and disadvantage could be claimed to each side in turn during the first four years. Of all the operational theatres, the boost war gives to science and innovation was at its most apparent here and it was when the Allies gained the upper hand both technologically and strategically that "the happy time" between 1939 and 1942 began to turn to days of failure for the U-boats.

The early British and other Allied losses and the vulnerability of the first transatlantic convoys led to a strategic rethink which centralized the routing of the ships, dispersed them over a wide area and strengthened the force of the escorts which protected them against the U-boats and other German assaults.

Apart from making attack more difficult, the new Allied strategy made the convoys much harder to find. To counter this, the Germans vastly increased their submarine numbers. After 1941 as many as 20 finished U-boats were coming off the slips every month. Helmut Benzing worked on U-boat construction, which was predicated on speed and a high turn-out:

> The U-boats were built in slices, pieces. These were brought in on small ships and in the shipyard, they were set one on top of the other, then they were pressurized and welded together. I suppose you could say they were put together like tin cans. We worked day and night and could launch one U-boat every 10 days.
>
> It was an ongoing production line, a system building process. Everyone had his own job. Where I worked, we built the flooding rods which allowed the flaps to be opened to let the air out and let the water in when the submarine had to dive. The rods ran the entire length of the boat up into the command centre and from there they were opened or closed. I built those, as well as parts of the diesel engines.
>
> It all happened quite quickly. When we'd got a boat ready, the sailors arrived and took it over. It went straight into dock, was tested, sent on trial and then out they went to war.

The Germans also modified their own strategy and the practice of making individual surface attacks on convoys increasingly gave way after late 1941 to the "wolf pack" technique. This required accurate intelligence and patient reconnaissance, in which the long-range Focke-Wulf FW 200 patrol aircraft prowled the Atlantic looking for likely prey.

Prior information enabled the U-boats to reach and patrol areas where convoys were expected well in advance. Once contact was made, there was no immediate attack. Instead the U-boats shadowed the convoy and signalled other submarines to come and join in the chase. Hunting in packs proved much more effective, and fruitful, than the lone forays typical of the early period in the war, and as the U-boats extended their range right across the Atlantic, the Allies had to take even more measures to protect their convoys.

Early on, escorts had been provided for convoys only in the Western Approaches to England, which covered the area south of Ireland, the southern part of the Irish Sea and the western section of the English Channel. The new wide-ranging area of U-boat operations required a greater span of protection, and escorts had to be provided for the whole of the transatlantic passage.

As a result U-boats began to avoid America and scour the open ocean for easier pickings. Even so they had to be very careful not to be detected by their prey. Werner Karsties remembers the precautions that had to be taken now that Allied expertise made it that much easier to locate an attacker:

> If a large convoy had been reported, then several U-boats that were nearby would be ordered to the area. If they were a long distance away, close to America, then it wasn't worth it, but those who were on operations nearby were instructed over the radio that a convoy was at such and such a position and ordered to go there straight away.
>
> But there was very little radio contact between U-boats during an operation. That would have enabled the enemy to detect them. They could discover through the radio signal alone that a U-boat was sending radio messages, and that "something" was in the vicinity. Then the people on deck searched even more carefully for German ships and the tops of U-boat periscopes.

The new Allied systems certainly provided fewer opportunities for the Germans on the notoriously difficult Murmansk run to northern Russia, where the destroyer escorts became more and more adept at keeping the U-boats away. Heinrich Schmidt was serving in one of the submarines which attempted to break the defensive ring: "From 1943 on, we sailed into battle against the convoys, the large convoys that sailed to Murmansk. But they were all well protected by destroyers, and U-boats couldn't get close and were forced away, so we usually came away empty-handed."

Wherever they were hunting the convoys now, the U-boats faced problems and the problems went on increasing. The Allies made major breakthroughs to claim the upper hand by means of advanced technology. The British introduced the high-frequency direction finder HF/DF, which allowed escort ships to get accurate locations for the U-boats from their radio signals. Usually called "Huff Duff", the apparatus was extensively used from the autumn of 1942, although not widespread until 1943, and could rapidly obtain a bearing even from a brief signal. "Huff-Duff" remained a secret from the Germans throughout the war and it was a great success, especially in the Atlantic.

So was another innovation introduced in 1941 – radar – which had been a vital factor in the defeat of the Luftwaffe in the Battle of Britain the previous year. During 1941–42 the mastheads of British destroyers became festooned with radar scanners and these forced more and more U-boats to operate underwater. This meant that their effectiveness was significantly decreased, and radar also gave Allied ships the advantage of more accurate navigation in areas of sea fog or limited visibility, by both day and night, although it was more limited in high seas.

At the same time the lives of U-boat crews were being complicated even more by the introduction of airborne depth bombs. Patrol aircraft were equipped with underwater bombs and search radar, together with high-intensity searchlights for use at night. All this enabled submarines to be detected on the surface at a considerable distance from both aircraft and ships. The "wolf pack" technique of U-boat attack was now at a disadvantage, since radar and "Huff Duff" on board convoy escort vessels provided very effective defence against surfaced "wolf-pack" submarines.

Like the Germans, the Allies instituted a rapid shipbuilding programme, which not only aimed to produce cargo vessels faster than the U-boats could sink them, but included increased numbers of anti-submarine patrol and escort vessels. These were equipped with new weapons, such as the Hedgehog and Squid missiles, which were thrown ahead of the ship. The Squid, which had a range of about 300 yards, was a depth-charge projector, developed by the Royal Navy, which consisted of a three-barrelled mortar. It was controlled from the ASDIC sound-range recorder and fired a depth charge with fins. The Squid's fuse was set automatically by information from the ASDIC depth-prediction gear.

The Hedgehog, which was more complex, involved firing 24 7.2-inch depth charges in a pattern ahead of the bow. The charges operated on a symbiotic system. They did not explode automatically, but only when one or more of them struck a U-boat. This was the signal for the remaining charges to blow up in their turn. The method took into account the requirements of the ship's sonar so that it would not be blanked out by random explosions but could hang on to its sound contact with the submarine. Charges were also thrown from the side and the stern of the attacking Allied ship.

The need for sonar devices for listening, echo ranging and locating submarines was grimly underlined in July 1942, when U-boats sank 96 ships worldwide. Sonar had been developed long before the war began, but now it became much more sophisticated to enable it to calculate the depth of submarines lurking underwater, detect the presence of incoming torpedoes and decide accurate ranges and bearings and the timing for firing weapons. Heinrich Schmidt remembers what it was like to be underwater, knowing that the sonar was looking for a U-boat and that an attack was sure to follow:

> You know what's going to happen when you hear the sonar coming closer and closer. Then it finds you and you have to prepare yourself. You can hear the sound of propellers and depth charges. They make eerie noises. The lights go out and parts of the engine shut off. Only someone who has been on a U-boat can describe the feeling. It's sad, a bitter noise, the noise of propellers everywhere above you and you can get terribly anxious. Are they going to drop depth charges or not? You don't know until it happens.

The Allies took some time to bring their new technological innovations into play. In the interim there were still insufficient numbers of long-range patrol planes based in Britain and America and the "wolf packs", some of them very large, were still able on occasion to overcome the convoy escorts. This situation continued even after the Japanese attacked the US fleet in Pearl Harbor on December 7, 1941, prompting the United States to enter the war. Hitler promptly declared war on the Americans and Admiral Dönitz responded by launching an immediate all-out attack on US merchant shipping. Initially he had only five U-boats to spare for this new war, but this increased to a monthly average of 20, and for six months, until June 1942, they made a killing ground of the American waters, sinking 500 vessels. It was if "the happy time" had suddenly returned, and U-boat crews made the most of it: "Once we sank an ammunition ship, it blew up, and from inside we heard the metal fragments banging against the side of the boat. When we surfaced, an axe on the boat had got stuck, so we made an emblem of this axe; we wore an axe on our caps with the letters "USA" – that was our emblem."

At this early stage in their war the Americans' inexperience in all-out warfare at sea was evident from the refusal to deploy even poorly protected convoys close to American shores. The Americans learned very quickly, however, adopting a policy of interlocking coastal convoys and continuous air patrols that made life much more difficult for the U-boats. Caribbean and American coastal waters were considerably safer for convoys after August, and the run of German successes came to an end.

By the latter part of 1942 the Germans had become wary but Karl Ohrt, who served on the U-595, remembers that playing safe was not always to their advantage:

> We located a convoy up in the St Lawrence stream in Canada. We had to obtain radio permission for an attack, from the High Command of the Wehrmacht. We wanted to start sinking ships, but all we were allowed to do was keep the convoy in sight at a distance of about 10 nautical miles. We were told to report locations continuously, together with numbers of the ships and so on, and had to continuously report locations, where we were, numbers of ships and so on. So we kept on reporting: "Now it's sailing in this direction, now in that direction, taking southerly course or northerly course." We sent in the report and the High Command tried to order other boats in to intercept and destroy the convoy.

It took a lot of time, and I think we hung around so long that we were detected. The people in the convoy knew exactly what we were there for, and that we were reporting back on their movements. So, during the night of August 16–17, we had 250 depth charges dropped on us. Afterwards we managed to return to Brest. The deep-water rudder and everything were damaged; repairs and maintenance took 14 days. It happened at other times, too. Every time we shadowed a convoy and reported its movements, we got a terrible thrashing.

Two weeks was not a long time for repairs. U-boats suffering this sort of onslaught, or simply breaking down, could be out of action for up to four weeks, and that was if the damage was not too serious. Hans Lange remembers that "there was always something wrong with the engines or something else on board" :

A damaged or defective U-boat was immediately taken to the shipyard. Damage lists were prepared about faults or the repairs we'd been able to make ourselves and we did this while we were still at sea. Once the shipyard had seen to the repair, there was a trial run, and it always took at least four weeks until the boat was ready to put to sea again. It was more if the damage was serious.

Even then, we couldn't always go out on another operation straight away. Very often the trial run out of the shipyard revealed that something or other was still wrong.

We had our boat repaired in the shipyard at La Spezia and the Italians gave us a completion date soon after we'd sailed in. We knew the Italians were supposed to be shoddy, careless workers, so we said, "Ha, ha! The Italians take twice as long!" But we were wrong. They were bang on time, the boat was back in top condition, exactly as they had said it would be. Afterwards our crew didn't need to pick up a spanner when they were out at sea, the boat was in absolutely top condition.

However, after 1943, four weeks for repairs or even two became a luxury for the U-boats. While they were laid up in dock, other boats that were, as yet, unscathed had to carry the extra strain. Extra work meant more time spent at sea and wider sweeps while there. To handle this situation the Germans set up a system for maintenance and supply at sea in 1942. Large ocean-going Type 9 U-boats were converted into supply vessels which acquired the nickname "milch cows". They were able to refuel, rearm and even repair submarines at sea. By this means the U-boats gained valuable extra operating time and greater efficiency, but it could be a perilous operation nonetheless. Herbert Lange was on board his U-boat when it was attacked:

> We were caught by English planes that dropped bombs and rockets on to us. One rocket shot through the tower, killing the duty officer and 12 men altogether, instantly. Meanwhile the boat was on fire, in the control room. The rocket had hit the oil-pressure gauge equipment, which contained about a ton of oil; it ran out and set off a huge blaze, although the central protection walls were closed quite quickly to prevent the fire from spreading. We had 20 live torpedoes on board. The might have started to burn and blow up, but fortunately we got away with it!

A U-boat attacked on the surface by an Allied aircraft meant a special drill if the wounded were to be saved. Clausdieter Oelschlagel describes what happened:

> During one attack on our boat, we had one man killed and seven injured from the flak gunners. The rest of us had to drop them down the open hatch – whoomp! – on to a large carpet or woollen mat. They fell down on to that and were rolled out of the way. Then those of us who were all right jumped down after them. You have to be able to do it extremely well, to jump in one after the other, because if a life jacket or a leather jacket got snagged on the way down, it could have had dire consequences. Our commander trained us specially to escape in this way. We practised for the whole day in the Ovik fjord near Narvik, up and down, up and down, again and again so that we were fit for the job at sea.

Karl Ohrt's U-boat had a remarkable escape, owing to the mysterious absence of Allied aircraft in an area – the Bay of Biscay – where they were usually numerous:

> We had to dive because the deep-water rudders were broken, we were stuck and only able to carry out a half-dive by going into reverse when we wanted to submerge. It was likely to take us 20 minutes to get from the surface down to the bottom. Nonetheless – and I haven't been able to understand it to this very day – we managed to sail through the Bay of Biscay into Brest without interference. We were in a really bad state, not being able to dive properly. Yet we weren't attacked by planes, English planes, we weren't attacked by destroyers or corvettes. That was normally a daily occurrence when a U-boat tried to reach harbour at Brest. We just sailed right through.

Kurt Wehling's last trip came to an abrupt end after his U-boat was forced to the surface:

> Depth charges didn't always explode on the boat 100 per cent of the time. They were spread about because the Allied ships didn't know exactly where our boat was. The depth charges were fired over the sides of the ships and spread around. If they exploded close to the boat, then they caused damage – the valves opened and water came in, that's what it was like. On the last trip we had to surface because the first depth charges were dropped quite close by and ripped the boat open. We weren't sunk by depth charges but by the ship's artillery, they got us.

On November 8, 1942 the Americans entered the European war when they participated in Operation Torch, the Allied landings in North Africa. The U-595 was in the Mediterranean and Karl Ohrt was on board:

> Our orders were to "prevent the Allied landings in Africa". That's how it was phrased, anyway. We were supposed to close off the harbour entrance at Oran. Around November 10 we sank a ship, not a big one, only 5–6,000 tonnes, and an Allied transport ship or something like that. We knew the enemy was using radar against us all the

time. We could hear it. It sounded like peas being thrown about in a saucepan, but we weren't too bothered about that. We were young, you see, so we didn't take it too seriously.

Then, on November 14, we got the order from Admiral Dönitz not to sail on the surface in the Mediterranean during the day. We knew the reason for we no longer had air cover; in fact, as we discovered later, we no longer had a proper air force. We set off shortly before 0800 hours, just as I was about to relieve the watch, and there was this unbelievable crash. The galley flap flew open, a bomb had exploded on top of it, the galley flap opened, and the alarm bell went off simultaneously. We saw this huge hole and through that we could see the sky. One of my shipmates – quite a tall fellow – grabbed hold of me and lifted me up. I got hold of the ring and then bang, the galley flap was shut tight again. There were four catches, and it slammed closed over them, but then water began to leak through it. We tried to twist it but we couldn't make it close down tight properly. Fortunately it stayed closed because the water pressure held it down.

The U-595 dived, but it was too badly damaged to remain for long below the surface:

We dived down and the pressure gauge in the engine room told us that that we had dropped over 250 metres. That was when water broke into the electric engine room. We were ordered to go to the front of the boat, then air was pumped in and we resurfaced. The whole episode lasted about five minutes, including diving and resurfacing. The starboard diesel was waterlogged, but the port-side diesel was all right and started up at once. We moved off straight away, but immediately we were attacked from the air.

All we could do now was defend ourselves and hope to survive. We were told to head for Spain, but the damage to the boat was too great for that and we were ordered to sail instead towards the African coast. We had a 2cm flak gun fixed on the deck and set up two machine guns which had recently been welded to the boat in the marine base at Brest. We were also carrying shells to use against armoured planes.

A little later we managed to get the starboard engine running again and we sailed towards Africa. Even though it was dangerous to be there, we were so exposed, many of tried to stay on deck because we knew that if the boat sank, we had the best chance of survival. If we'd been down below, our chances wouldn't have been too good.

Being on deck also gave Ohrt a grandstand view of the opposition they were facing:

On deck, we saw planes all around us, at least nine of them. Gerhard Horn, who was manning the flak gun, was a trained artillery man and he let the enemy planes get close, up to about 250 metres, before he began to fire. The rest of us packed the cartridges for the gun so that he wouldn't run out of ammunition. Although there were so many aircraft, they didn't come in to the attack in groups. They always attacked one at a time, so it was that much easier to see them off.

What I didn't find out until after the war, when I met two of the pilots, was that they were scared stiff of our armament. They said they had been much more scared than we were, because they didn't know what what we were hitting them with. That's why they stopped attacking us and so allowed our boat to sail on towards Africa. But we were in a terrible state. The back of the boat sank, water had broken into the electric engines, and the boat became heavier and heavier at the stern. It went up at the front and down at the back and suddenly we only had eight or 10 metres of water beneath the keel.

The order came: "All men overboard!" and then out we went, and then we sank the boat. When we were in the water – we were defenceless, of course – a plane came over and shot at us. But it only made one run, thank goodness. No one was seriously hurt except one man, Walter Holdorf, who was shot through the thigh.

Ohrt and the rest of the crew of U-595 had not not yet finished their adventures. Onshore, on the North African coast, they were attacked twice, from the air and then from the sea:

We managed to get ashore and you won't believe this when I tell you. Another aircraft flew over and dropped leaflets on us. The pilot said that if we didn't stay where we were, then he would fire at us. Well, we ran off, he returned and opened fire, but we had all hidden ourselves behind stones and no one was hit. He flew off after that. The next thing we knew, there was a destroyer offshore bombarding us with artillery. We were lucky again, because only one salvo was fired, it didn't hit anything or anyone, and then they stopped.

Because Holdorf was injured, we signalled the destroyer to send a boat to fetch him on board. Holdorf became a prisoner, but at least he was well looked after and his injuries tended. The rest of us marched off in the direction of Oran. We met a French policeman and asked him if he could help us, we wanted to get dry and all that, and he said that we could spend the night in the school. But you know how it goes: the English got to hear about us and radioed the Americans to say that a German U-boat crew had landed, go get them. Four American tanks rolled up and took us prisoner, the only U-boat crew to be captured by tanks.

We were taken to Oran, where we were presented to the population as a German U-boat crew, they stood us up in the town square and told everyone that we were criminals. Well, that's how they regarded us. After that we were taken to the citadel and if you didn't already have lice or fleas then you caught them there from the bedclothes.

On his voyage to captivity, Ohrt saw for the first time the immense power of the Allies at sea:

That same night we were sent on board a ship called the Brazil, a 20,000-tonner, where we were stowed in the engine room, and taken off to America. After three days were we allowed on deck for the first time. I've never seen anything in my entire life like that, such equipment. An aircraft carrier, six destroyers with smaller ships in attendance, even a cruiser, I think. The convoy consisted of perhaps 14 ships, all sailing towards America.

Being forced to surface, like Ohrt's submarine, naturally put the vessel in much greater danger of being attacked. The severe damage and ultimate sinking of the U-595 proved what happened when a craft was obliged to abandon the comparative safety of the underwater depths. To enable U-boats to remain submerged for longer, at a time when air and surface ship radar were already making life very difficult for them, in February 1944 the Germans introduced the snorkel, a hollow, retractable mast which contained tubes to take in fresh air and to vent the engine exhaust.

Heinz Reiners's father-in-law helped to design the snorkel, which was fitted to the U-boats after 1944. As an experienced submariner himself, Reiners was well aware of the advantages of the snorkel, but also some of the disadvantages:

> The air inside a U-boat was dreadful, so when my father-in-law helped to design the snorkel, he was doing U-boat crews a great favour. You could unfold the snorkel's long tube and while we stayed submerged, only the top of the snorkel, where the air was sucked in, was above water. Before this, we'd always had to surface to charge the battery and air the boat, but now we could do it underwater. We could keep moving, too while we were doing it.
>
> But the snorkel didn't work so well if the water was choppy and there were waves on the surface. The check-valve would snap closed and then it sucked diesel fumes from the engine room, resulting in negative pressure. In the galley, if the cook, the "Smut", as we called him, was bending over his pots, they flew up into the air. It drove you mad, the different pressures when the snorkel was out.

When the snorkel was first introduced, Allied radar was not yet advanced enough to pick up the end of the mast as it poked up above the surface. Later radars had this capability, however, so that the snorkel became yet another method by which U-boats could be detected and attacked. Reiners recalls being targeted:

> You always knew when the sonar was after you. The sound comes closer and closer and then it found you and you knew what was going to happen next. We had to prepare ourselves. We could hear the sound of ships' propellers approaching and the sound of the depth charges. Depth charges and destroyers make eerie noises, the lights go out and

parts of the engine too. Only someone who's been on a U-boat can describe the feeling. It is a bitter and sad noise when the destroyers and depth charges are coming, the noise of the propellers everywhere above you, they can get you very, very anxious...

Werner Ziemer, too, found the propellers noises thoroughly unnerving: "They sounded like 'sshh-sshh'. You can hear each blade slicing through the water. Nowadays the propellers have multiple blades, in those days they only had three. You could also hear the sonar echoing inside the boat. It went 'tick tick tick tick tick – tick tick tick'. It was unnerving, really unnerving."

Increased Allied vigilance and more success in destroying U-boats had a knock-on effect on the U-boat war. Werner Karsties observes how the U-boats were denied time to update their equipment in harbour:

Naval technology advanced a great deal during the course of the war, not only on the German side but also in England. The English ships were faster, more accurate and could find us much more easily than they could in the early years. As a result our losses increased and those U-boats which survived had to do more work than before. We were continuously in action at the front. Boats could only be improved when they returned from operations against the enemy. The commanders were supposed to report what they had experienced through being intercepted by the enemy, and told the technicians on land what had to be done. But after 1943 there just wasn't enough time for this to be done properly.

U-boat crews had to be careful, too, how the hatch was closed before diving. Werner Ritter von Voigtländer explains the problems this caused when, later on, the U-boat had to surface:

You can't get the tower hatch open after surfacing until you have established pressure equalization between the air outside and the air inside. It used to happen that if someone fastened the tower hatch too tightly when they dived, they couldn't open it again once they were on the surface. Even when the pressures were equalized, you could do

what you liked, the rubber ring was so tightly sealed that they could-
n't get it open again! The only thing to do was to dive again straight
away so that you could get some pressure on it and loosen it before
resurfacing. After that you could open it.

Equalization of pressure causes steam, anything that is wet suddenly
evaporates into steam and the whole boat is filled with mist, sometimes
a lot, sometimes less, depending on the position. The ventilation had
to be turned on immediately. We really couldn't afford mistakes like
this when there might be Allied aircraft prowling around ready to drop
bombs on us while we were more occupied with opening the hatch than
firing back at them.

Constant vigilance was a must for U-boats, which could be attacked
at any moment, and in the later part of the war, von Voigtländer remembers, a double watch system was introduced:

Towards the end, on the Type 21 U-boats, the previous triple-shift
system – eight hours on watch at a time – was abandoned and the
double watch system replaced it. On the Type 21 we had two watch
periods, which weren't that dramatic, because for the most part the boat
travelled underwater. When we were submerged, two men were at the
deep-sea rudder, one on the rudder working the levers, and once the
submerged boat had been set on course by the chief engineer, after the
diving procedure, then the duty officer took over the responsibility and
we continued to travel underwater. He sat in the control room and made
sure that nothing happened while the others slept and two or three men
looked after the engines. Otherwise we were on watch every four
hours, and believe me, when we were on the surface, there wasn't much
sleep to be had. We had to reckon the enemy could appear and attack
us at any time.

In this tense situation U-boat crews had to protect themselves in any
way they could, even if it meant attacking civilian targets. Werner
Karsties's U-boat was in the eastern Mediterranean, close to the coast
of Palestine, when the fishing boats common in the area came under
suspicion:

During the last days of my service in the Mediterranean, we sank lots of small fishing boats with the 88mm gun. They were really harmless fishing boats around Haifa and Jaffa and in the early days of the war – "the happy time" – we probably wouldn't have touched them. But later we thought that these boats might pick up something on the radio and we knew they had some very modern equipment, these harmless fishing boats. They could radio to the shore immediately and it wouldn't be long before enemy planes arrived. That was why it was necessary to sink them immediately without bothering to search them or investigate them.

German anxieties in the latter half of the war were exacerbated by the very punishing casualty rate suffered by the U-boats. In all, around 60 per cent of all U-boat personnel were lost during the war and it was not unusual for U-boats to manage only two sorties before they were destroyed. There was a dearth of young officers and battle-hardened crew and many submarines had to put to sea commanded by inexperienced young men in their early twenties. Several U-boats, and their young crews, were lost on their very first voyage.

Werner Karsties remembers that U-boat commanders had their own solution to the problem of inexperienced crews. It worked, but only for a time:

Every commander made an effort to keep the core crew, with which he had taken over the boat from the shipyard, with him for as long as possible. This had always been our practice at least until the middle of the war. If a boat was in for repairs, and you knew how long the repairs would take – four, six, eight weeks – a U-boat crew wasn't dispersed.

Of course, it was possible that someone or other would be ordered away, someone on another boat in the flotilla would become ill, and then the first duty officer or the helmsman would go out with that boat as long as, theoretically, he could get back on his own boat when it was ready.

The U-boat flotillas used to organize all this between themselves. There was also a flotilla reserve – men on standby in La Rochelle, in

Bordeaux, or wherever, who were assigned to duty if someone left a boat or became ill. But essentially the core crew remained together.

Later on, though, that was no longer possible because of the losses, which led to men being ordered away to other boats or to NCO training. These NCOs were sent to other boats and were replaced by new men from the U-boat training schools. So commanders could still end up with inexperienced crews.

The U-boats themselves were not always in the peak of condition and inexpert handling made the situation worse. Werner Ritter von Voigtländer was serving on the U-415 when a potentially fatal accident occurred:

Three days after I reported for duty at Kiel, our U-boat suddenly went crashing down to a depth of 250 metres because of a mechanical failure during the dive. I sat on my deep-sea rudder box and thought: "It's not that great on this boat, is it?" The ship was leaking water, which dripped down on everyone, and nothing worked.

Fortunately our people managed to get the boat back up again, but there were so many mechanical failures because of the "top deck tubes", as we called them. We found that the water pressure had been so great that it had squashed the reserve torpedoes flat. It was a close call at that depth.

Towards the end of 1943 the U-415 was back in action, and on Christmas Day the boat became embroiled with a destroyer:

The destroyer wanted to ram us and came thundering towards us. We were at periscope depth and had to dive at once. We released an acoustic torpedo from our tube five, kept right on target and the destroyer was hit and sank. We managed to rescue about four casualties from the destroyer, but it was all very unpleasant. It was Christmas Day, not a day for killing and destruction.

The U-415 returned to Brest to rejoin the First U-boat Flotilla and then von Voigtländer was ordered to retrain for service on the Type 21 U-boats, which represented a new concept in U-boat construction:

> The 21s were welded together in three shipyards; those with the numbers 25 in Hamburg, those with the number 30 in Bremen and those with the number 35 in the east, in Danzig. We were sent to 3001, but it wasn't put into service because it had some very bad technical defects.
>
> The Type 21 was the first attempt to make a U-boat by shoving together, pushing and welding together, different parts. The ducts had to fit together and if someone forgot to remove a flange, then nothing worked. Later, when the 02 was put into service, we got quite a few surprises. The 02 was lost because of a breakdown in the harbour at Kiel. We got the propellers tangled in the nets that were designed to catch the torpedoes.
>
> Ours was the first boat of that type to arrive in Kiel. We went into reverse in front of the bunker so as to be able to sail in slowly, which caused the stern to sink a little and then – whoomp! – we got entangled in the thing and the boat was unfit for service. We were towed away by another boat to the docks in Flensburg, where they discovered that it was hopeless, it couldn't be repaired quickly.

The Kriegsmarine had now entered a fatal spiral. Allied shipbuilding was climbing far above Allied losses at sea. On the U-boats, reducing experience and rising losses meant that young greenhorn crews were going to sea in what had become almost a "turkey shoot".

Long-range aircraft, such as the British Short Sunderland flying boat and the American Liberator fitted with long-range fuel tanks and radar, were able to seek out the U-boats as never before. Surfacing became even more dangerous: the U-boats could come under attack immediately from Allied aircraft patrolling the skies above. However, not surfacing also had its perils. Kurt Wehling was involved in a depth-charge attack that forced his U-boat to remain submerged for eight hours. Eventually, despite the dangers, the boat was obliged to surface because the crew was having trouble breathing: "We were short of air, critically short, in fact. So we had to surface, come what may. We were lucky on that occasion. The enemy was nowhere to be seen, but everyone lay on the floor with respirators, gasping for air through our apparatus. We were able to air the boat, and what a relief that was, I can tell you!"

By mid-1942 the Allies had developed, although not until a year later perfected, their compact airborne radar system, which enabled them to detect a surfaced submarine several miles away. This gave them the advantage of surprise. U-boat commanders could suddenly find themselves confronted with a heavily armoured aircraft swooping down out of the clouds and flying straight at them on a bombing run. Clausdieter Oelschlagel was on board one U-boat that was attacked in this terrifying fashion:

The Liberators came tearing down 40 or 60 metres above the sea. On July 17 we were attacked by a Liberator bomber and were lucky enough to hit it on approach. We shot that one down, but two days later another Liberator arrived. We were taken by surprise, confused, and didn't know whether we should dive or not. We remained on the surface and the Liberator raked us very badly. One man died and seven were injured on the bridge. We managed to dive several hours later, catch our breath and recuperate a bit, and then went staggering off back home.

By this time the Allies already had an advantage of which the Germans were unaware. In 1941 the Royal Navy had managed to get hold of the top-secret Enigma code book from a crippled German weather ship. All signals to U-boats were coded and could be decoded only by means of this book. It was now an arduous but straightforward matter to crack the German codes, and one of the benefits was that the Allies were able to identify the positions of the U-boat "wolf packs".

By this time the Germans had had the Enigma machine for enciphering radio transmissions for 20 years, and during the Second World War they changed their codes every day. Different branches of their armed forces used different codes, and the Germans came to believe that the system was foolproof. They never realized that French intelligence had helped Polish mathematicians and cryptanalysts build copies of Enigma, which they had handed over to the British and the French before the war began. The capture of the Enigma code book in 1941 was also unknown to them and so was a similar incident that occurred in 1944.

It happened off the Cape Verde Islands, when an Allied force on patrol captured the U-505. The submarine's code books were seized intact, enabling naval experts to decipher the German naval code even faster than they were then doing. Werner Karsties recalls what happened after the Allies got their hands on this invaluable secret:

> They should have thrown the logbook into the sea, those people on the U-505, but either they forget or weren't able to. So the Allies got hold of it and then the code machine also fell into their hands. The code machine was used for decoding the radio messages which were not in "clear". They were encoded – A was B or C was E; not as simple as that, of course, but you get the idea – and the code was changed every 24 hours. The message had to be decoded on board the U-boat and then handed to the commander. But the Allies got hold of all this and, according to one story I heard, they sent false coded messages ordering U-boats to a certain point and when they got there they bombed them.

The breaking of the codes, combined with new sonar, radar and other weapons, produced an even more dramatic rise in German U-boat losses. In one month – May 1943 – 37 boats were lost. Another 34 went down in July. Werner Ritter von Voigtländer's craft, the U-415, was one of those that managed to escape this massacre, but it was a very close-run thing:

> It was May 8, 1943, a day I'll never forget as long as I live. Four-engined planes came down at us from out of the clouds – huge machines. We knew that if enemy aircraft looked the size of mosquitoes on the horizon, then the boat could dive and you were safe. But these planes were big, big, big, and we had no chance. In any case we had orders to remain on the surface and fight them off from there. It may sound strange, but there was good thinking behind it.
>
> You see, bombs from the air sink to perhaps five metres below the surface before exploding and if the boat is down at 12 or 15 metres,

then that's it, it's finished. Kaput! The depth charges were specially adjusted to explode much deeper – at 50 or 60 metres below the surface.

If the U-boat had dived, the aircraft saw a big whirlpool and they'd take their time and aim. There was no one to disturb them by firing at them, and they dropped their depth charges in this whirlpool. If the U-boat was in the diving phase, and down, let's say, up to 80 metres, with all the hatches open, the catches open, then the depth charge exploded right beside the boat and blew it to smithereens. That caused huge losses, of course, so that's why we were told to stay on the surface. We just had to sit there and take it until the aircraft had finished dropping their bombs or until they had withdrawn to a distance, perhaps in order to make a fresh approach. That gave us time to dive down to a safe depth before they came back, but we had to dive well over 80 metres or they'd get us the second time.

We didn't have much of a chance, though. On the U-415 we had just one weary old 2cm and they had lots of on-board guns, machine guns and heaven knows what. We tried to manoeuvre out of danger. We went right and left at full speed ahead, hard to port, hard to starboard, trying to get out of it. It was useless. All the things they threw at us – bombs, depths charges – all the damage!

One of the depth charges exploded right under the stern and the boat practically stood on its head. We closed the tower hatch but it didn't lock. It wasn't hermetically sealed. There's a click spring to close it from outside, so the hatch was open a way. We were strapped in with our broad belts and the steel straps for stability in the waves and the boat sliced down to about four or five metres. In other words, we were roped on to the bridge and then there were perhaps five or six metres of water above us.

When the boat tipped up and stood on its head because of the depth-charge explosion, our chief engineer at once realized what had happened. He could see where the boat was from his depth gauge. He immediately had the water chambers discharged, let pressurized air into the flood tubes and drove the whole thing back up. But for one or two minutes we had to hold our breath. I saw nothing but green and more green, and spluttered. I thought: "The show is over" and then, pppffff!

Suddenly everything became lighter and we were out. We'd been lucky.

If the sea was being made dangerous for the U-boats, there was no much more security in dock. Karl Ohrt's submarine was berthed in Hamburg when it got caught up in the last raid on the already flattened city in 1943:

I was on watch at the time. It was a daytime raid and there was no air-raid siren to warn us. I heard the bombs falling and I sent the crew members who were still on board on watch duty into the bunkers as fast as possible. I remained on board with one or two others. The bombs fell into the harbour and our diving tanks were badly damaged. We were towed into the bunker at Rohwald, but the damage was so serious it couldn't be repaired.

Werner Karsties remembers how U-boats crews being depth-charged received some assurance in their predicament from a fail-safe procedure that could save them even if their ship were lost:

We could get to the surface from quite far down, from from perhaps a depth of about 60 metres. Everyone had a respirator on his life jacket and the control room would be flooded so that the pressure would be equal to the outside water pressure and the tower hatch could be opened. You then had to open the valve, not too quickly, so that you moved upwards, but slowly. Unfortunately far too many men panicked, opened up the valve and shot up to the surface. Then they were poisoned by the nitrogen, so that blood flowed out of their mouth and nose. No, when escaping from a U-boat, you needed to keep calm. It was a great reassurance for us. We knew that there was a way to get out even if the boat was doomed.

Kurt Wehling's U-boat was doomed when his U-boat set out for a foray in the Mediterranean and ran into a powerful convoy escort:

We were in front of a convoy and sank one ship. But immediately afterwards the first depth charges fell and hit us. The boat had cracks in it and we had to creep away, keeping absolutely quiet inside the boat. There were three destroyers above us, three! They searched and searched and searched with their equipment, "Ping-ping-ping-ping," we heard it. The small pinging sounds meant they hadn't found us, but if the ASDIC went "Ping – P-I-N-G!" when it bounced back, then we were in the soup.

Another destroyer sailed up after the first and dropped more depth charges. By this time it was 2000 hours. We crept forwards in silence and they kept on searching, but somehow we managed to get away with it and they gave up.

After another two hours we had to surface because too much water had leaked into the boat. Once we had surfaced, the duty crew immediately went up into the tower and manned the twin 2cm machine guns. Good thing, too! We had hardly emerged from the water before we were caught in the searchlights of three destroyers. They opened fire immediately with their artillery. The crew on duty on our U-boat answered by opening fire on the searchlights.

One shell hit us directly in the tower and there was a stench down at the bottom of the tower from the explosion, the stink of dynamite. My role down below was to pass on the commands – they weren't given through a microphone, each command was passed from man to man. The chief engineer in the control room suddenly shouted, "Everybody out", probably because he hadn't received any more orders from the tower. The commander was no longer there because of the direct hit. I stood between the control room and the commander's room and was one of the first four men to get out.

I got up on deck; there were searchlights all around us. It was as light as day and the guns on the destroyers were still thundering away. We had one-man rubber dinghies that were distributed all around the boat and in an emergency everyone could grab one, tie it around himself like a little briefcase with two cords. I took one and once I was out and in the water I turned on the little pressurized-gas bottle. It went "Shhhhhh!" and out came the boat. I draped my arm into it and paddled away on my own.

It was very dark. Each of us had a whistle so that all those who were nearby could gather together. I heard the first whistle but I didn't answer. I thought: "Stay on your own, stay on your own. Who knows what's going to happen, you've got a one-man rubber dinghy, you can paddle." But it didn't take long before a wave threw someone over, then there were two of us, and in the end there were four of us with two rubber dinghies.

The dark was a blessing because after a while the destroyers returned to their convoy. Then a searchlight appeared on the horizon, came closer and closer and some English sailors fished us out of the water. They set boats down and I remember there was a big black man – the first black man I'd ever seen. He was a big, strong fellow. He grabbed hold of us and pulled us out of the water.

We were taken back to the destroyer and went on board. We were well treated. They showed us immediately to a room where we could have a shower. Each of us was given a Red Cross parcel in which there was a pair of pyjamas, toothpaste, socks and shoes, felt slippers, that is. We went into another room and found the table was set with ham, bread, packets of cigarettes and heaven knows what. It was all very welcome.

German losses were at their highest in the Atlantic, where the only victories they scored were usually pyrrhic victories. In October 1943, for example, the U-boats sank one escort ship and three merchant ships, but lost 22 of their own craft. This was in sharp contrast even to the flawed success of a "wolf pack" six months earlier when the U-boats attacked convoy ONS-5, en route to Newfoundland, and sank 13 merchant vessels for the loss of six submarines.

Ultimately the cost became too great for the service to bear and Admiral Dönitz was forced to order the complete withdrawal of the U-boats from the north Atlantic in May 1943. Nevertheless, the U-boat menace was not at an end. When the Allies sent the largest amphibious invasion force in history across the English Channel to land in Normandy on D-Day, June 6, 1944, 43 German U-boats were sent to attack them. However, it was to be their last concerted stand, and all but 19 were destroyed. By this time the Allies were also wrecking the U-boats at source, in the submarine pens. Werner Ritter von Voigtländer was about to sail in a new U-boat when the Allied bombers came over:

> Two days before we were due to sail there was an air raid and the
> boat sank, right beside the pier. One of our men was inside, to the rear.
> Twenty-four hours later we still hadn't got him out. It just wasn't possi-
> ble. We tried to pull it up with a tugboat but all the cables tore, we
> couldn't cut it open because he would have drowned in there. He
> was quite a young NCO, but he didn't know Morse code. He just kept
> banging madly on the walls of the boat. But it was no use. He died.

Despite their desperate situation, the Germans were still introducing
new methods of promoting the underwater war. One of their technological innovations was the Type 5 acoustic torpedo, which was designed
to home in on engine noise. Clausdieter Oelschlagel had a poor opinion of the Type 5, which U-boat crews nicknamed the Zaunkönig, the
"wren":

> In my opinion the Zaunkönigen weren't much good because the
> convoys soon had a defence against them. The sloops or corvettes
> would tow a "rattle" buoy at a distance of about 200 metres behind
> them. It was a noise-making buoy. That attracted the T5 torpedo and
> the stupid thing headed towards the sound and exploded there. It was
> such a simple method they used, but "poof!" in a moment a marvel-
> lous weapon on which many engineers had worked for years went up
> in smoke!

Oelschlagel took part in the last operation undertaken by a German U-
boat against a British warship when the destroyer escort Goodall was
sunk off the Kola Inlet on April 29, 1945:

> We had a report from the first officer on the Gudel [Goodall] which
> we were given after the war: apparently 117 men were lost with the
> ship. That was my last trip and after we had sunk the Gudel we were
> heavily attacked with depth charges by other destroyers and sloops in
> the area. Our attack periscope was hit, flooded with water, so that we
> only had the second, the air periscope or "knee-bend" periscope.

That's the one you see in films when the commander stands at the periscope and goes up and down. We called it the "knee-bend" periscope, whereas the attack periscope was automatic. That was still intact, but had the disadvantage of an enormous head that could easily be seen. On the return trip to Narvik following the April 29 attack, we spotted another convoy on our starboard side, but it was far away, and we were ordered to sail into harbour and not attack any more, just defend ourselves if attacked. We sailed into Haarstad in the Lofoten Islands, where there was an important naval office, and on to Narvik.

On May 4, 1945, five days after Oelschlagel's last U-boat voyage, Grand Admiral Karl Dönitz, now German Head of State since Hitler's suicide on April 30, issued an order for the submarines to cease hostilities. Dönitz was highly respected by the U-boat crews and, to judge from his final words to them, the feeling was mutual:

> My U-boat men. Six years of warfare lie behind us. You have fought like lions against a crushingly superior force, but you are unbroken in your warlike courage. You are laying down your arms after an heroic fight without equal. In reverence, let us think of the many comrades who have died. Comrades! Maintain your U-boat spirit with which you fought most bravely and unflinchingly during the long years.

Since 1939 733 U-boats had been lost, together with 79 Italian submarines. A total of 2,919 Allied ships of 14,557,000 gross tons had been sunk.

Clausdieter Oelschlagel was still in Narvik when Nazi Germany surrendered on May 7, 1945, and he remained there for nearly three weeks more:

> We were still in Narvik on May 25. Our boat was lying in one of the fjords, but no one came. We were then given permission to transfer to Trondheim, where the Flotilla was and where we had our belongings. We got as far as the entrance to the fjord at Trondheim, where we met a Canadian fleet and they ordered the U-boats to go to Scotland. Half the crew were taken off there, and the rest of us sailed to Lisholly near

Londonderry in [Northern] Ireland.

After that we were all sent to England, where we ended up in a tent camp at Butterly. On the way we officers were locked in the ladies' toilets at Hampton Court Palace – well, it was one way to get a look at a royal palace, I suppose!

Werner Ritter von Voigtländer's war ended in a much more curious fashion. His U-boat was at sea when the surrender of Nazi Germany was announced, but the crew knew nothing about it:

We were halfway across the "big pond", heading for America. We didn't know that the war was over because our special long-wave radio equipment wasn't working. The reason for that was the capture of the big transmitter near Magdeburg by the Allies. So we were cut off from the world.

We didn't surface, we were a full-snorkel boat, which meant we could sail for hours underwater. Then we started to intercept some strange messages – or at least, we thought they were strange. There was one from a stoker in Wilhelmshaven who was sending greetings to a female naval assistant in Oslo. What a load of rubbish! we thought.

Then the English sent an open radio message, saying that we should deliver our boat to Loch Eribol up in Scotland, hoist the black flag, throw the ammunition overboard and surrender. We thought it was a rotten trick. We weren't going to fall for that, we said. But just the same we suspected something was wrong, we didn't know what, so we decided to sail back to Norway. Three quarters of the way there, when we were heading towards Bergen, it occurred to us that maybe the Russians were there. That was something we didn't want – not under any circumstances! So we changed course again and decided to go home to Germany through the Baltic Sea. It was risky, because we didn't have any mine charts for the Baltic.

Then, suddenly, we heard a dreadful noise under the water and our sound detector picked up signs of an entire fleet sailing by. We looked through the periscope and there was an English invasion fleet sailing across to Norway. Cruisers and battleships one behind the other. We watched them calmly, and submerged a little.

It was only then that we realized the war was over. It had finished two days earlier, and no one knew our U-boat was in the area. Well, we had 24 torpedoes on board, and we could have fired them, one every 30 seconds at a depth of 70 metres. It was a completely new technique which had never been used. But we didn't use it. Instead we worked our way through the minefields around Scargen, and while we were doing that we were sighted by an English plane.

We were in a fix. We thought the plane might bomb us. Our signalling equipment – a small spotlight – was destroyed, so we couldn't report the number of our boat that way. Instead we had to write our number – 3008 – on the metal deck with some chalk. That seemed to satisfy the English pilot and he flew away.

Next thing we knew, we were being ordered into Friedrichshouen, in northern Denmark. That was difficult. The water was too shallow for our draught and we couldn't get in, so we set ourselves on to the anchorage and waited to see what they intended to do with us. We waited for two days, and then a fleet formation arrived from Kiel, a torpedo boat or corvette or frigate or whatever, one in front, one behind. They put us in the middle to keep an eye on us and escorted us into Kiel. We arrived there on Whit Sunday 1945, just about the last U-boat of the war to surrender.

CHAPTER SIX

The Defeat of the Luftwaffe
1943–44

The battle for Stalingrad is frequently cited as the bloodiest, most hard-fought and most destructive struggle of the Second World War, and the Luftwaffe's part in this monumental contest was always gruelling. They played many roles, not only attacking targets, but carrying out reconnaissance and patrols, gathering information and airlifting supplies. Hermann Goering's boastful opinion of his Luftwaffe had remained unchanged and when the Sixth Army was encircled and trapped inside Stalingrad in late November 1942, he assured Hitler that the air force was able to provide the supplies needed to sustain the Germans and enable them to keep on fighting. The amount required was about 550 tons a day. It proved to be an impossible target, given the ferocity of Russian anti-aircraft activity. The result was the near-destruction of the Luftwaffe's transport arm.

In these circumstances any role the Luftwaffe might play on any particular day was dangerous and nerve-racking. Horst Ramstetter considers his missions at Stalingrad the hardest he ever flew in his entire career as an airman: "Undoubtedly the most difficult mission was Stalingrad, because the concentration of defences was so enormous, more than at any time from the beginning to the end of the Russian campaign. For me at any rate, it was an enormous effort to reach the various points that had been chosen as targets there, fly there and do the job."

The job entailed pounding Stalingrad with such damaging raids that the water mains were destroyed and large areas of the city were left burning. Many of the buildings had to be pulled down to stop the blaze spreading. Dar Gova, in the south of Stalingrad near the River Volga, was obliterated, leaving its rows of neat bungalows a mess of smoking wood and ash. At the nearby sugar plant, now in ruins, only the grain elevator remained standing.

Before the battle began, the younger German airmen had not realized what they were in for. Horst Ramstetter remembers the excitement and anticipation of 18-year-olds facing their first battle, and how quickly these feelings changed:

When our advance on Stalingrad began, everyone said, great, we're moving, marching, everything's fine. Then they realized too late that the Russians had no intention of losing. To them, Stalingrad was a sort of "show town", an object of prestige. Some of the pilots were only 18 and had never flown a mission. They'd had their heads filled with "Führer, Volk and Vaterland – we'll storm onwards, we heroes will win the war!" But the real thing was very different. They came back crying their eyes out. They were ready to drop, they hadn't been prepared for such an operation, or for an enemy as ferocious as the Russians. The raw reality pulled them back down to the earth.

Ramstetter remembers how he discovered that the Russians had broken through the German defences:

> Romanian troops, our allies, were fighting with our forces. They were positioned to the north of Stalingrad. Two of us flew a mission over the area. We were supposed to find out what was going on because the front line was a bit confused. I looked down and saw these greyish-brown uniforms. "The Romanians!" I thought, and decided to check it out.
>
> I dived down, but I was fired at. I said, "Those crazy Romanians, why are they firing at us, we're allies." It wasn't the Romanians, it was the Russians, but what were they doing there? I immediately flew back to base at Pitomnik and reported: the Russians have broken through. Where? I showed them where on the map. "That's impossible," they said. "That's where the Romanians are." "Yes, exactly there," I said. And once the reconnaissance had flown over and confirmed my report, we prepared the airstrip ready for defence.
>
> We knew that if the Russians kept advancing like that, they'd be on top of us in a day. We had nothing, no infantry, nothing. We had already been forced to evacuate our airfield, because the Russians were too near. Now they were coming close again and all we could do was sit in the trenches and wait until they arrived. We lay there all night and at first light, at dawn, we climbed into the planes and flew up over the airstrip. The Russians were already there, and they fired on us.
>
> We flew 15 or 16 missions. We were reloaded with ammunition and bombs while the engines were still running and then we had to take off again.

By October 1942 the battle for Stalingrad had already become a battle of attrition. Russian resistance was so fanatical that General Paulus, in command of the German Sixth Army, lost four battalions in exchange for capturing a block of flats. On October 14 five German divisions were sent to overrun two factories, supported by 3,000 sorties from the Luftwaffe.

In December 1942 Horst Ramstetter's squadron was transferred to Nichechieskaya, south of Stalingrad. They wanted to celebrate

Christmas with a sing-song but instead found themselves in the thick of battle:

> We heard: "Alarm! Alarm! The Russians have broken through." Thank God we had an 88 flak unit with us, one that had been pulled back from the front. The 88 was the best anti-tank gun of all, although it had been intended as an anti-aircraft gun. But it kept the Russians off our necks and we were able to take off and fly over Stalingrad, which was already under siege. Army Group South were supposed to relieve the Sixth Army with their advance tanks. We thought, "Great, thank God!" But it didn't work out that way.
>
> General Paulus, with his 150,000 soldiers, sat there in Stalingrad. The supply lines weren't working. They'd been told, "The Luftwaffe can supply you, you can hold out." But that didn't work. They went hungry, they had no ammunition, no fuel, and they ate the horses that were lying around dead. We saw the front line of the relieving army and saw the signals from the besieged pocket. The distance between them was 40 kilometres.
>
> The men on the ground had been told, "When a German soldier stands there, he does not yield one centimetre of ground." These stupid orders, the glorification of heroism. Madness! Suddenly the relieving army halted. What's wrong now? we wondered. I'll tell you: the Russians broke through the southern wing and soon Russians and Germans were fighting house to house. Sometimes they were on different floors. When we flew attacks on Stalingrad, we couldn't tell our troops from the Russians.

For Ramstetter, total war on the ground at Stalingrad was translated to total war in the air:

> We carried many injured men, picked them up directly from the medical stations near the front lines, we flew very close to the front, but at low level. We were often able to avoid the flak because we knew roughly where the flak batteries were. But over Stalingrad we used to fly very low because the light flak, which was operated by women, was very accurate and low flying meant they couldn't track us so easily.

The heavy flak was quite a different matter. The Russians had set up their flak, and before you got to Stalingrad, you saw what looked like a wall of fire. Shells detonated, it looked like darker and lighter balls of cotton wool. And we had to fly into them! There wasn't time to be afraid because we were so preoccupied with keeping our planes in the air, but when I returned to base I felt I had just been dragged across an obstacle course. We didn't have much respite, though. We were soon in the air again, to reconnoitre the Russian troops' supplies.

On one such mission, disaster nearly overtook Ramstetter after his aircraft was shot down. He narrowly escaped the Germans' worst fear in Russia: being captured by the communists:

I was flying an FW 190, and discovered a Russian train loaded with war material. We attacked and destroyed the engine, but my aircraft received a massive hit and I had to make an emergency landing. I came down behind the Russian lines.

We carried emergency rations of a bar of choco-cola and weatherproof matches and Dextrose. We had the machine gun on board the plane and were carrying our own handguns. I got out of the plane, saw a corn field and ran into it. I heard the troops rolling past somewhere in the distance and I said to myself: "If the Russians should come now, you've got seven or eight rounds in your gun. You can try to get the Ivans with seven of them and the last one you've got left will be for yourself." But I thought again and said: "Nothing doing! I'm not going to kill myself."

I had my compass with me and knew in which direction I had to go. I set off, always keeping myself hidden. On the second night I arrived at a German border position on the front line. I swam across a river and ran across a field and shouted, "Don't shoot! I'm a German pilot!" But just as I reached the position safely, a Russian fighter-bomber appeared and dived down on us. Everyone threw themselves to the ground and some men jumped on top of me. They saved my life. They were hit by shrapnel, but I survived, but I thought, "I'd rather volunteer for 100 combat missions than go through another day like this."

Aerial combat with the Russian fighters was a traumatic experience for Detlef Radbruch:

> It's an awful moment to see six planes fly towards you all at once. It was frightening. We didn't know what was going to happen. But when you were fighting, operating the gun and firing it and hitting your opponent were the only things that mattered. When we had flown difficult missions, we called it birthday celebrations, we celebrated our birthday, for having got through it.
>
> We flew in formations of up to five planes and each had three machine guns. We had agreed on the tactic of firing at the first Russian plane that approached us and mostly we managed to shoot it down or damage it badly so that it turned away. When that happened, the other five Russians turned away as well. Except, that is, for the pilot we called "the Commissar". You always knew there was a fanatical communist piloting that plane, because he'd attack us even though we outnumbered him. We were hit many times. Once, our undercarriage was hit so that we had to land on one wheel and make a crash landing. Fortunately all of us got out in one piece.
>
> We were very lucky, but many others weren't. It's a terrible thing to see a comrade shot down. During transport flights over the Kuban bridgehead in the Caucasus, we had escort planes. They kept the Russian fighter planes at a distance but several of them were shot down. When we saw that, it was a great shock every time. At Stalingrad some 488 planes were shot down and more than 1,000 airmen were lost. It had taken a long time to train them – a year for radio operators and about as long for pilots, but all that could be lost within a few minutes.

Despite all the efforts of Radbruch and other German pilots, the 550 tons a day that the encircled Sixth Army had been promised by Goering never materialized. It was difficult enough for the Luftwaffe to deliver 100 tons a day, and even that was rarely achieved. The transports were frequently ambushed by Russian fighters, which had special orders to destroy German supply aircraft flying to Stalingrad. On November 24, four days before the Russians completed their encirclement of the Sixth Army, Luftflotten 4 lost 22 out of 47 of their Ju-52s. Another nine were destroyed the following day. General Baron Wolfram von Richthofen, a cousin of the famous "Red Baron", realized how crucial this rate of loss was: "We simply have not got the transport aircraft to do it," he said. By December losses among the Luftwaffe transports had risen to 30 per cent of all flights attempted.

The Luftwaffe fighters, too, came under threat and Richthofen was forced to move some of his fighters into Stalingrad in order to protect them. He admitted: "We have not been able to master the Russian fighters absolutely and, of course, the Russians can attack our forward airfields any time they like. We have been able to fly in only 75 tons instead of the 300 tons we were ordered to deliver."

Richthofen had only 550 bombers, 350 fighters, 100 reconnaissance planes and his few transports against the Russians' 1,250 planes. The standard of servicing was low and the intense cold damaged the fabric of the aircraft, causing many of them to crash. Supply lanes that managed to land safely were plastered on the ground by Russian artillery and roving T-34 tanks and bombed and strafed by Russian fighters. Unloading them had to be done at speed, the wounded were embarked and the aircraft would have to run the gauntlet again to take off safely. The casualties in men and aircraft were massive and Pitomnik, the principal supply field for Stalingrad, was full of bomb craters, snow and wrecked planes.

Despite all this, Goering's orders to supply the troops inside Stalingrad with 550 tons a day or more still stood. Richthofen realized the part played by ego and politics in Goering's refusal to see sense. "Orders are orders and we'll do our best to carry them out," he commented. "But the tragedy is that no local commander on the spot, even those who enjoy the Führer's confidence, can any longer exercise influence. As things are, we commanders, from the operations point of view, are now nothing more than highly paid NCOs."

When he first arrived in Russia, Detlef Radbruch worked at the direction-finding station that regulated the air traffic supplying the German pocket at Stalingrad, but he had been told he should get some flying experience, and at the end of January 1943 he flew with a night mission over the city:

The pilot of our aircraft had already flown 11 missions to Stalingrad, so that was a lot of practice and we were going to be very grateful for it. But it was extremely dangerous, the temperatures were below -30 [Celsius] and the distance to the airfield at Stalingrad was over 300 kilometres, so it was going to be a big effort to return to base.

The Russians had set up very powerful flak around the Sixth Army in the pocket at Stalingrad. General Paulus had already surrendered, but there was a detachment to the north of Stalingrad still holding out. We reached it and dropped our cargo – bread in sacks, sausage and ammunition. One crate, containing special ammunition, got jammed in the door and the parachute dropped out and opened. Two of us were able to cut the parachute free but it became entangled in the tail-fin aileron and the pilot had to struggle to keep the plane flying. Because he was an excellent and experienced pilot, he was able to get us back to the airstrip. This was the last aircraft supplying the Sixth Army at Stalingrad.

Many of us thought the disaster at Stalingrad was Goering's fault. We didn't think a great deal of him. At Stalingrad there were between 260 and over 300,000 German soldiers Our planes brought out 40,000 wounded but at least 160,000 fell during the battle, and about 100,000 were taken prisoner. Only about 6,000 came home after the war. The Russian losses at Stalingrad were double or three times ours. They lost over half a million soldiers. In that dreadful battle, over half a million young people or more died because of the madness of two dictators – Hitler and Stalin.

General Paulus surrendered in Stalingrad on January 31, 1943, and the following July the Germans attempted to recompense themselves with the massive tank assault on the Russians at Kursk. They were beaten again and this weakened their already fragile position on the eastern front. The Luftwaffe, flying in support, was hammered by the Russians and lost 1,400 aircraft. After that, Horst Ramstetter recalls, many planes were grounded owing to lack of supplies: "We'd been given all sorts of promises, about wonder weapons and miracle armaments, but it was all nonsense. What actually happened was that our supply line broke down and we couldn't get off the ground. We had to leave the planes standing, or blow them up because we didn't have any fuel."

A scarcely less violent struggle was continuing in the Mediterranean, where the Luftwaffe were striving to keep the supplies lines open to the Afrika Korps. This imposed so much strain on the Luftwaffe pilots that one of them, a sergeant by the name of Mosbach, lost his nerve. He told his commander, Hajo Hermann, that he had decided not to fly:

> We'd been fighting against the Royal Navy and the battles were very hard. RAF fighter planes were there as well, and everyone was under terrible pressure. This Mosbach was a very capable, skilful pilot, but one day he came up to me and said, "Sir, I have to report that I don't feel well. I think I'm going to be shot down on this mission." I replied, "Have you gone off your head? What's the matter with you? You're not an old woman." "No," he said, "I know that I'm making myself a laughing stock, but I have such a strong feeling, that I just can't do it today."
>
> I just stared at him for a bit and said, "Well, Mosbach, I've known you for a long time and I've never experienced anyone like you come up to me in this way." I was a bit angry, but I told him, "Stay at home then!" So he stayed at home. But he was shot down during another mission and floated around in a rubber dinghy until the British came and picked him up. But the terrible thing was, he was badly burned and lost his sight.

On May 9, 1943 the German and Italian troops in Tunisia surrendered unconditionally and Erwin Rommel, the original commander of the Afrika Korps, was said to be relieved that his men were now Allied prisoners and far beyond the reach of Hitler, who would have sacrificed them rather than capitulate. The last German resistance in North Africa, at Cape Bon, was extinguished on May 12, when, together with his entire staff, Colonel-General Jürgen von Arnim, commander of Army Group Africa, was captured at an inland camp on the peninsula.

The invasion of Sicily took place on July 10, preceded by 100 sorties by American Mustang fighter-bombers. They bombed and strafed behind the German defence lines, plastered troop concentrations with cannon fire and left transport, bridges, locomotives, railway yards and barracks burning and in ruins.

The Luftwaffe was now subjected to the same treatment it had meted out in Poland or Russia. The Allied air presence, which included attacks by Liberator bombers, was so overwhelming that German pilots were unable to get their planes off the ground and within only a few hours the Allies had command of the air. The Sicilian campaign ended with the Axis surrender on August 17, 1943, and less than two weeks later Allied forces invaded Italy.

After his service in Russia, Detlef Radbruch flew missions in Italy in support of the German troops on Sicily and as preparation for the invasion of the mainland:

> We were withdrawn from Russia and flew on special orders to southern Italy, where we were to bring the Division Hermann Goering, an infantry division that was part the Luftwaffe, to Naples. After the surrender in North Africa, we flew around Italy for three weeks, bringing troops to Sicily and Sardinia because the Allied landing on Sicily was expected.

One day Radbruch was on the airfield at Naples-Cappodiccino when he heard and "unbelievable" sound of engines. He looked up and saw 16 Me-323 Gigant troop transports above him. The size and capacity of the Me-323s was reflected in their name. The Gigant, which flew on six engines, had a length of just over 92 feet, and could carry 130 troops and 21,500 pounds of freight, three times the capacity of the Junkers-52. Despite their formidable appearance, they were far from impregnable. Gigants were slow-flying and vulnerable and in April 1943, during the last days of the war in Africa, a Polish Fighter Wing serving with the RAF had downed most of a flight of 20 Gigants, sending tons of much-needed supplies into the Mediterranean. The Gigants Radbruch saw were going to meet a similar fate:

> I saw these planes and immediately thought: "Oh God, that's not going to work, because the Allied air superiority is too great." In the evening, after an Italian flight, I returned and went into the casino. A captain sat at the bar shaking his head and getting drunk: he had seen

the death of the Gigants. All of them had been shot down. Each Gigant was carrying 20 tonnes of fuel, which was to be taken to Tunis. The captain said he saw the sea burning, he was very shocked.

Detlef Radbruch had his own dangers to face in Italy:

> We fetched German troops from Livorno and brought them to Sicily and Sardinia. These flights were very dangerous. We had to fly very low because many of our aircraft were being shot down at that time. The twin-engined Lightnings found our Junkers all too easy to destroy. We flew very, very low, because the fighters can't operate down there, and apart from that, we hoped that if we flew over the sea and were hit we could make an emergency landing in the water and be saved.

In Italy, the Luftwaffe scored a surprise success on the night of December 24, 1943, when 105 Ju-88s attacked the Adriatic port of Bari, where the First British Airborne Division was based during the transfer of Allied Forces from Sicily. The attack was entirely unsuspected. There had been no attempt to blackout the port. The docks were brilliantly lit as the Luftwaffe swooped in on the 30 ships in port, and blew up two ammunition ships which caused the loss of another 17 vessels.

One of these, the John Harvey, was carrying a secret supply of mustard gas as insurance against the chance that the Germans might resort to gas warfare. She blew up in a massive fireball that threw debris and her deadly cargo hundreds of feet into the air. The crew died instantly, and among the rest of the estimated 1,000 casualties, more than half, 628 people, died of mustard-gas poisoning. Large areas of Bari were reduced to rubble, and the capacity of the port was severely curtailed for the next three weeks.

The raid on Bari resulted in supply shortages to the Allied Fifth Army in Italy and the losses sustained there prevented the US 15th Air Force from participating in raids on Germany for another two months. However, the raid was not a sign of renaissance for the Luftwaffe. It was more of a final sting in the tail of a once-deadly scorpion. The Luftwaffe was, in fact, in a desperately decimated state by the time the Allies invaded Italy. There was a serious decline in number of pilots and their effectiveness naturally suffered. The Luftwaffe retained its esprit de corps and its camaraderie, but these were small advantages compared with the enormity of the task facing it after 1943. Preserving planes and pilots became an important consideration. Horst Ramstetter was one Luftwaffe pilot who had to judge whether or not it was wise to attack:

> We had to think about whether the risk we were taking was worth it and what would happen if an attack went wrong. Sometimes we'd attack a position four times and blaze away at it with everything we had. The problem then was that the enemy fighters arrived, and our weapons went "Click!" – there was no ammunition left.
>
> After that you had to start thinking about whether you'd get back to home base or not. There was, though, a trick we used to use. We called it the "pilot's fart". There was a stopper that you could pull out and you got an extra burst of speed through an additional injection of fuel and went 40 or 50 kilometres faster. The snag was that when you had pulled that thing, it virtually destroyed the engine. You could fly for perhaps five minutes and then it was over. But in an emergency, you hoped that the five minutes enabled you to escape.

In spite of such ploys, the situation of the Luftwaffe worsened steadily: "The pilot training periods were reduced, and because the new fighter pilots had no experience, they were the first to be shot down. As the war went on, we were no longer capable of flying missions over manufacturing plants while, at the same time, Allied bombing raids on Germany were hurting us a lot."

One important setback for the Luftwaffe was that the Allied planes had made the Me-109 obsolete. Not only was it outclassed, but the version introduced at the end of 1942, the Me-109G, carried so much firepower and extra equipment for protection against Allied attack that it was unable to operate successfully. The Luftwaffe's operational strength fell to a mere 4,000 aircraft, with no reserves. Thereafter the numbers fell consistently, leaving the Germans no more than 1,800 aircraft during the rest of the war. Besides this, the Allied bombing campaign on Germany reduced the Luftwaffe to a defensive role, something for which it had never been designed.

The Allied raids went on round the clock. The United States Army Air Force (USAAF) Flying Fortresses and Royal Air Force Lancaster bombers took turns, the first bombing Germany by day and the second by night. The cities as well as the factories of the Fatherland were targets. The Luftwaffe was short of night-bombers, and the Ju-88, built as a light bomber, had to be specially adapted to cope. Heinz Philip was a gunner with one of these Ju-88s:

> As the night fighting became acute, when the English started to come more and more frequently at night – we didn't have any planes specifically for the night. At first the Me-110 was equipped and put into operation as a night-fighter but it couldn't fly for long enough and didn't carry enough guns, so in order to be able to use more weapons the Ju-88 was used. Trials with other planes were made, but they proved ineffective.
>
> We didn't carry bombs. When the plane was constructed there was a space intended to house bombs and this space was filled with a tank, an additional tank, so that we were able to keep flying for four hours.
>
> I sat at the guns on the Ju-88. There were four 2cm guns at the front and the magazines were in such a position that I could remove them when they had been emptied, that was my job, and I had to fix new magazines to the back. That was something to occupy me, but I didn't do it continuously. And when the English or the Americans attacked, that was during the day, they defended themselves and I looked at them head on. To look head on at a machine gun that is firing at you, that made me very nervous, and the pilot was busy with his plane while I just sat beside him and didn't know what to do. That happened the first time, but the second time I took my camera with me and from then on when we flew during the day, I took photographs so that I had something to do, to distract myself.

Hannau Rittau served on one of the Luftwaffe anti-aircraft batteries defending Berlin from the Allied raids:

> Our battery had four guns, one rangefinder and one radar. There were

about six people operating each gun, another six to operate the rangefinder and five on the radar. Our job was to protect the Heinkel aircraft factory at Oranienburg, a suburb in the north of Berlin. The light anti-aircraft couldn't come into action at all because the Allied aeroplanes flew far too high. We couldn't reach them because we could fire no higher than 3,500 metres or thereabouts. But the planes usually came over at almost twice that height – around 6,000 metres – and only the heavy anti-aircraft could deal with them.

Berlin was bombed almost every night, well, perhaps not every night, but very regularly. The worst of it came in 1944, when the Allies started their 1,000-bomber raids and 1,000 of them came over at one time. The sky filled with planes, and during these raids I was at my rangefinder. I had to pick up the aeroplanes and get all the data, which was transferred to the guns so that they could fire at the aeroplanes at the right height. There was no time for training. We learned on the job.

Our battery was on the outskirts of Berlin. Most of the anti-aircraft guns were on the outskirts, except for two anti-aircraft towers which were located right in Berlin, one of them at the Zoo. Berlin looked very, very damaged, houses came down and collapsed in ruins. But you got used to that after a while, you get used to everything after a while. But we didn't like getting it every night, that was horrible.

The raids on Berlin normally started at around 2200 hours and Rittau's anti-aircraft was alerted by radio:

We were told where the bombers were, and were in action for three or four hours as they unloaded their bombs. Unfortunately our flak wasn't very effective. Our battery shot down a total of eight planes, which wasn't much considering how many raiders there were. We used to put a ring on our guns for every aircraft we shot down.

We thought of the pilots up above us and wondered how they felt, being fired at. I don't suppose it felt very good when you sit in an aircraft and see all this firing going on around you and know the next shell might hit your plane. I think that we damaged some of the planes and didn't think they would get back to England. Some of them came down over the Netherlands or in France. On the other hand we

Eckhart Strasosky (right) in Russia in 1940.

Eckhart Strasosky (far left), who was sent as an officer at the age of 22 to fight on the Russian Front. "Hitler thought we would conquer Russia in one year and had not even remotely considered equipping the troops with winter clothing."

Strasosky outside the Grossdeutschland Division's barracks in 1941.

A half-track advancing across Russia.

A German anti-aircraft gun is put through its paces on manoeuvres.

Being entertained by an accordion in front of a Russian cottage.

A steam engine stranded on a destroyed railway bridge.

The poignant sight of German soldiers' graves in Russia.

The detritus of battle. Russian light tanks, armoured cars and the corpses of draft horses litter the field.

A German unit on manoeuvres, practising with range-finding equipment.

Herr Kosak of the Waffen-SS. "We were exhausted … we had been sleeping in the woods, and I woke up because someone was shaking me, and there stood the Russians in front of me."

Herr Kosak today. "I joined [the Waffen-SS] because my Reich Labour Service platoon commander had a very nationalistic attitude and 1 wanted to get out anyway."

An officer of the Waffen-SS prepares to join an attack with a hand grenade. During the coming months in 1939 the Waffen-SS were responsible for many instances of bravery, but they were also associated with unbridled brutality.

The German infantrymen paid an enormous price for the battle of Stalingrad, but their losses were eclipsed by the Red Army, who lost over one million men in the defence of the city in 1943–44.

In the closing stages of the war the Luftwaffe had practically disappeared from the skies above Germany, and so troops had to remain in a state of constant vigilance for attacks from the air.

Alfred Wagner, Luftwaffe fighter pilot. "I volunteered for the Luftwaffe when I was 17. To me, it was a marvellous adventure… If we were asked to volunteer to fly somewhere, I was always first in the queue!"

Karl Born, a Luftwaffe pilot. "The Russian air force was very bad. They hurled all sorts of stuff down, stones, bits of iron. It was all very primitive."

A wing of Junkers-87 Stukas escorted by a Messerschmitt 109. These were the
aircraft which heralded the days of blitzkrieg.

Countless Russian towns and cities would be reduced to shattered rubble by street fighting which grew in scale and intensity as the war went on. The conflict in Russia was to reach a terrible climax at Stalingrad.

Grenadiers marching into the front line during the summer of 1941. The optimism and sense of adventure can be seen in the happy smiles for the cameras.

Weary Grenadiers during a short pause in the fighting for Stalingrad.

A German prisoner wearing a camouflaged smock is taken into captivity by a US infantryman. The smock was generally issued to snipers, and in this case the young man was probably lucky to have escaped with his life.

German prisoners are made to confront the evidence of maltreatment of Soviet prisoners in German captivity. One Soviet guard recalled how the Germans marched slowly at first, but as more and more grisly remains were encountered, they began to move faster and faster until they were almost running through the camp.

Berlin, 1945. Ollech and his comrades preparing to defend the German capital.

Digging in the guns and spotlights around Berlin in 1945.

Ulf Ollech, a 16-year-old flak helper in Berlin in 1945. 'Everything that had two legs and two healthy hands and could carry a weapon was mobilized.'

Soviet tanks and other heavy equipment in front of the Brandenburg Gate in Berlin.

The shattered streets of Berlin made a strong defensive position.

Moscow 1945 – destroying captured German standards.

were the ones being bombed, so we were very glad when we were able to shoot down an Allied plane.

Rittau's world during a raid was a world of noise and flames:

You hear a humming sound all the time – that comes from the bombers flying overhead. We used to watch through binoculars to see when the bombs came down. Of course, you could figure out roughly where they were going to fall and sometimes, if it looked too close, you had to dig in, duck your head. and pray you weren't hit. It was terrible, I mean it was a terrible noise, you would see flames over the place. We were scared, no question, all of us, but fortunately our battery was never hit by a bomb.

Hajo Hermann was flying over Berlin in his Me-109 on August 24, 1943, while one of the Allied raids was going on. The raid was not a surprise, for Air Chief Marshal Arthur "Bomber" Harris had already announced it. The Germans were well aware that Harris's strategy was to win the war by bombing them into submission – a mistake Goering had already made about the British during the Battle of Britain. Hajo Hermann had already survived several brushes with death. This mission came the closest to costing him his life:

We were more or less prepared for the next attack that Harris had announced. It seemed to cause a certain amount of panic. The people, women and children above all, were evacuated from Berlin, and I stood ready to join in the fight. I flew during the night of August 23–24 from Bonn-Hangelar to Berlin, and from a distance I could see that over Berlin an enormous firework display was under way. The flak shells and searchlights were shining and I noticed the first planes being shot down. Then I went into action.

There was a bomber in front of me which I fired at, but it escaped by spiralling away. I wanted to be more accurate with the next one and flew very close to it. But, stupidly, I flew so close that I was lit up by the German searchlights below. So was he, and we fired at each other at almost point-blank range. I could see the whites of his eyes, so to speak, and I suppose he could see mine.

His plane started to burn and the crew had to bail out. He fired and hit my engine. Smoke began to pour from it and I had to bail out, too. I fell into a lake, wearing full war gear – in other words, an overall with the parachute but without anything such as a life jacket. I had to struggle to keep my head above water, and with great difficulty managed to swim ashore, where I met one of the British crew. He was quite friendly. Later on another member of the bomber crew was sent to a nearby hospital and I visited him there. What happened to me was a rather stupid affair, but at least Harris's bombers didn't return to Berlin for another two months, except in very small groups.

In January 1944 the RAF staged a big attack on Hitler's headquarters. Once again the Germans knew about it in advance, having intercepted the British coded messages. When the raid took place, Hajo Hermann was in action again and once again brushed with death:

The weather was quite bad. Nevertheless, I got my man in my sights and hit him. His plane started to burn, but just then a large area of defensive lighting spread out over the clouds. I was more interested in seeing if the plane was going to crash, and while that was going on I became visible as a silhouette against the light beams.

From behind me to the left, a Mosquito fired a salvo into my engine and everything was smashed up inside it. I got shrapnel in my leg and it was very unpleasant. At first I didn't notice that I was bleeding. I noticed it only when my leg became cold. I grasped it and saw what had happened. Well, I told myself, you'll have to do something to get down fast, and I flew towards the west because the weather looked as if it was better there.

I managed to reach an area around Hagen in the Ruhrgebiet, near Dortmund, but I hardly knew what I was doing. I was in a very bad state, with bouts of blindness, and thought I was going to fall unconscious. I said to myself, before I crash down below with the plane, I'll bail out and that's what I did. I came through the clouds and snow storm and landed on the ground, but in really dreadful condition. I came down in a forest clearing, at about six o'clock in the morning, a door opened somewhere, some light shone and I called out, and some people quickly picked me up and drove me to a hospital. Fortunately the hospital wasn't far away.

The Mosquito that shot down Hermann belonged to the squadrons that were ranging virtually at will over German territory in the latter part of 1943. The Luftwaffe tried desperately to inflict losses and reduce the onslaught, but all that happened was that the Allied planes came over in increasing numbers. They were using new techniques – the "pathfinder" system, which located and marked targets by radar, and the strips of metallized paper known as "window", which, when released in the air, jammed and confused Germany's own electronic defences.

The Luftwaffe could do little or nothing to prevent the systematic destruction of German cities, towns, factories and airfields. Hamburg was destroyed in July 1943, in a raid privately described by Minister of Propaganda Josef Goebbels as "a catastrophe the extent of which simply staggers the imagination". The RAF bombed Wilhelmshaven and Peenemünde, where the V1 and V2, Hitler's "vengeance" weapons, were being developed. The USAAF attacked the oilfields at Ploesti in Romania and the important ball-bearing factories at Schweinfurt.

Albert Speer, who became Hitler's Minister of Armaments in 1942 and took total charge of war production the following year, relocated and camouflaged factories and other important installations in an attempt to halt the severe disruption caused by the Allied bombing. The disruption nevertheless continued. Manufacturing capacity was decimated and the development of new weapons, such as the Me-262, was almost brought to a standstill.

Goering was still criticizing the Luftwaffe, this time for not being able to stop the Allied bombers. Heinz Philip, by now a fighter pilot, was one of the objects of his ire:

When we were confronted with American air superiority, we practically became the hunted, we fighters, and because we hadn't shot down enough planes and the Americans arrived with the bombs and so on, Goering stood up and said, "My fighters have become cowards." In consequence the entire officer rank removed their decorations and insignia and went around without their insignias of honour – Knight's Crosses and so on, all gone.

I couldn't stand Goering even before I was in the Luftwaffe. I regarded him as a vain, dressed-up fat man who performed like a theatre puppet. He wore fantasy uniforms – once he arrived in a snow-white uniform. He arrived in the morning, had a midday meal, inspected us, in the afternoon he did something or other, he changed uniforms two or three times in that time. He was a vain caricature – the highest decorations, highest-ranking marshal and God knows what else. I know of one incident when he was urgently needed but couldn't be found. Eventually he was discovered at Karinhall, his palace. At Karinhall there was a gigantic model railway in the cellar. Two or three men from the Luftwaffe had been assigned to him just to look after this railway, and there he was, playing with it.

Early on in their campaign, RAF and USAAF bombers had been vulnerable because of the lack of fighter escorts that could accompany them all the way to Germany and back. This problem was solved in 1943 by the introduction of the P-51 Mustang fighter, and with these guards to protect it the USAAF was able to resume the daylight raids that had been abandoned in 1943. This new Allied capability was typified by the "Big Week" of early 1944, which saw continuous, round-the-clock raids in which RAF Bomber Command took over from the Americans at night. Between February 20 and 26 the Allied air forces struck at the German aircraft and anti-aircraft factories and assembly plants in Leipzig, Regensburg, Augsburg, Fürth and Stuttgart. The Luftwaffe's attempts to halt the raids destroyed 244 heavy bombers and 33 fighter planes, but cost it 692 aircraft in the air and many more on the ground.

This was only part of the attrition suffered by the Luftwaffe and its pilots. By May 1944 the Germans had lost 2,442 fights in action and another 1,500 through accidents and although their air industry was not destroyed, the numbers of trained pilots lost were irreplaceable.

The Luftwaffe attempted to cut off the onslaught at source, by attacking airfields in England. Heinemann made two of these flights:

We were sent on night-fighter raids, with the bomber formations. We found the airfields in England were lit up brightly. I suppose they thought there would be no more Luftwaffe raids. We were supposed to give them some bother over there, but it proved much too dangerous. The raids were cancelled because too few of our planes returned.

Meanwhile the shortages occasioned by Allied attacks on Germany's oil-production facilities meant that training new pilots was curtailed for lack of fuel. Many Luftwaffe pilots going into battle for the first time at this late stage in the war were inadequately equipped to face the Allied challenge and all too often they were soon shot down by the bombers or their fighter escorts.

Anton Heinemann, one of the Luftwaffe's night-fighter pilots, remembers the sheer impossibility of the task that faced them:

Once the massing of the Allied planes began, you could theoretically shoot down perhaps one plane every half an hour, but the other 90 or 100 had already flown on, heading for their target. Our actual rate of "kills" was no more than six bombers shot down in one night. We thought that was quite a lot. Once we shot down three, which was not so good.

The problem was the opposing fire we encountered from the rear gunners on the Allied planes. So our aircraft were equipped with two guns facing vertically upwards. The rear gunners found it much more difficult to get at us as we flew under the bomber and fired up into its right side in order to make it burst into flames. That worked quite well. We were also given a follow-up round which was belted on to the gun so that we could destroy a bomber's fuel tanks. We used to pierce the tank, use an explosive shell which increased the size of the hole we'd made and another, incendiary, shell to start a fire.

We used to fly mostly in a right-hand curve. The thinking behind this was that in our own aircraft the pilot sat on the left and we assumed that it was the same in the enemy plane. When a plane caught fire the Allied pilot wasn't going to turn on to the side that was burning. So mainly they flew away to the left, in order to keep the fire above and not below, and I think that gave the crew a chance to bail out.

The way we'd fired at the Allied planes was something of a secret weapon. I heard it reported that they were shot down by flak because they didn't know how we'd shot them down. I always hoped that the crew survived, but for us it was important that the plane and its bombs didn't get to its target.

Heinemann himself had the experience of being shot down and bailing out to safety:

In December 1943 my plane, a Junkers-88, was hit during one of the daylight missions we had to fly. We were going after a formation of American Boeings and were somewhere between Heligoland and Schleswig-Holstein. There were about 50 American aircraft and they had such firepower at the rear that one of our engines was soon on fire, and we had to bail out

It isn't difficult to make the decision to bail out when your engine is burning. All you know is the urge to escape. The Ju-88 had a hatch in the bottom, but when it was thrown open and produces such enormous suction, that if you just held out your boot, then pphhtt! you were gone. We had been trained to count to about 30 before pulling the cord and then the parachute would open. On this occasion, I don't know why, I wasn't able to count to 30. I got to about 10 or 12 and then I pulled the cord. A rush of air got hold of me and I was pulled out of my felt boots. I remember seeing them get smaller and smaller down below, because they were flying faster than I was with my parachute, and disappear into the clouds.

Then came the interesting question: was I going to fall into the North Sea or land on the coast? Luckily there was quite a strong west wind and I landed in the area of Itzehoe, north-west of Hamburg, in an empty field. A man came rushing up. He was wearing a yellow badge which meant he was a Polish labourer and he said, "Anglees, Anglees?" He thought an Allied invasion had begun and that he would soon be free. He was very disappointed.

By the time Heinemann's Ju-88 was shot down, the American Eighth Air Force had opened up a new avenue of attack on Germany. Its P-51 Mustangs were let loose to search out the Luftwaffe fighters, embarking on a run of some 200,000 sorties during which they shot down 4,950 German aircraft and destroyed another 4,131 on the ground.

The Luftwaffe reeled before this onslaught. So many Luftwaffe aircraft were lost to this new strategy that Adolf Galland commented: "The day the Allies took the fighters off close escort duties and allowed them to roam free to engage the Luftwaffe fighters in the air and on the ground was the day we lost the air war."

The Luftwaffe was in no shape to challenge the greatest of all onslaughts during the Second World War: the D-Day invasion of Normandy on June 6, 1944, when the greatest amphibious force ever known to warfare assaulted Hitler's Fortress Europe. The air arm of the invasion carried out no fewer than 11,000 sorties and enjoyed complete superiority in the air from day one. Alfred Wagner was on his first combat mission when this mightiest of air umbrellas imposed its presence over northern France:

When we heard that Allied paratroops and glider-borne forces were in Caen, just before the main Normandy landings, we were stationed a long way away, at Biarritz, near Bayonne on the Bay of Biscay, close to the Spanish frontier. We were woken early in the morning and heard the news and were told we were going to be transferred north straight away.

We were taken there on lorries, because we didn't have enough planes to fly there. On the way we were attacked continuously by English fighter planes, but managed to reach our destination while it was still dark. That was when I saw real, live war for the very first time. The fireworks, they were impressive and frightening at the same time. We were all very young and we couldn't really comprehend it.

We were quartered in a château, quite a comfortable place. There was a landing strip nearby and it was from there that we flew our missions. We flew in four planes in the direction of the front line. The flak came up at us, and you heard the detonation right next to your plane, and saw mushrooms when the shots exploded, directly beside you. It was a very unpleasant feeling. I don't know if it was enemy flak or "friendly fire", but thank God, I wasn't hit.

Then suddenly the enemy planes were there. I saw a Spitfire flying directly in front of me, but I managed to get away. I got separated from the other three planes and landed back at our airstrip on my own. That was my first mission and it had been quite easy, I suppose, except for the flak, of course.

But later things got really hot. We had to fly to wherever Allied fighters had been reported. We sighted them, and then it began, the swerving, the diving, like some terrible ballet we were performing. It was very nerve-racking. You had to have eyes everywhere, otherwise you could be "jumped" by an enemy and that might be the end of you.

Once we had to attack a formation of Liberators directly head on. That was very dangerous because from head on, you had only about three seconds – two to fire your guns and then you had to make sure you got away. The Liberators or the Boeing B17s were so heavily armed that there was barely a blind angle to hide in. That's why we had to fire quickly when we attacked and get away fast.

On one mission an American Thunderbolt appeared in front of my snout, as they say. He tipped himself away to the right so that I could see the pilot quite clearly. He was black! A black American! We looked at each other, I pressed the trigger, there was an explosion and … he was gone. But I never forgot him. We had been eye to eye, opposite each other and that left a deep impression on me. It was frightening, and you said to yourself that the war was such madness; every war was. You shot down people you didn't know and would never know. It was terrible.

Wagner discovered the hard way that the propaganda fed to the Luftwaffe pilots was totally untrue:

At the beginning of 1944 we'd been told that the Luftwaffe had a superiority in numbers of 10 to one. The prospects looked good, especially after I'd shot down seven of those 10. But it was all a lie. When I was shot down myself, we were being attacked by three or four Allied planes at one time. So much for Luftwaffe superiority!

On that occasion my plane had problems on the ground. The engine was over-revving, and I noticed that the switch on the control equipment was on manual, when it should have been on automatic. The flight mechanic had been careless, I thought. I switched to automatic and the number of revolutions dropped considerably. There was a huge wall of dust in front of me from the planes starting before me. I took off, but soon afterwards reported myself out of service. I wanted to return to the airstrip, but then I looked up and saw a large formation of Thunderbolts above me.

I didn't want to face them with a defective engine and looked about for somewhere to land unnoticed. But the Thunderbolts had seen me, and before I could do anything a couple of them came down after me. I was hit from behind and saw flashes sparking from part of my wings. The wings were shredded. I felt a stab in my right foot. It must have been an explosive shell and my foot was shredded, too.

My plane started to burn and I had to get out. I ejected the cockpit hatch, but couldn't push myself out properly because my right foot was useless. I managed to push myself out with my arms, and as I did so my right arm struck the bodywork and the bone broke. Somehow or other, I don't know how, it must have been instinct, I pulled the ring of the parachute with my left hand – not something you normally did because you were taught to use your right hand. But if I'd tried to do that, I wouldn't have been alive now. I still can't understand how I managed to pull the parachute cord with my left hand. It was instinct, I suppose.

The air battles in France took place quite close to the ground and my parachute had only just enough time to open. I managed to land all right, but quite far off in the distance I saw the mushroom cloud of smoke rising from where my plane had crashed.

I was lying on the ground, fearing I would be shot while I was lying there, helpless. I shouted for help like a madman, and a French farmer came up over a nearby hill. He asked, "Soldat allemand?" – German soldier – and all I could say was, "Oui, tout de suite, hôpital!!" He said, "Doucement, doucement" ("Gently, gently") and went away.

I went on screaming for help and another, older farmer came up and he asked, "Soldat allemand?" I replied again, "Yes, quickly, the hospital!" This one ran away, too. After an age, or so it seemed, a car drove up and two military policeman and the second French farmer got out. The policeman was carrying a machine gun. He was only two or three metres away when he started firing. I screamed, "You stupid animal!" "Oh," he replied. "I thought you were an English Tommy." They wrapped me in the parachute, carried me to the car and brought me to the hospital.

Wagner's injuries were very serious. His right foot had gone and his right leg had to be amputated below the knee. He had lost the middle bone of his left foot and the fourth toe was missing, but he was alive, an outcome he ascribes to a certain spiritual resilience that surfaces at times of great danger. "I think that at such moments the human being is capable of superhuman achievement, superhuman strength."

Men at war have always had to live with the proximity of violent death or, perhaps even worse, crippling injury. Hajo Hermann had his own way of dealing with it:

> You may think the entire bird is going to fall to pieces, the plane's going to break up and that will be the end of you. But you just can't be continuously eaten up with such emotions. When something goes wrong, of course you get a big shock, but I used to say to my people, "If there is a bang and bullets start shooting through the cabin and the wind howls in, well, you can still think, you can still act. All right then, let's keep going. None of this trembling and dirtying your pants!"

During an attack on British ships at Le Havre at the time of the D-Day invasion in 1944, Hermann witnessed at first hand what could happen when nerves and anxiety took over:

> I'd borrowed this man from somewhere because my own navigator was ill. When we were about to make the approach run, he would keep saying, "Are there barrage balloons? Is there going to be any flak? There are so many searchlights" and so on. Was I going to make a horizontal approach to the target? he wanted to know. No, I told him, that won't be any good, we won't hit anything. I'm going to dive on the target.
>
> He said, "Then I might as well bail out now!" "Please do," I told him. He stayed on board, of course, but he made a grim face as if he

wanted to murder me. Afterwards, when you pull the plane up and see those fat barrage balloons above you, then of course it's a bit frightening, but you have to say to yourself that the balloons aren't everywhere, you'll be able to get past them. This man moaned and groaned all the way back to base. We didn't fly into any wires, but frankly that was pure coincidence.

Heinz Philip knew what it was to be afraid, though he, too, developed his own method of keeping the fear at bay and even acquired a certain detachment about death in the air, whichever side in the war was doing the dying:

You can't hear the flak exploding all round you, but you could see light. There was so much light when you're flying at around 3,000 metres. You could read a newspaper by it and the flashes of explosions and tracer bullets. That's what it was like up there. You had a very empty feeling in your stomach and there were wet trousers, too, sometimes, There are people who said that they weren't afraid, but I was afraid and most men were afraid too. "Glorious, you just fly through it," we used to be told. Not at all, that's just Latin, as we say in Germany, airmen's Latin.

You just can't get away from the fact that you could be killed at any moment, so you try to distance yourself from death. When a comrade is killed, you try not to think about it too much. I was once playing a game called skat with three other Luftwaffe men. I had a marvellous hand, and so did one of the others. We kept on bidding and it was so exciting that other people in the room stood around watching us.

Suddenly there was an alarm. We threw down our cards, saying we would continue the game later. I was the first one back, so I sat there, cards in my hand, waiting for the other three to arrive. They never came. Then we were told that the pilot had crashed after take-off and all three had been burned to death. Maybe it didn't really register, but I said, "Well, there must be someone around here who can finish this game." There was, and so we finished the game.

It worked both ways, for our opponents as well as for us. We never thought – at least I didn't and neither did our crew when we talked about it – we never thought that, if we shoot down an Allied plane, then we are going to kill 10 people who are sitting inside. For us it was: "We are not killing the people, we are shooting down the plane." That is an enormous difference. For us the plane was the adversary.

In the last week of July 1944, after seven hard-fought weeks, the Allies broke out of the Normandy beachhead. By mid-August the German forces were escaping eastwards, with the prospect that the Fatherland itself would soon be open to invasion. Meanwhile, on August 15, 1944, two months after D-Day, the Allies landed in the south of France. Heinz Phillip had his worst experience of the war as the Luftwaffe tried to prevent this second invasion:

It was at Coulommières in the south of France. We'd been fighting all through the the Allied disembarkation at night. We'd flown low level attacks on the beaches, and we returned to base and wanted to land. But when we were about to touch down, an English night-fighter caught us at our most vulnerable moment. When the undercarriage and the ailerons are out, then the plane is as helpless as an old duck. The pilot of the night-fighter was a very good shot. He was directly behind us and when he fired, the radio operator was hit several times in the chest. Our aircraft was still able to fly, the engines were still running and our pilot retracted the ailerons and the undercarriage, accelerated and climbed back up into the air.

But we were burning up, left and right, the wings – there are fuel tanks in the wings, too, and they were on fire. We wanted to bail out, I jumped, but my parachute got tangled in the plane. I was outside and the parachute was up there somewhere, so that I was just about able to look inside. The pilot, who was preparing to get out himself, saw that I was hanging there and he went back to the cockpit, set the plane straight and then he tried to kick me free with his foot. But that didn't quite work. He bailed out and the plane exploded. Only then was I free and although my parachute was rather shredded, I managed to land all right. But I landed very heavily. The time it took me to get from up there until I arrived down on the ground, it was only a few minutes, but it felt like an entire lifetime.

In December 1944 the Germans made a desperate attempt to halt the Allied advance towards Germany by attacking the American Seventh Army and other forces through the forested plateau of the Ardennes, on the border between Belgium and France. This brief but doomed campaign saw the last major offensive by the Luftwaffe, on January 1, 1945, when some 800 of its aircraft attacked airfields in France, Belgium and the Netherlands, destroying 156 Allied planes. It was an attempt to disrupt Allied air support, but it failed, with heavy losses. The Ardennes offensive cost the Germans a total of 1,600 planes and the Luftwaffe was finally broken.

The Me-262, the world's first turbojet fighter, which first flew in combat in September 1944, came too late to save the Luftwaffe, or Germany. Its remarkable speed of 540 miles per hour, 140 miles faster than any conventional aircraft of its time, was wasted by Hitler when he ordered it to be used as an attack bomber rather than a fighter. Besides this, the Me-262 had cardinal faults, including engines with a service life of only 25 hours, and there were too few of them at this late stage in the war to make a difference to its outcome.

The moment the Luftwaffe and the Wehrmacht had struggled so hard to prevent came on March 7, 1945, when troops of the US Ninth Armoured Division broke into Germany across the Ludendorff Bridge over the Rhine at Remagen. German engineers were just preparing to blow it up when the Americans arrived. Heinz Philip had volunteered for a mission to destroy the bridge. It was the only time his Ju-88 dropped bombs:

> Some volunteers were wanted and I took part. My pilot was always way out in front and I wasn't always filled with enthusiasm, but I had to go with him. A five-hundredweight bomb was attached below each of the wings left and right, and we were meant to drop them on the bridge at Remagen. Four or five planes in all went on this mission, which took place at night. But of course the Americans had gathered everything together at the Rhine crossing, everything they had, to defend themselves against air raids and it was quite some firework display that was staged there.
>
> For us it was not very good because we had drawn number three –

in other words, we were to be the third plane to attack. Each plane was given a time, and we knew, now the first one is attacking, and then there was a fireball and he no longer existed. Then the second plane went in, that became a fireball too, except that it was a little lower down, and then it was our turn.

You can image what our feelings were. It wasn't exactly lovely. But we made it. Admittedly we didn't hit the bridge, our bombs fell beside it, but we got out of it in one piece. But I'll never forget it, we had 88 bullet holes in the plane by the time we got away.

CHAPTER SEVEN

The Closing Battles:
From Stalingrad to Berlin
1943–45

Stalingrad was the watershed of the Germans' campaign in Russia. After that, the tide of the war turned irrevocably against them. In February 1943, as Field Marshal Paulus and the remnants of the Sixth Army began their Russian captivity, there was still a great deal of killing, dying and destruction yet to do, but the way back to Germany and the Götterdämmerung of 1945 were already marked out.

The Russians went on the offensive immediately after Stalingrad and within a fortnight of the German surrender there, they had captured

Rostov and were attacking in the Ukraine. Herr Rönner remembers being subjected to the power of the Russian assaults:

> We had to take up positions in southern Ukraine. The Russians were only 500 metres away. It was relatively quiet during the day but as soon as anyone moved slightly the Russians fired their "ratch-boom". The shells had a flat trajectory and the Russians fired at anything that moved. At night the antiquated planes we called "sewing machines" flew over. If the moon was bright enough, you could see them in the sky. We managed to shoot one of them down with a machine gun.
>
> At the end of October 1943 a Russian shock troop – about 11 or 12 men – arrived in front of our position, an advanced position we had set up. The Russians shot up our front line, but we didn't attack them. A battalion near us used up all their ammunition firing at these Russians.
>
> The Russians were very strongly armed. They had their "Stalin Organs" and their T-34 tanks were standing on the top of small hills. We were in danger of being cut off. Then I was wounded. I had diffi-culty loading my gun because of the bad weather and the mud, and I was just opening my mouth to complain about it, when a shot hit me. It went right through.
>
> I reported myself off duty and met a group of 20 or 25 men who had also suffered injuries. I found out that they were the replacement who were supposed to close up the front line!

The Germans' response to the defeat at Stalingrad was an attempt to gain some recompense with a fresh offensive which would also capi-talize on their capture of Kharkov in March 1943. It turned out to be their last major offensive in Russia. The focus of this effort, code-named Operation Citadel, was Kursk on the River Seim, where the plan was to encircle and destroy the Central and Voronezh Fronts.

Hitler proclaimed that a German victory at the battle of Kursk, in revenge for Stalingrad, would "shine like a beacon to the world". In private, however, he had grave misgivings. Colonel-General Heinz Guderian put it to him that an attack at Kursk, or anywhere on the

Russian front that year, would be a retrograde step.

"I know," Hitler replied. "The thought of it turns my stomach."

His stomach had good reason to turn. The impending defeat of the Afrika Korps in North Africa meant that an Allied invasion of Sicily would take place very shortly. Sicily was the stepping stone to Italy and, with that, the western Allies would make their first major intrusion into Hitler's Fortress Europe. Heavy losses of men and materiel in battle had become the norm in Russia, and Kursk was very likely to waste a great deal of manpower and armaments that would soon be urgently needed in southern Europe. Hitler was not the first, nor last, national leader to make public pronouncements that were contrary to his private opinion, and while realizing the facts of the situation in mid-1943, he was also aware of the propaganda value of a victory at Kursk.

So was Colonel-General Kurt Zeitzler, Chief of the General Staff, who had his own reasons for supporting the campaign. Zeitzler's relationship with Hitler had been soured by his resentment of the Führer's criticisms of the Sixth Army at Stalingrad. Zeitzler wanted to show that the Wehrmacht in Russia was neither faltering nor inept and insisted that an attack at Kursk was the logical next step after the capture of Kharkov.

It was certainly logical. Capturing Kharkov had created a large salient south of Orel. Kursk lay at the centre of the salient, with Belgorod as its southern base. The Russians could see the logic of such a move just as easily as Zeitzler. They were, besides, informed of Hitler's plans by agents of their "Lucy" spy network in Germany and by the British, who had used their Enigma machine to decode messages from German radio and pass them on to Josef Stalin. The news was confirmed after a sapper captured by the Russians told them the date and time of Operation Citadel: 0300 hours on July 5. Another sapper, a Slovene who deserted, told them the same thing.

The original date for the attack had been May 4, 1943, but this was postponed so that the new Panzer and Elefant tanks would be able to take part. The collapse of the German front in Africa and Soviet partisan attacks caused further delay, and the new date was fixed for July 5.

The Germans assembled 50 divisions for Citadel, comprising about 900,000 troops supported by 2,700 tanks and assault guns, 10,000 pieces of artillery and 2,000 Luftwaffe aircraft. The Luftwaffe, once again playing its traditional role as "air artillery", opened the proceedings at 0245 hours on July 5, with a 10-minute attack by Ju-87D Stukas in which an area around Butovo of 2.3 miles square was intensively dive-bombed. That done, the German artillery on the ground opened up against the Russian positions, and the Germans began to advance. The initial assaults achieved limited success. The Ninth Army, attacking on a 35-mile front along the Orel-Kursk axis, breached the Russians' Central Front and, on a 30-mile front west of Belgorod, the Fourth Panzer Army penetrated the first Russian line. The Germans – and their "success" – ended there, brought to a halt by the Russian artillery and mines, although on the night of July 3 sappers had cleared and marked paths through the Russian minefield. This was a very dangerous procedure, which involved prodding the ground with bayonets and removing 2,700 mines by hand. Nevertheless, these efforts proved insufficient and the extensive Russian minefields were another obstacle to bring the German advance to an end.

Ultimately the battle of Kursk resolved itself into the greatest armoured battle yet fought. On July 12, near the village of Prokhorovka, Germans and Russians fired at each other at almost point-blank range, and the battlefield was soon obscured by thick, black smoke as some 600 tanks from both sides were blasted into twisted metal and set on fire. When the two sides disengaged at the end of the day, the Russians had lost twice as many tanks, but the German attack had failed.

Herr Senneberg was at Kursk and remembers all too vividly the experience of being under heavy artillery attack:

> In the area of Orel and Kursk, the Kursk bend we called it, a final attempt was made by the German army to go on the offensive. To the south of us the greatest mass of our tanks was collected, and then it started. They wanted to attack, but the Russians intended to do the same thing, and one offensive met the other. But the Russians were stronger in materiel and had greater numbers of men.
>
> Before we advanced on this offensive, first came a dreadful barrage. I knew in advance what it was going to be like, because my father, who had been injured at Verdun in the First World War, described it to me. He knew what it was like to be at the mercy of the big guns – and in

1943 the Russians had many big guns. My father said that he had had to jump into shell holes. The ground looked as if it had been ploughed up. It was the same for us in Russia. You saw on the left or the right of you that there was a new shell crater, so you jumped into that one and then the next one. This went on for three hours before the actual fighting began. And that's what we did too. The barrage ended after three hours and the fighting began. But our offensive collapsed, the Russians were superior and we had to retreat. Further and further we retreated. Fortunately we were protected by a German tank named Ferdinand, the biggest and heaviest tank that I had ever seen. It was so big that the ground was practically shaking when it was three kilometres away. Not even the Russians had one like it. But then there was this thunderstorm and it began to rain and rain. The ground went soggy and that was the end of Ferdinand. The motors were damaged and the tank broke down.

Kursk was another decisive defeat for the Germans and the losses incurred there crippled their future ability to carry on the war in Russia. About 49,000 Germans were killed or wounded. The Russians' losses were even greater – 70,000 killed and around 110,000 wounded – but the initiative was undoubtedly theirs. After a week, by July 14, the Germans were withdrawing, and they continued to fall back as the Russians embarked on a sequence of advances that pushed their opponents south of Orel by August 4, and from there spread out along the entire fighting front. On August 5 the Russians captured Orel and Belgorod. Kharkov was retrieved from the Germans on August 23. After that the Germans were systematically driven back across southern Russia towards the Balkans.

Heinz Frauendorf was in the rearguard of his regiment at Kharkov when the staff sergeant told his men to retreat. However, a lance-corporal objected to the order and though he did not get his way, there was a disturbing sequel:

Before we could radio through the news that we were retreating, our set received a direct hit. The man who was carrying it on his back was lucky. The radio was in pieces but he was alive. Now that we had lost contact, the staff sergeant took over and said, "Let's get out of here." There were 20 of us.

Now, there was this regulation which laid down that even when a higher-ranking man was in command, a retreat could be cancelled, even by a lowly private, if he believed we could still succeed and should stand our ground. Well, we had one of these idiots in our group. This man was a lance-corporal. He came from Upper Silesia and we called him "the dog-eater". He said, "We are staying here, what's going on? We have a motorbike and we can drive up there and back." We told him, "You are off your head" and drove off.

Three days later this lance-corporal arrived and brought Russian prisoners with him. We were all put in front of a court martial for dereliction of duty or something like that. The court decided that the staff sergeant, as commander, had to be executed by the rest of us. We were given five live rounds and a blank. So we had to execute him. If we hadn't, we'd have been shot ourselves. A pity. I didn't like the man, but he was a capable leader and highly decorated.

Herr Kosak, a radio operator who had been at Kharkov since the previous February, also took part in the retreat from the city six months later:

When the thunder of the guns at the front came over, I can remember very well, it was an awful feeling to realize that you really were in danger. I was with the divisional staff in my unit, and so was not directly involved, but it was played out in front of us and it was terrible.

This was a war on the move, and the groups, friend and foe, became confused. One of our groups was wiped out. In February 1943, I think it was, the Russians – one or two tank corps – succeeded in retreating as far as Kharkov. The town changed hands twice at that time, I think. We went in and then the Russians took it back and then we reoccupied it.

By the time summer came, the front line was at a standstill. We took up positions in a suburb of Kharkov, where we were quartered with Russians. I remember that we played chess with them and because they had nothing to eat, we gave them food. There were casualties in the fighting, and many radio operators were lost in Russian air raids, except for me. The Russians had superiority in the skies and came over in fighter planes. Once I had to drive my car into a small wood to keep myself safe from them.

Kosak took part in the battle of Kursk, and the subsequent German retreat:

We heard that we had lost at Kursk because our plans were betrayed. We had to retreat a long way to the south after that, over the River Dnieper. We reached Kiev and then we set up a front line. That was in the winter of 1943–44, and in January 1944 I was lucky enough to go on leave back to Germany. Hamburg had been heavily raided by the Allies six months earlier, and I saw the destruction. That gave us an awful feeling, it goes without saying.

Not all the Russians the Germans had to contend with after Stalingrad were in the Red Army. Partisan groups were also active, and Rudolf Oelkers saw their handiwork:

We had to go on guard duty around the village at night, because of the partisans. I was the SMG gunner in a support post, and the partisans were all around us. Small groups of German soldiers used to come to the village from time to time and one day, when four of them had arrived, we heard some shooting. Nothing else, just guns firing. But the four Germans had disappeared.

The support post consisted of a platoon, which was alerted, and we were sent to the village. But it was as silent as the grave, there was no one around, everyone was gone. Partisans had driven even the civilians away. The civilians had to prepare the food supply convoys for us, and the partisans came at night to requisition the food. We went there in the afternoon, no one to be seen, as I said, but in all the houses the fires were still burning in the hearths, so they could not have been gone for long.

We found a dead Russian who had a Kalashnikov rifle. I took it from him, but by that time it was getting dark and we had to go back to our post.

Next day we went back to the same place and this time our whole company came. Everything was as before, but the Russians were gone, though we could see about four people some distance away, perhaps three or four kilometres. We fired at them, but I don't know whether we hit any of them or not.

We realized we had to supply our own food now, so we found a pig and took it back with us. We tied to to our sled and slaughtered it with a machine gun. Soldiers have to do such things in war.

Oelkers and the rest of the company at the village were ordered to hunt for the partisans and came across some grisly evidence of their fighting methods:

We tramped through scrub and bushes for about two weeks, in water most of the time. It was pointless to try and get our boots dry. We had sporadic contacts with the partisans. One episode from that time upset me terribly. The Russians had captured one of our reconnaissance patrols, four men. Three of them were old hands and they quickly scampered off and were gone, leaving an 18-year-old behind them dead on the ground. I was only 19 myself at this time. The Russians had not only killed him but absolutely massacred him. His whole brain hung out of his smashed skull.

We also went on night marches, hunting the partisans. Once, when we came to a clearing, partisans suddenly jumped out of the wood and started firing at us. We returned the fire, of course. But one of our sergeants was hit in the neck and killed.

Soon afterwards Oelkers's company was withdrawn from the post at the village, and was sent with the 18th Panzer Division to Orel and Kursk:

Stalingrad was over by this time and we were in action at Orel and Kursk. Some of our men had to go in a beika, as the Russians call it – a big hole in the ground, sometimes up to 40 metres deep. From above the opening of the beika was visible, but nothing else. The men in there thought they were safe, but the Russians poured in mortar shells and most of them were killed, about 90 per cent, I think.

Later I became driver's mate on one of our cars. Our company had moved away from Orel to the north of Volkhov and when our car drove up – it was near Briansk – a sergeant-major appeared and started yelling, "What are you doing here! Have you gone mad? What do want here anyway?" The Russians were firing at us from about a kilometre away. We were in Briansk for about another two weeks, and when we returned to the front line, we found it had collapsed.

Herr Meding was wounded in September 1943, when the impetus the Russians had gained after Kursk was already bringing German resistance close to a state of collapse:

My battalion attacked a village. I had become a group commander by this time. My second in command was killed, he simply fell into my arms, and so I was alone. I said to my comrades, "We have to get through this." So we attacked, and suddenly, in a field of maize, I got a blow and felt that on my left side I had been shot in the stomach. The bullet came out one centimetre away from my spine. Two comrades, to whom I owe my life, carried me out from the field. There was a field hospital set up nearby, outside in the open, and there was a medical transport. It was already full up, but I was loaded on to it. There was so little room that my head hung over the edge on the spare wheel. You must not drink, I was told, because you have a stomach wound and if you drink, your life is over. I travelled through Russia and Poland, back to Germany.

By January 1944, when they at last raised the 900-day siege of Leningrad, the Russians prepared to advance in the west and in the south, where they were intent on clearing the Crimea of German forces. The result was a swift run of success in which Sevastopol was retaken in only two days and the Germans were thrown out of the peninsula within four weeks in April and May.

German losses were appalling and many prisoners were taken, among them Herr Räde:

> The retreat in the Crimea took place under an indescribable artillery
> bombardment, without the least possibility of help from elsewhere or
> from among ourselves. I was running for my life away from well-
> aimed rifle and machine-gun fire. It hailed down around me like rain
> against window panes. Before that, during the flight towards the coast
> road on the Black Sea, I found myself suddenly totally alone at night
> in the mountains in the middle of a partisan-held area. All about me
> Germans lay scattered on the ground with their limbs cut off.
>
> I was lucky. I was captured on May 8, 1944, near Sevastopol. With
> a great deal of luck I arrived in captivity on May 8 near Sevastopol on
> the steep Maxim Gorky coast. We then marched for three days with-
> out a single bite to eat, drinking filthy water from the puddles on the
> way. We were beaten, there were executions and suicides. Everything
> we had was stolen, including our boots. Thank God I was wearing
> shoes! Only a few Russian officers refrained from such outrages.

By the late summer of 1944 the Russians had advanced beyond the
bounds of their own country and were driving into Poland and heading
for East Prussia.

Hitler's allies in Hungary and Romania were now in grave danger and
already, on March 19, 1944, he had ordered the occupation of Hungary
by German forces. Werner Reuhs was in Hungary with them:

> We were sent to Hungary, by way of Vienna. The place was full of
> our troops – SS divisions and the Third Tank Division, together with
> other Tank Divisions. I was in a Panther tank along with 14 others. We
> were the reserve. Two men were assigned to each tank. They sat on top
> at the rear because they were afraid of the Russian infantry and if they
> saw them, thought that, in that position, they had time to take cover.
> We travelled at night because we had night-vision equipment and
> were able to see just as well in the dark as we could in the daytime. Our
> tanks were very good, almost new. We had 10 of them. I was acting as
> a company messenger because our radios had failed, and we had to
> jump from vehicle to vehicle to deliver messages.

We reached the railway embankment at a place called Serigelius, but couldn't get any further because there were Russians in the way. We had to drive off the road and that was when we suffered our first casualties. I was only 19 years old, and it was a great shock to me. You're all excited at first, but after the first deaths occur, then it's different. But we had to do our duty, of course.

I had been trained as a medium-wave radio operator, but had to act as a gun loader after our gun loader was badly wounded. When this happened, we were trying to tow another tank that had lost its right-hand caterpillar track and broken down. It was all very dangerous. My best friend was killed at the railway embankment. He hadn't wanted to sit on top of the tank at the rear. He told me, "It's too dangerous. I'm an only son. If I get killed, my parents will have no sons left. Let me go to the rear somewhere." So, with about 20 other soldiers, he was allowed to get into trenches in front of our tanks. His trench suffered a direct hit and he died there. Later I had to identify him. It was a terrible moment, terrible.

Russian fire was coming from every direction, forwards and backwards. We were fired at from the air by the Russian planes. They told us lies – that we had broken through the Russian lines and so on – but the fact was that most of the time we were retreating. Then all 10 of our tanks ran out of fuel. But we could still fight. We positioned ourselves behind a hill and within 20 minutes we had destroyed five T-34s with our own tank. Every shell hit. We could fire quite accurately, that was our advantage. The Russians were numerically superior, but our fire was accurate, and they couldn't get at us because we only had the turret visible behind the hill. But then all 10 of our tanks ran out of fuel and we had to blow them all up. A very expensive exercise.

On March 21, 1944, two days after the German occupation of Hungary, German divisions were sent to Romania. The Germans seized important locales in the capital, Bucharest, and went on from there to take over key points and communications in neighbouring Bulgaria. By this time Russian forces had crossed the line from which the Germans had invaded them in 1941. In the north, East Prussia – German territory proper – came under threat in mid-July when the Russians captured

Pinsk, the fortified base in the Pripet Marshes and the railway junction of Volkovysk. Herr Strasosky, a lieutenant serving with the prestigious Grossdeutschland Division, was determined to keep the Russians out of the Fatherland:

In 1944 we were in Romania, and the Romanians, unfortunately, were our allies. That summer, at the same time as the assassination attempt on Hitler took place at his headquarters, on July 20, 1944, the Romanians deserted to the Russians with all their armaments. Suddenly we were on our own again.

In the meantime the Russians had marched into Estonia and Lithuania and were threatening our eastern border. So it was high time to prevent the Russians up there from invading German territory. The entire division was loaded on to the train and taken from Romania up to Lithuania. Unfortunately, by the time we got there, the Russians had occupied German territory, and had succeeded in breaking through to two large German towns, Memel and Tilsit.

We arrived resolved to nail down those Russians. I was proud of my personal intervention to save Germany from annihilation, without regard for the losses we were going to suffer. We didn't have any choice. Either we defended ourselves to the last, or we would be crushed, but it was very hard, fighting the Russians. We of the Grossdeutschland Division were an elite division, but even we couldn't work miracles. Look at it this way. The Russian front line was on one side, our own front line on the other. The Grossdeutschland Division was in the centre. To the left, there are soldiers from other divisions, and to the right on the other side it's the same situation. Now, the Russians attack with a massive superiority, and the Russians on the left and right of us are able to drive back the German soldier to the right and left of us. Our division remained in the middle as a single block, and defended ourselves desperately. But, because of the Russian superiority on both our flanks, we were forced to retreat as well. If we had remained where we were, the Russians would have encircled us and we would have all been taken prisoner. And we did not want that to happen.

Strasosky was impressed, as many Germans were, by the Russian T-34 tank, but the Grossdeutschland Division had their own way of defeating them, though at great risk to themselves:

The T-34 was just like our Tiger tank, and we in Grossdeutschland had the Tiger tank and the King Tiger tank, which was even more powerful. If a Russian T-34 tank drove through an area, our sappers sat in the house cellars. The tank drove past outside, and once it had driven by, the sappers came up out of the cellar, climbed up on to the tank from behind and placed a wooden box filled with dynamite on the tank track. The tank only drove a few metres further before the track blew out, the tank was immobilized, the turret flap opened and the Russians emerged from out of the turret. Then our sappers threw hand grenades into the turret opening. Or they used the machine gun and arranged the deaths of the Russians. If you can imagine that, it takes an unimaginable strength to do that, will power, because during an attack like this no one was certain whether the act of dynamiting the Russian tank to make it immobile would succeed, or whether he would bite the dust in the attempt; would meet his death or would be shot by the Russians. The risk was huge.

Strasosky escaped death at the hands of the Russians on several occasions:

I was wounded three times, the third time in the knees through artillery shrapnel in an artillery attack on our position. As a tank commander, I was at the front in the trench in order to observe the Russians and find out whether there were tanks or artillery guns drawn up behind their lines, ready to destroy us. At that time the Russians had guns which we called "ratch-boom". We only heard the discharge, and the explosion in our lines occurred seconds later. And the Russians' "Stalin Organ" was a really murderous weapon – 12 barrels, six above, six below, on a mobile artillery frame, and all 12 fired simultaneously. Whooo-oooo-boom! Like a rocket. The Russians used to adjust this sound so that it would have a demoralizing effect on soldiers who had no courage or guts, who were, well, feeble, who were already beaten down.

We were operating at Heiligenbeil, near Königsberg, in East Prussia. Mehlsack and Zinten were the other places where we were operating, trying to stall the Russians. We received a direct hit in the trench from a tank shell, and after the smoke had disappeared I looked left and right and there lay my comrades beside me, corpses. Twelve of them. All killed at once by that shell. I was the only one still alive. They had fallen over, dead, killed by the shrapnel that had penetrated their bodies all over, and some of them had fallen on top of me and that is partly what saved my life.

The German medics did not dare to come out during the day to retrieve the wounded. Strasosky lay in the trench for some seven hours before they arrived:

In the afternoon, when it became dark, at about five o'clock, I was taken out of the trench by the medics, and sent to the main dressing station. It was only 400 metres away from the Russian snipers. Anyone who let himself be seen would be immediately shot dead.

As I lay in the hospital the chief medical officer came up to me and said, "Don't go to sleep, lieutenant, because there is a casualty transport leaving tonight and we only take those men with us who report to us. If you go to sleep, you'll stay put, then you will probably be taken by the Russians."

Strasosky stayed awake, and was sent to Danzig on a medical transport to join the casualty ships berthed there. There were dramatic scenes as deserters attempted to board the ships:

We were sent to Danzig, in the medical transports, where the casualty ships were. They lay in the harbour, connected to the land by heavy ropes. We were taken to the quay, we were all lying on stretchers, and a crane was extended from the interior of the ship, and took us up into the air on our stretchers and into the freight bays inside the ship. The medics were there and released us from the stretchers, took us to wherever there was room.

But there were many deserters, and these deserters who had left the troops through cowardice now tried to get on board the ship by climbing up the cables. Our field gendarmes – they were the police, the army watchdogs – they all had large sheets of chest armour. And once they noticed that the deserters were all trying to get on board, they took out their sub-machine guns, shot them down, and they dropped into the water and drowned. It was the only way.

Wolfgang Reinhardt was in the middle of officer training when he was suddenly called to the front on the Russo-German border:

I was in Posen [Poznan], in training at the war academy there at the start of 1945, when the Russians were approaching the borderlands between Germany and Russia. Our training was immediately cancelled, we were given rifles and sent out to fight the Russians. Luckily I was a radio operator, assigned to a battalion commander, so I escape being killed. We suffered enormous losses, though.

We were relieved in February and were sent to Dresden, from where we received the order to march to Klagenfurt in Austria. Our training was supposed to be resumed – we were studying to be officers – but that plan collapsed. Instead we were assigned to two newly formed divisions in the south-east of Berlin, in a defensive position on the River Neisse We were there until the beginning of April 1945, and we were then moved on to the town of Lüttenmensprey. At Lüttenmensprey, I had my first real experience of war. We were in the front lines, eyeball to eyeball with the Russians, but we felt ourselves to be inferior even then, because we were not particularly well equipped, had no heavy weapons. I had a direct confrontation with death, when the man operating the machine gun beside me was shot from only two metres away.

Reinhardt was shocked by this experience, but another shock awaited him when he came face to face with a Russian:

I was a platoon commander in this troop. It was difficult to get a clear view of the area, and I said to the sergeant, "I'm going over to the left to see if the enemy is there." I was armed with a "storm rifle", a kind of sub-machine gun but heavier, with a magazine containing six or eight rounds. I held it in front of me as I went through this area where there were small houses. At the corner of a small house I suddenly found myself standing in front of a Russian solder. I can still see him in front of me. I was 20 at the time, he was perhaps 18. His fur hat was crooked and he had a brand-new military coat which was too big for him. His belt was also crooked and his rifle was upright in front of him, with the very long bayonet which the Russians had.

I had the presence of mind – and in war the one who shoots first survives – and I pressed the trigger, but my gun didn't fire. I no longer remember whether it jammed – the guns were not very well constructed – or whether I had forgotten to release the safety catch. But there I stood, and at such moments your life rushes before your eyes like a movie. I was afraid this Russian was going to take advantage of his situation. I know that we looked at each other, and then suddenly, in a flash, he was gone. He suddenly vanished. Just went, disappeared. I'm glad that it happened like that. I would never have been able to forget it if I had killed him. I believe he thought that I wasn't going to harm him – maybe he didn't think my gun had jammed – and perhaps he made the decision not to hurt me either.

Fred Angerstein originally went to Russia to serve with the Luftwaffe, but once the air force ran out of fuel and weapons, he found himself fighting on the ground, with the army. Like Wolfgang Reinhardt, however, he was not well equipped:

We had carbines and the disadvantage with the 98 carbine was that we could load five rounds into the magazine, with one round in reserve, but we had to reload each time. I had this thing that was only half finished and I always had to hit it with a stone to get it to close and finally it didn't work at all.

The Russians stormed our front lines, our positions, and we ran off, retreated with everything we could carry. There were many deaths. One man ran beside me carrying an anti-tank grenade. I said, "Throw the thing away!" "I'm not allowed to, I can't," he replied. I said again,

"Throw the bloody thing away." He ran on and at last threw the grenade away, but he was shot, fell down and was certainly dead. My comrade said to me, "You're bleeding here." I'd been shot through the uniform but I hadn't noticed it. We came to a cemetery, where we hid ourselves behind the gravestones.

Shortly afterwards Angerstein encountered a very young SS officer who tried to commandeer him as his personal protector. Another man buttonholed by this officer had his own answer to this demand:

This very young SS officer came up to me and asked, "Where do you come from?" I said, "Don't you know? From our front line. Our entire company has been wiped out and we've retreated." And he said, "You are staying here for my personal protection." Just then an old non-commissioned officer came out of the bushes and he said to me, "This is true what I'm telling you. He kept me here for his personal protection as well, but the Russians are going to kill him anyway." "Yes," I said. "What shall we do then?" The NCO said, "Move away a little. I'll shoot him myself." "You can't do that," I said. But he did. He killed him with a bullet in the head.

Angerstein and his comrades had not yet escaped from the Russians. They were chased into a ruined town, where they hid in the cellars:

I remember there were lots of potatoes in this cellar. The Russians began to break in because they suspected we were there. They stopped one cellar door away from ours and went away. Luck was with us, it seemed. We took to marching at night and during the daytime we crept into hiding somewhere. Then in one village we were approached by a Czech, who said, "You're Germans, soldiers, aren't you?" I didn't answer and told my comrade, "Keep quiet. Don't say anything." But he kept following us and I said to him, "Get lost, you idiot!" He ran off, not to leave alone, but to betray us to the Russians. A Russian sub-lieutenant came up and went, "Bam, bam, bam" over my head with his rifle. "Hands up," he said. "The war is over."

Already, by 1944, the Germans' allies were falling away. Fascist Italy had surrendered in September 1943, soon after the Allied invasion. Romania surrendered in August 1944 and Finland the following month. Like the Italians, the Romanians subsequently declared war on Germany.

In October 1944 the German Army Group North was driven back and became trapped in the Kurland bridgehead near the Gulf of Riga, on the border between Latvia and Lithuania. In the light of these disasters the Ardennes offensive launched by the Germans at the end of 1944 briefly revived memories of the blitzkrieg penetration of this forest plateau four years earlier, but it was a swansong and delayed the inevitable end by only a few weeks.

The final assault on Germany itself began in southern Poland on January 12, 1945. The advance of the First Ukrainian Front swept through Poland, to reach the border with Czechoslovakia by the end of March. To the north, the First Belorussian Front swept aside the newly formed German Army Group A, and when March ended, Russian troops were positioned at Kustrin, only 50 miles from Berlin. As Berliners waited for them to arrive, a grim joke was doing the rounds: "Enjoy the war while you can, because the peace will be terrible."

Nevertheless, there was no question of the Berliners hoisting the white flag and surrendering on their own account. Even in this twilight of Nazi power, the Nazi state still functioned. Hitler was still in command, giving orders for the defence of Berlin, and the SS and the Gestapo secret police retained their control. Ernst Henken saw certain proof that the retributive nature of Nazi rule was still alive, even in the ruins of Berlin:

> I saw two bodies hanging from the street lamps in Berlin. I have never forgotten them. I went through the streets with two officers. The bodies had a sign hanging on them saying something like: "I have to hang here, because I, as a lieutenant, didn't come back from captivity." I believe that they were left there for several days as a deterrent for anyone who might have felt like giving up.

During the Soviet advance into Germany, many German civilians, already in dread of the Russians long before they actually arrived, saw their worst fears come true as the invaders embarked on an unrestrained orgy of looting, murder and mass rape. Russian officers did nothing to restrain them: this was revenge for the atrocities the Germans had committed in the areas of Russia they had occupied after 1941.

By April 1945, in front of Berlin, German losses had been so great that they had 1,519 tanks to the 6,250 the Russians could put into battle. According to one estimate, Hitler may have had one million men to deploy in 1945, but the Russians had two and a half million by the time they encircled Berlin on April 24, 1945.

Nine days later, in the west, American forces reached the banks of the River Elbe. From the south, the Allied forces which had fought their way up the long "leg" of Italy were approaching the border of Austria.

Herr Poemüller had experience of fighting against the Americans on the Italian front, though he just missed confronting the Allies in Normandy, on D-Day:

We were sent to Lüneburg Heath, where we were formed into fighting units and were sent from there to France, where we helped set up the coastal defences against the Allied invasion. We planted big tree trunks in the mud flats so that the landing boats couldn't get in, and we laid mines in some places. Well, we waited and waited for the attack across the English Channel, but it didn't happen. So, we were put on to trains and sent east towards Russia. Then, just after we reached Nuremberg, we heard that the cross-Channel invasion had begun, on June 6, 1944.

We were told, either go straight ahead, towards Russia, or turn to the right, to Italy. We chose Italy. In the assembly camp, there were Croatians who were there to build the assembly camps but they hadn't got them ready, so that when the Allies were about to attempt their next breakthrough, we were thrown in to meet them. The last units came back, an SS unit marched through before us, although we were told, "There's nothing in front of you but Americans." We heard the SS arrive at night in march step, German march step, with hobnail boots. Could only be Germans. We let them march through. Suddenly there was shooting and we were surrounded. The Americans had an armoured helicopter and fired on us from above while we were in the vineyards.

That was it. We were taken prisoner by a group of Americans, small men in American uniforms. They started hitting us and threatened to shoot us. I could speak some English, so I protested, "Is that fair, how you're treating us?" They answered, "Fair? What d'you mean, fair? You shot our comrades, shot them from behind and now we kill you. You killed them and now we kill you." It was a bad situation, but an American chaplain came down the hill looked around, and asked, "Anyone speaking German?" Yes. We all spoke German and that was an opportunity to ease the situation. Besides, I don't think the Americans would have killed us while the chaplain was there.

With Allied forces advancing from the west, east and south and a northerly route of escape cut off by the sea, the noose was finally closing around Hitler's "1,000-year" Reich. Berlin, of course, was to be the scene of final destruction and in the last two weeks of the war in Europe the Germans prepared to defend their capital as best they could.

The east side of Berlin was strongly fortified, with three separate lines of anti-tank defences. In the city centre, every street was to be turned into a strong point. Hitler had hoped to make Berlin into a fortress and it was certainly given many of the relevant features. Ringed around the city were three structures which echoed the castles of medieval times. These were the flak towers, three huge concrete structures with walls so thick that not even the heaviest artillery shells could penetrate them. The first, known as the Humboldt Tower, after the famous German oceanographer, was located just off the Brunnenstrasse in the north of Berlin. The second was just to the east of the city centre, on Landsberger Allee, and the third was in the south-west of the city centre, at the Zoo.

The original purpose of these flak towers had been to serve as anti-aircraft gun platforms to protect Berlin against the frequent Allied bombing raids. Each of the enormous gun towers had a satellite tower a short distance away from where artillery observers controlled the anti-aircraft fire. After the Russians beat off a last desperate stand on the Seelow heights east of Berlin, pouring down such a weight of artillery fire that the defenders had to retreat, the last natural obstacle into the city was open to them. Now the onus was on the defence ring hastily thrown up around Berlin and on the flak towers, which were virtually impregnable.

In 1945, with the dreaded Russians almost at the gates, these defences were to protect not only Berlin, but also the heart of the Nazi regime, located in a bunker close to the Chancellery building on Wilhelmstrasse. They were also meant to preserve the nearby key city landmarks of the Brandenburg Gate, the famous Unter den Linden and the Reichstag on Königsplatz.

In his bunker, Hitler was obsessed with dreams of glory that would never come true. At the start of 1945 he had dismissed as ridiculous fantasy the idea that the Red Army was about to launch a major offensive into Germany and even at this late hour clung to the illusion that forces commanded by SS Lieutenant-General Felix Steiner were going to link up with the surviving German forces north of Berlin and strike a decisive blow against the Russians. Steiner had no more than a ragbag of forces, the grandly named Group Steiner, that was incapable of even scratching the Russian advance. The Russians simply brushed them aside as they completed their encirclement of the Nazi capital.

Another saviour in the deranged mind of Adolf Hitler was Field Marshal Schörner, one of his close confidants. Schörner did not let his loyalty to Hitler blind him to realities and his main concern in the closing days of the war was to prevent needless bloodshed among his troops. Leo Mattowitz, who had recovered from his injuries sustained in Russia and returned to duty, was serving under Schörner at this time:

> Four weeks before the end, we were supposed to be used in Berlin, but after the capitulation our plans were changed – not by Hitler, but by Schörner. He ordered us away from Berlin, and we headed through Czechoslovakia towards Karlsbad, where we intended to give ourselves up to the Americans. General [sic] Schörner led us into Czechoslovakia. There we found a lorry belonging to the Todt Organization – they built roads. They used to wear brown shirts, and there was a bundle of brown shirts lying on the ground. I had not had on a clean shirt for two months, so I took one of them and put it on.

Unfortunately, before we could reach the Americans, we were captured by the Russians. They said, "Fascist! You are a fascist!" For the Russians, anything brown was fascist. I told them they were wrong. I had never been in the SS, but they wouldn't listen. So I was sent to a camp in Czechoslovakia, where there were SS officers, Nazi functionaries and me, with my brown shirt.

Finally, Hitler turned to Colonel-General Gotthard Heinrici, commander of the Army Group Vistula, including the Ninth Army, which, he fancied, was going to march into Berlin any day and save the Reich and its Führer from the communist devils. Heinrici was an experienced professional from a family with a military tradition going back eight centuries. He was supposed to be responsible for the defence of Berlin, but he knew a lost cause when he saw one. Like Schörner, he ordered his troops away from the capital, advising them to surrender to the British or the Americans. Hitler ineffectively dismissed Heinrici on April 28 and returned to his illusions. He spent his time moving flags on a large map, apparently believing that they represented real military forces. He remained unaware that his new mighty "armies" consisted of a few small groups and defenders holed up in Berlin's flak towers.

Hannau Rittau was a gunner in the Zoo flak tower. He was prepared to do all he could to defend Berlin, his birthplace, but like Heinrici, he knew it was hopeless:

You could see what was happening, the Russians were drawing closer and closer to Berlin and when they started firing on Berlin with their artillery we said, "Well, this is the end!" But I was born and raised in Berlin and we had to defend our home, just as we had to defend our country. That's what we tried to do.

I was lucky to get into the tower at the Zoo. There was an army and an air-force hospital on one floor, though in the end we had wounded solders and civilians on all the floors. I think there were 3,000 people in this tower. My job was to drive the ambulance and bring the wounded to the tower from outside, so it was easy for me to stay there.

The tower came under determined Russian attack for two days and two nights. Despite the safety Rittau and the others had found in the tower, it was a frightening experience:

> The Russians were firing at the tower all the time. The noise of the exploding artillery against the walls was terrible, the walls shook all the time. They couldn't get through because the concrete of the tower was so thick and strong.
>
> Even so, at one o'clock in the morning of May 2, the tower was surrendered to the Russians. We were told to stay at our stations, which we did. The first thing I remember after that was the door opening. A Russian tank driver came in and said, "Everybody kaput, everybody kaput, ja? Everybody kaput, ja? Don't be frightened, Russian soldiers are good. The bad things you've heard about us were all propaganda." And out he went again. That was our first contact with the Russians.
>
> A few hours later the Russians came round looked at everybody. The wounded soldiers were lying on the floor, we had no beds, the wounded were on blankets on the hard floor. The Russians started stealing their watches, as they did with everybody. They were very interested in watches. We looked after the wounded, as we had done before. We had enough food in the tower because there was enough food storage in there for the whole of Berlin.

Although the Russians did not appear to be particularly dangerous or violent, Rittau decided to escape from the tower:

> I tried to get out, because we hadn't seen any fresh air all the time, you never saw daylight in this tower. I was on the third floor. I went downstairs and there was just one Russian standing on guard there. I gave him a cigarette. That seemed to please him. I was in hospital dress, all in white, so that he could see that I was a member of the hospital team. I looked around, and then went back into the tower again.
>
> During the next two days, all of a sudden they starting making lists. The Russians came around asking, "What's your name? What's your grade? What was your last regiment?" "Oh, oh!" I thought to myself.

"This is getting dangerous. I'd better get home!"

It was May 6 by now. The Russians on guard were so used to seeing me that they didn't notice when I slipped out of the tower. It was easy. I did the same thing again, I was wearing my uniform, but I had removed all the insignia. I pulled on my white hospital dress over it, went out the door and walked away, just like that! Of course, I tried to keep out of sight of any Russian soldier in the street who might ask me, "Where is your pass or your pay book?" or goodness knows what, and I walked home. Although my parents' house was quite close to Berlin, I didn't arrive until seven in the evening, after 10 hours. Walking all the way, it took a long time because I tried to avoid any Russians wherever I could see them. I just ducked away out of sight and waited until they had passed by.

Ulf Ollech, formerly of the Luftwaffe, was in a rather more exposed position than Rittau. He helped to man an artillery battery in the environs of Berlin. Members of the Volkssturm, the citizens' militia, were also there. This body, consisting of Hitler Youth and older men up to the age of 65 or more, had been specially trained with the Panzerfaust, also known as the Faustpatrone. This was a deadly anti-tank weapon which fired a hollow-charge projectile effective at 33 yards. In the battle for Berlin, groups armed with the Panzerfaust went hunting for Russian tanks and destroyed so many of them that the wreckage littering the streets actually obstructed the Russian advance.

Ollech was, however, disturbed at the idea that the Panzerfaust and their other weapons were going to kill people:

I was only 17, but suddenly I had to shoot at human beings in order to preserve my own life. We were trained with artillery, and were stationed on one of Berlin's arterial roads, the Prenzlauer Allee, it was called. Work began at 0700 hours – practice with the artillery and training, training, training. Then we were transferred further to the northeast, to the eastern edge of Bernau. We set up positions on the road, but were then transferred at night to a place called Malchow, where we had a free field of fire on the road closer to Berlin, near the Weissensee – a free field of fire towards this road.

The Volkssturm troops were in the trenches in front of us. Behind us were residential areas with trees and houses and gardens, so that we were well camouflaged; and we expected, quite rightly, that the Red Army would come along this road straight past us. We had to be patient. During the course of one day, in terrible weather and soaking rain, walking through the trenches meant that you carried the mud and filth with you. We spent the night there, half awake, half asleep, and the next morning, when the sun rose, we heard they were advancing along this road. Because it was an asphalt road, the Russians could see exactly whether or not someone had been laying mines there. But it was free of mines and so they advanced.

Four T-34s, two Shermans and an assault tank came along. The road had a small bend and before the first tank had reached this bend, we started firing. We had an artillery gun, which had a velocity of 1,200 metres per second, the only gun in the world from which the shell left the barrel at such speed. That meant that the discharge and impact, especially at a distance of 200, perhaps 300 metres, was so short that you thought the discharge and the impact were the same sound. The tanks were all destroyed and the Red Army infantry at the rear of the tanks dispersed.

The wrecked tanks glowed red throughout the night and the ammunition inside exploded. We spent that night there, and the next morning the weather was dry, we discovered that the infantry units, in the shape of the Volkssturm, had gone, vanished. They were supposed to be in front of us and we had seen them the day before, but now they were nowhere to be seen.

That, of course, scared the wits out of us, because we knew that if the Red Army infantry had come at us overnight, we could never have fought them off. The next morning we ate a little and drank some tea, and then we got the order to retreat with our unit into the town proper, because the Red Army, primarily the infantry, but also the tanks, had already gone around us and broken through into the suburbs.

Ollech's part in the battle of Berlin ended in one of Berlin's flak towers, which was under siege by the Russians:

We retreated and retreated and we finally ended up in a flak tower – there were three of them in Berlin – and we got ourselves over to one of them. It was surprisingly comfortable. The food was good – I had the most glorious pea soup I had ever tasted in my life – and each of us had a plank bed, a cupboard, and everything was in first-class condition. We kept guard outside for four hours, then two hours inside.

The Russians started firing at the tower with their tanks. You could hear them. Their shells went "Clack-clack" as if someone was knocking on a door. That wasn't good enough for the Russians, so they brought up some 15cm howitzers. They managed to make tiny holes in the concrete. There were windows which were closed from the outside with heavy steel doors, I imagine that they weighed tons, and the Russians succeeded in hitting the upper hinge of one of the doors, which burst. One of them broke off, twisted off the other one and hurtled downwards. Apart from that, the flak tower wasn't badly damaged at all.

They then brought up a light artillery piece. A tank attack at night followed; they knew that we were lying in relays in the surrounding trenches. We had never experienced a tank attack at night before, and that was perhaps the most awful experience, because they attacked and we sought cover, and fought them off. Next morning we saw Russian corpses hanging over the edges of the trenches, with their machine guns dragged halfway. The Russian MGs were on wheels. You could hear when they were being pulled across a street because they rattled, "rat-a-tat-tat".

Then came April 30, when we learned that Hitler and his wife had committed suicide. Hitler had once said: "I am National Socialism, if I no longer exist, there will be no more National Socialism; in other words, everything was focused upon him. We young men were very upset. We'd believe him when he'd said that. We'd grown up with it. We felt he had let us down. It was like losing an all-powerful father. What was going to happen to us now? we wondered.

It seemed hopeless for us to carry on. On May 2 we surrendered the flak tower.

That same day, Berlin capitulated. Or rather, the Germans finally gave up its rubble and ruins to the Russians.

What was Berlin like at the end? Ruined, destroyed, incinerated. The civilians were in the cellars, scared to death, old people, women and children. They left the cellars only to fetch water and maintain a minimum of hygiene. It was just the same in the rest of Germany. Scarcely anything to eat, and living in constant fear.

The dead were too many to count. It was an enormous number. We were standing in our trench one day. What we feared most of all, justifiably feared, was street fighting. The Red Army were not interested in the house and the interior, they went into a house up to the top floor, opened up the attic flap took their telescopic rifle and looked to see where they could dispose of a few German soldiers.

We tried to eliminate them, too. I had a telescope, and our staff guard, he had the rifle with telescopic sight. We tried to eliminate those who were firing from high up in the houses. There was a church which is still standing today, yes, it wasn't damaged; the Russians brought their wounded in there, they had to do something with the wounded, and look after them, and one of the Russian snipers was in the church tower where they took their wounded. We were in the trenches and hadn't noticed that our escape route ran directly towards this church. When you are standing in the trench you only watch what is happening opposite you, what surprises you can expect from there.

It's very strange, what happens. We were all together, then suddenly, intuitively, you notice that something's happened, someone's missing. You look across and there he lies, shot through the head, and you couldn't even hear the shot that had killed him. Only then do you realize, "My God, that's the line of escape, our way out of here and a sniper's there!"

There's a lot of sadness at such moments. We had all been so close. We slept beside one another, we ate together, we were out there together in this misery, together we experienced the shock of hearing Hitler had shot himself. Now the man was suddenly gone, and the sniper was already searching for his next victim. Who would it be? we wondered. Until it happened we would never know.

Ernst Preuss, a specialist radio operator, was in Berlin with his unit as the Russians approached, but he never saw them. The unit was ordered out before the Russians could catch up with them. Preuss was highly relieved. Like many Germans, he had been afraid that the fight for Berlin would be like Stalingrad – street by street, house by house:

> We were in the Olympic Village – the village built for the competitors in the Olympic Games in 1936 – and waited for our orders. Suddenly we were told that we had to get out of Berlin because Berlin was going to be attacked. We drove through the city by way of the Kurfürstendamm, the famous shopping street, and headed for Mecklenburg. We heard a lot of firing, of course, but we didn't see any soldiers.
>
> We were glad. We'd all been afraid that there would be street battles, like Stalingrad, but that didn't happen. We expected Hitler to demand that we fought that way, but he was probably no longer in control of himself and didn't give the order. Down in the bunker, though, I think they believed we could attack Berlin and save the situation, but we knew it was too late.
>
> I have very sad memories of Berlin from this time. I knew Berlin in peacetime. It was a beautiful city and now it had been bombed. As we drove through, I saw the ruins of the Café Kranzler, a very famous place, very fashionable, but now completely wrecked. It seemed to have all disappeared so suddenly. We had been in front of Moscow, and now we were in Berlin. What a contrast! All that bombing, all that destruction, all those deaths, all those homeless people and all for nothing. I'd been a soldier for about seven years and I'd fought for nothing.
>
> In 1945, you would have had to be an incorrigible optimist to believe that the war could still be won. The war could not be won. Everybody with any sense knew that. Of course, all the armies that fought wanted to win the war, but it wasn't us.
>
> My wife was in Hamburg and she wrote: "Everything has been destroyed here, you have survived the war in one piece and now you will be taken prisoner by the Russians and they will send you to Siberia." That didn't happen, thank God! But it was a very sad time for us.

The defence of Berlin, however hopeless, was conducted with fanatical ferocity. The struggle saw the house-to-house fighting the Germans had so feared, and the battle was carried on below ground in the cellars and along the underground railway. The Russians had to bludgeon their way towards to their prime objective, the Reichstag building, along the Landsberger Allee and the Frankfurter Allee. The Russians fixed crimson victory pennants at every hard-won vantage point. The shelling, the constant rifle fire, the explosion of hand grenades and the huge fires in places like the Tiergarten, Berlin's park, threw a pall of smoke into the air so thick that Russian transport drivers had to switch on their headlights to see their way through it.

The most vicious resistance came from the SS troops. They knew perfectly well that they had no chance of survival if they fell into Russian hands. The Russian had already adopted the practice of shooting SS personnel out of hand and even the British, who had a reputation for fair play towards prisoners, regarded the SS as "animals" exempt from the provisions of the Geneva Convention. British or American captivity had always been preferable to falling into the hands of the Russians, but even the Americans dealt sternly with the SS. Alfred Wagner of the Luftwaffe was in hospital at Wasserburg when the Americans arrived:

> The rumour went around that the Americans were looking for members of the SS and flight personnel from the Luftwaffe. I thought, OK, but then, as they came closer and entered the annexe to the hospital, we heard that an SS man had been shot in the annexe. I must confess that I was a bit cowardly and I destroyed all my decorations, my armband and everything. I flushed them all down the toilet.
>
> Then the door was kicked open, there were eight or 10 of us wounded lying in the room. An American soldier came in and asked if we were SS or Luftwaffe. He checked the others, and I then showed him my wallet with photos of my girlfriend. "Oh, very good," he said. He grinned at us, winked at us and the checks were over. I regretted it a bit, of course, having destroyed everything, but what else could I do?

On April 30 the Reichstag was stormed by the Russian 150th and 171st Rifle Divisions. Here the defenders had bricked up the windows and doors, and had to be prised out, corridor by corridor, room by room. The fighting was still going on when two Russian sergeants planted the Russian flag as a victory banner on the Reichstag roof.

That same day Hitler committed suicide by shooting himself through the mouth in his bunker. On April 29 he had married Eva Braun, his mistress, who had chosen to join him. She took poison. The announcement made on German Radio at 2230 hours on May 1 revealed that Josef Goebbels's Ministry of Propaganda was game to the last, obscuring the truth about Hitler's death and holding him up as a valiant opponent of Bolshevism:

> It is reported from the Führer's headquarters that our Führer, Adolf Hitler, has fallen this afternoon at his command post in the Reich Chancellery, fighting to the last breath against Bolshevism and for Germany.
> On Monday the Führer appointed Grand Admiral Dönitz as his successor. Our new Führer will now speak to the German people.

"German men and women, soldiers of the German Wehrmacht!" said Dönitz. "Our Führer, Adolf Hitler, has fallen. The German people bow in deepest mourning and veneration. He recognized beforehand the terrible danger of Bolshevism and devoted his life to fighting it. At the end of this, his last battle, and of his unswerving, straight path in life, confirming his death as a hero in the capital of the Reich."

A week later, on May 7, 1945, Nazi Germany capitulated, but the Germans in Czechoslovakia refused to accept it and fought on until May 13. The Second World War in Europe was over.

Ernst Preuss remembers his reaction to the news that Hitler was dead:

> We heard the report that "Our leader, and Chancellor of the Empire, Adolf Hitler has been killed in action at the front line in the service of the Fatherland." Our first thought was: "Thank God, the end of the war." We didn't regret the fact that he was no longer alive, we didn't know whether he had committed suicide or not, but I can't imagine that

he fought. We were relieved, we had known for weeks that the war was lost, and we wanted to get out in one piece rather than lose our lives at the very end.

Ernst Henken and his comrades were given the chance to go home once the news of Hitler's death arrived:

I kept a diary and the entry for May 2, 1945 was: "Now the Führer has been killed in action, and if the Führer has given up, then Germany is surely lost." We were in a large clearing in a wood. The Americans were 12 kilometres away, the Russians were 17 kilometres away. The whole divisional staff had been gathered there.

The commander said his goodbyes and told us, "The Führer has been killed in action, and you are therefore released from your personal oath of allegiance to him. Each of you can now head off towards home." So we did. We had plenty of food and other supplies. They had been intended for Rommel's army in Africa, but never got there. We had chocolate, cola, sugar, drinks and food, salami sausages, survival packs and cigarettes. I don't smoke, but there were 1,000 cigarettes in my car. Our commander ordered that there should be no more firing, although the war wasn't officially over yet.

We hid ourselves in the wood, and at night we crept out along the pathways. One night we heard voices, talking English and German. We said to ourselves, "We're all right here. It's not the Russians." Either the Americans or the English were nearby, but they speak different kinds of English and we couldn't tell the difference.

But we'd got tired of creeping around and hiding. The following day we decided to give ourselves up. We had a lorry, which was disguised as a refugee's car. It was covered with a white bed sheet which I'd taken in March 1945 from an empty flat in Stettin. I must have realized even then that the war couldn't go on much longer. A white sheet's very useful if you decide to surrender!

Like Leo Mattowitz, Henning Kardell became a prisoner of the Russians. Kardell had taken part in the humiliating retreat from Leningrad, which began on January 27, 1944:

We were pushed back through the Baltic states, through Estonia, Latvia, Lithuania, White Russia. By August 1944 we had been forced to retreat to the border of Lithuania and East Prussia. Then East Prussia was surrounded. In January 1945 we tried to break out towards Danzig. I was wounded during this manoeuvre, I was wounded often, I had become an officer in the meantime, leading a company, sometimes a battalion, and earned the Knight's Cross at Leningrad. I was wounded three times before I was taken prisoner by the Russians and lay in the field hospital for a long time until the end of the war in May 1945.

Heinz Frauendorf ended his war with the Russians in much more dramatic fashion. Nazi Germany had already capitulated at 0241 hours on May 7, 1945, but the following night Frauendorf's unit was involved in a battle with the Russians in Kurland, between the Gulf of Riga in Latvia and the Lithuanian border:

We were warned by the Russians through loudspeakers that if we didn't surrender, then not one of us would survive. I was with a mortar unit as a messenger. I crawled to the commander's bunker, and was totally astounded and shocked to see that he was gone, together with his cronies, without even telling us. I crawled back, grabbed hold of the casualty messenger and said, "Come on, we're getting out of here."

It was better to risk being killed than fall into the hands of the Russians. We had a horror vision of Siberia. The proof of it came from the soldiers at Stalingrad who were taken into captivity. Only 2 or 3 per cent of them came back. Fortunately we were clever lancers and battle-hardened corporals, so we took our chance and managed to reach the harbour at Lvov by motorcycle.

One glance around the harbour showed Frauendorf and his comrades that a large number of others had had the same idea. A formidable queue to escape had already formed:

There was this mass of people, bigwigs and "Golden Pheasants", as we called them, paymasters and top officers who were all going to disappear with the steamers that were moored there. It looked as if there was no chance of getting out. But luckily I happened to overhear a conversation in Hamburg dialect. I come from Hamburg, so I understood every word. That was how I learned that there were SS men from Latvia already on board one of the ships.

Fortunately they agreed to take us with them. We sailed along the Swedish coast, along the three-mile zone, and a Swedish guard boat came past with German soldiers on board. They warned us against going to Sweden. "The Swedes will deliver you up to the Russians," they said. That was too much for some of the men on board. As I've said, Russian captivity was their worst nightmare. Several committed suicide.

Our ship turned back, and eventually, we managed to get into the bay at Kiel. We found hundreds of ships of every shape and size berthed at the quayside. We were the very last ones to escape from the Russians.

Werner Reuhs was on the border between Austria and Hungary when the war ended, but the way there had been dangerous and the Russians were always close:

When my best friend was killed, we had to leave him behind because the Russians were pressing in and we had to get away from them. We retreated to the Steiermark in Austria and wandered through Hungary for four days. At the border with the Steiermark, we were collected together and formed into a tank grenadier unit. That was in April 1945. We were stationed near the castle at Fürstenfeld in the Steiermark for a while.

The Russians were in front of us. We could see them, but we didn't always shoot at them. In the first week of May no one knew what was going to happen to us. Late in the evening of May 7, that is the day of the surrender in Germany, we were in our position, with the Russians only 200 metres away. At night they made a lot of noise. They were drinking themselves silly with vodka.

I was on watch at five o'clock in the morning, when the Russians attacked. Luckily we had a machine gun and defended ourselves as much as we could, although we eventually had to retreat because the Russians were numerically superior. That was on the morning of May 8. A few brave stragglers kept on skirmishing with the Russians. We managed to get through several of our tank barricades and there was an SS division on our right – the Vikings. They said, "The war is over." We were totally astonished.

The unconditional surrender of Nazi Germany, which took place on May 7, was completed by the final act of military capitulation by the heads of the Wehrmacht, the Kriegsmarine and the Luftwaffe at 0016 hours on May 9 at Karlshorst, a suburb of ruined Berlin. Air Chief Marshal Arthur Tedder of the Royal Air Force oversaw the signing of the nine surrender documents, three each in English, German and Russian.

The setting for this historic act was appropriate. Only Berlin could have provided a vista to illustrate how totally the Germans had been beaten. The scene was one of utter destruction, desolation and death.

"If you want to know what war means," said Air Chief Marshal Tedder, "come to Berlin."

CHAPTER EIGHT

Prisoners

Being taken prisoner in war is shocking, shaming, frustrating, but for many a welcome escape from more fighting and the chance of death or injury.

Germans who were captured by, or gave themselves up to, the British or the Americans believed they would receive fair and honourable treatment. However, prisoners of the Russians were much more certain that it would be a difficult task, or simply good luck, to live through their captivity. Except for the Japanese, the Russians were the harshest and most retributive of captors, as might have been expected from a people who were so hard on themselves.

In his post-war assessment of the Russians at war, General Erhard Rauss concluded that they were able to absorb more punishment than any other opponent the Germans encountered. In Rauss's opinion, they had little regard for their own lives and safety, and would climb over the bodies of their own dead if it meant they could get at the enemy. They were contemptuous of death and were able to endure the most extreme hardships. However many of them were killed in a battle, and no matter what destruction the Germans wrought on their armaments or defences, the Russians had a terrifying ability to rise from the dead, as it were, and deliver fresh and lethal assaults. Compared with this remorseless approach, the war in the West had been a gentlemanly and well-behaved business.

The Russians had never signed the Geneva Convention of 1929 on the treatment of prisoners in war. With other Allied prisoners whose countries had signed, the Germans usually acted according to the rules. By contrast, they treated their Russian captives with great cruelty, and often exploited them as forced labour. Hundreds of thousands died. It was mutual, though, when Germans became prisoners of the Russians and, short of death or crippling injury, Russian captivity was the most dreaded fate Germans faced on the eastern front. Henning Kardell was one German prisoner who was made to confront this fate. He remembers the moment he was captured:

> Everything was in flames, farm buildings were burning, everything was glowing and burned to the ground. We came to a road and suddenly I found myself standing five metres away from a Maxim gun – that's a Russian machine gun from the First World War. Two of my comrades were with me, walking behind. They released the safety catches on their machine guns and wanted to fire. I said, "No, throw them away, it's over." We would have been riddled with holes if they had fired.
>
> I agreed to negotiate with a Russian officer and we weren't supposed to bring our guns with us. But he had his gun in the back pocket of his trousers and shot me through the arm and shot me in the heart, here.

There's the hole in the heart. Here, you can see. I lay down as if I were dead, but then I got shot in the shoulder, and afterwards I was shot in the thigh.

Once captured by the Russians, Kardell was brutally interrogated:

There were interrogations over a 10-day period and by the time they were finished, I had blood-poisoning in my arm. During an interrogation I was told, "You will be sent to the field hospital if you give us a statement. I didn't make a statement, but I tore off the bandage and smeared it over my interrogator's desk, blood and pus and rotten flesh and so on. But I was sent to the hospital just the same.

At the hospital Kardell was surprised to find that he was well treated, even after the commanding officer, Colonel Alexander Trafkin, tried to get more information out of him but failed:

I was called in to see Trafkin and had to show him on the map in blue and red – that's the way it is in the military, where friend and foe are depicted. I was supposed to give away the German positions, but I said, "What would you answer in my position, as a prisoner of the Germans?" I expected him to say, "I am not a prisoner, you are, so tell me what I want to know." But he didn't say that. Instead he told me, "I understand you. When did you last eat?"

I was in a very sorry state. I had my arm in a sling and and I was walking with a stick. I had a bandage around my head from a head wound I had received, and this gentleman asked me, when did you last eat? I was surprised. I replied, "I don't know, it might have been three or four days ago." He said, "First of all you must eat something." We were given corned beef from Oscar Meier from Chicago – deliveries, everything was Oscar Meier, this corned beef, and the Russians gave me a half-litre bottle of vodka.

The medical superintendent, a Colonel Pakovnik, a professor from Leningrad, came to see me and took great care of me. Perhaps because I had the Knight's Cross, they thought I was a brave man and gave me a lot of brains to eat. The professor believed it would give me strength.

Kardell remained in hospital for several weeks until, at the end of April 1945, he was sent to Vilnius in Latvia, under arrest by the NKVD (People's Commissariat for Internal Affairs). This could have been the prelude to more interrogations, perhaps even more brutal than before, but just over a year later he contrived to escape:

> We had a woman doctor, a very good Jewish doctor, and there were two German doctors who became my friends. I asked them, "How high is the death rate in here?" and they replied, "Two a day, 65 or 66 a month." There were 3,000 of us in this prison and I calculated that the death rate was 25 per cent. Those were not exactly good odds.
>
> Besides, I already knew how long the Russians intended to keep us in captivity. When I was taken prisoner, I asked a Russian general how long I would have to stay. He said, "You have to rebuild everything that you destroyed, but as you are hard-working people, I guess it will only last 15 years." That was in my head and I said to myself, "Fifteen years in my young life is too long." So I escaped.
>
> It was very difficult. My feet were frozen but I was helped at first by Lithuanian farmers and then Lithuanian partisans, who do not understand much about the art of war. I was a great help to them. These partisans used to say, "We have 10 men here and 15 men there and there 60 men, so let's attack a post office or a train carrying freight. But they suffered great losses fighting this way because they had no leadership.
>
> So I said to them – I could speak Lithuanian – "I can help and advise about how to carry out an attack." They had a colonel, but he had no understanding about infantry. He was a very clever man, an engineer, and he spoke German, French, English, Polish and Russian. But he had no concept of how to fight in war. I stayed with the partisans for some time, and was injured again, in an attack. I have a bullet wound in my neck, it came out beside the spine, it was as big as a hen's egg, but I survived.

Leo Mattowitz, who was captured by the Russians wearing a brown "fascist" shirt, received some very harsh treatment after he was mistaken for a member of the SS:

They kept on saying, "You belong to the SS, don't you? I kept on replying that I had never been in the SS. They didn't take any notice. "You are wearing a brown shirt," they said. "You are a fascist."

After that I was given no food for three days, no toilet, nothing at all. And me, poor devil, got put in there where only the Nazi criminals were and where I didn't belong. But at least on the fourth day we got something to eat. It wasn't much, just a mug full of rye. It tastes like sugar if you haven't eaten anything for three days.

By this time the war was over, but not for Mattowitz and the other prisoners. They learned that they were going to be sent to Siberia, the last place on earth they wanted to be. Mattowitz, however, was going to avoid that fate. Like Henning Kardell, he was going to escape:

"Oh good God!" I thought, "that's going to be great, Siberia!" A lorry arrived and set off for the station, where we were to be loaded on to freight trains. On the way, though, someone called out in broken German, "We need a mechanic. The lorry's broken down." This was my chance. "Go on, volunteer!" I said to myself. "Perhaps you'll get a piece of bread if you help them."

An officer called Potbolkovnik came up, a Kirghiz, and opened up the bonnet. All the Russians were drunk. They'd been celebrating their final victory, so they couldn't have fixed the lorry even if they'd known how. I took off the filter, but there was no smell of petrol. "Not petrol." "Not petrol!" said Potbolkovnik. "Sabotage, sabotage!" The soldier who was supposed to have filled the tank with petrol was summoned, and he was beaten up. Potbolkovnik kept hitting him, swearing loudly in Russian.

But it wasn't sabotage. There had been about 40 barrels of petrol for filling up cars and lorries, but among them there were a couple of barrels of diesel. Unfortunately for him, the soldier hadn't realized that and when he was told to fill up, he pumped in diesel. The lorry was driven a short way, and then it stopped working. Instead of trying to find out what had gone wrong, they kept on trying to start and went on until the battery was flat. We got a couple of cans of petrol, and I took out the carburettor, the petrol pump, cleaned the plugs, out with the diesel, in with the petrol.

Potbolkovnik was grateful, but Mattowitz was unable, quite literally, to stomach his gratitude:

He came up with a bottle of vodka. "For heaven's sake," I said. Nothing in my stomach for three days, and then a drink of vodka. He put his hand in his pocket and took out a bit of yellow, rancid pork. And he was an officer! That's how the Russians lived and that's how the officers lived. Like pigs, if that's not too much of a joke.

After I'd fixed the petrol, the lorry had to be push-started. I was driving and the Russians pushed and pushed until their tongues hung out. The plugs had become so saturated with diesel that it was running out of the exhaust pipe. Suddenly the engine started, and there was a big, blue cloud of smoke from the diesel. It was getting dark by this time. I came to a crossroads, and I saw once again how primitive the Russians were. There was a Russian woman with a white flag and a red flag. Red means stop. White means go. As I approached the crossing, she was waving the red flag for the other vehicles on the road, but for me she waved the white one. This wasn't a clear road, you understand. It was full up with prisoners, it was so packed you could barely drive. Then we came to a complete standstill. There was a large paving stone, a tank barrier, across the road.

This was an unlooked-for chance to escape, and Mattowitz took it:

I jumped out and left the lorry standing in the middle of the traffic, jumped into a ditch, into a hedge, across a field to a house. It belonged to a Sudeten farmer and he and his family spoke German. The first thing I did was to get rid of my shirt, so that I didn't have a brown Nazi shirt on any more. I was given a shirt by a farmer. I was very grateful to that man, and visited him after the war. I managed to get through to an American base across the River Moldau, thrashed my way through, you might say. It took enormous effort. I slept in the fields at night, in barns and in the deepest night I swam across the Moldau, the Americans were on the other side, that's where I wanted to go. They would ask me, "Where were you in captivity and how did you get out?" I must have had a guardian angel to help me escape the Russians and escape Siberia.

There was no escape, however, for Eduard Stelbe, who had served with the Luftwaffe. His Russian captivity, which began in 1944, lasted for four years after the end of the war. By the time he went home in 1949, after five years as a prisoner, he had endured many hardships and some terrifying close shaves with death:

In January 1944 we arrived at the Pripet Marshes at Brizhima and took up fixed positions. It was all ice and snow. The ground was very soft, a mound made of snow. There were two men on each mound, with only a canvas sheet to protect them from the cold. We got stuck there, unable to move. If we had moved, the Russians in the high woodland above would have shot each one of us like rabbits. Russian snipers had no mercy and we thought there were plenty of them there.

I was lucky to get away for a while, on leave. By the time I returned to my unit, the Normandy invasion had already taken place. The Russians broke through just under three weeks later, on June 21, 1944. Just then we found there had been some sort of sabotage, or maybe just a mistake. We didn't have the ammunition we needed. The tanks got artillery ammunition and the artillery got tank ammunition. The chaos was terrible and when the Russians broke through, our units were helpless. They were scattered and destroyed. Our company suffered frightful losses: out of 120 men to start with, only nine were left.

There was nothing for us to do but move around between the two front lines, but we never reached the German front line, because the Russians got there first. On July 6 I was one of 20 men in hiding on a hilltop during the day. It was dangerous to move during the day, so we moved at night. Or so we thought. There was a road running past this hilltop and lorries carrying soldiers came along it. They set up positions and machine guns and a detachment of them came marching towards our hill. As they approached, our lieutenant told us, "Fire only when you get orders to fire." But it was hopeless. We couldn't defend ourselves and I suppose the lieutenant knew that. He shot himself.

Everyone else ran off right and left. I said to my friend, "You know what, Hermann, before I let myself get shot to pieces, I shall surrender." I took out my handkerchief, we stood still, a first lieutenant joined us and there were then 15 of us, all prepared to give ourselves up. Everyone else had disappeared, some got shot.

A Russian officer said, "Does anyone have a cigarette?" Yes, of course we had. We handed him a cigarette and smoked one ourselves and he said to us, "The war is over, you'll soon be home." Wonderful. If only it had been like that. The Russians took us to an assembly camp where there was a Jewish man from the NKVD. We emptied our pockets. I had wonderful pictures of my family and I wanted to take one or two of them back. I didn't think the NKVD man was looking, but he saw and jumped at me. He would have hit me if the Russian officer hadn't also jumped up and pushed him aside and said, "Not like that, my friend. They are prisoners now." That made me think. That was all right. Maybe these Russians aren't so bad, after all.

We were lined up, there were 700 of us by this time, and we were going to march to an assembly camp about 100 kilometres away. We marched for four days all over the place. I think the Russians wanted to show us that they were the victors, the rotten way they behaved. Some of our shoes were taken away from us.

On the way we encountered a Russian women's battalion. They were ferocious, those Russian women. They fought just as savagely as the men and were greatly feared. Several of the women came up, they had pistols hanging from leather straps, and we didn't know that they had emptied the pistols. They approached us and cocked the gun, held it up and click... click... They were torturing us. Ever heard of Russian roulette? You don't know whether the next bullet is live or not. But they didn't shoot anyone and no one was hurt. It was just a little show of sadism.

Despite this experience, Stelbe learned that the Russians were also capable of kindness:

We marched on and the same day, five kilometres further on, we were lying in a ditch when a tank battalion drove past, Russian T-34s, and they stopped. An officer called the staff sergeant over and asked, "How long is it since these prisoners last ate something?" "Well," he said, "they haven't had anything to eat for two days." Then the officer said, "Send 10 men over to our quartermaster." The quartermaster had 20 sacks, such big sacks, one hundredweight of dry bread, there were thick slices, and he gave them to us.

Later on we were resting in a ditch. It was very hot. I was lying to one side and had a stick which I had rammed into the earth. I had hung my jacket on it and lay with my head in the shade. I was dozing off when I felt something against my ribs. I looked up and there stood an old lady looking at me. She asked if I would like something to eat. Then she fumbled under her apron and produced a plate full of potatoes and thick milk. It was unbelievable, impossible to forget. After all, we were enemies. We had done many bad things. It was all very well for soldiers to do their duty, but the civilians, like this old woman, were the ones who suffered.

Eventually Stelbe and his fellow prisoners arrived at Smolensk and were put into a large assembly camp. Where they were going to be after that was something they did not know:

The officers were separated from the men and we were put into 60-tonne wagons, 100 men to each wagon. Off we went. We were given a little food, there was warm soup sometimes, American tinned soup, it tasted good, with bread. One loaf between four men. That was something. We travelled for 10 days but had no idea where we were going to land up.

On August 10 we arrived in Turinsk in the Urals, where a camp was situated. Two and a half thousand men were housed there. I was there for five and a half years and everyone was unfit to work four months in every year because of infections that came off the marshland. We were exhausted for most of the time and the food was absolutely appalling. We got warm soup three times [a day], it could hardly be called soup, it was warm water with a couple of cabbage leaves or peas, a spoonful of peas, that was the soup and then 200 grams of bread for each meal.

We had to work according to the productivity norm and if the norm wasn't fulfilled, then we got 200 grams of bread less, and that was very hard. In January 1945 there was an International Red Cross Commission investigation and of the 2,500 men, 1,000 were declared unfit to work. They were given American food for four weeks. They recovered a little, didn't get fat, but they were mentally better and after four weeks they had to go back to work.

It went on like that for three years, but then in 1948 there was a new danger. When I was in the Luftwaffe, we had our blood groups tattooed under our left arms. Unfortunately the SS had a tattoo in the same place and the Russians didn't know the difference. In 1948 the Russians started asking where we came from, where we were born, where we'd been in action during the war and so on. If they got the idea that we came from Lithuania or anywhere near the Baltic, that meant 25 years' hard labour. So I told them I was born in Danzig, which was Germany territory, of course.

I'd taken the precaution of burning off my tattoo with a cigarette end. It hurt like hell, but I managed to remove most of it, except for one small piece. We were made to put our hands up and, of course, the burn mark showed up. I said it was an ulcer. I had had an ulcer on my lower arm, which had been treated, and in my papers its location on my arm wasn't mentioned. So I got away with it, or I thought I had.

Shortly afterwards a Russian NCO came up to our brigade commander with a list of all those who had to report to the political officer. My name was on it. "Now I'm in for it," I thought. When I came before the political officer, he said, "You don't need to tell us anything, we know that you were in the SS, in such and such a sector and you did such and such." I said, "Sorry, none of that is right. I was in the Luftwaffe in an elite division, and I have burned away the blood group here." "Why?" "Because I knew that you would not like the blood group." I was hit in the face left and right for being too outspoken.

Many of the other prisoners believed that if they became ill they would be released. So they made themselves ill. They drank water with salt in order to get swollen legs, but the Russians weren't fooled. When I finally got home to Germany I was somewhat the worse for wear. That was not surprising! The SS prisoners were all sorted out and kept back, but the rest of us were loaded on to wagons. There was a stove so that we could heat up water, and a field canteen and some straw to sleep on. But at least we were going home. We arrived in Friedland on December 15, 1949, and we were all released.

Edmund Bonhoff had to work for the Russians in the mines after he was taken prisoner in Kurland:

In Kurland we had a commanding officer who seemed to live on hope. He told us that we should stick it out and the English and the French, they will help us conquer the Russians and we have to persevere. But he didn't believe what he said. Eight weeks before the surrender, in March 1945, he ran away, just leaving us there. Then we were taken prisoner. We were collected in East Prussia, where we were told, "You will all be going home, it's not so bad, we just don't have any capacity on the trains. We still have the battle around Berlin, and when that's all settled then you'll be going home. It was all nonsense.

At first, in the prison camp, we were guarded by soldiers. They weren't so bad because they understood what it was like in war and had something in common with us. But later on they were replaced by youngsters carrying rifles as big as they were. They were terrible, really hard, brutal kids. Whoever was unable to walk had to sit for a quarter of an hour in a puddle. They beat us all the time. The only way to get away from them was to get ill.

I was ill and a doctor took me home with her. It was a relief. The entire area was a punishment area. Even the Russians who were there were all there for punishment. But I was lucky. I got ill. The doctor treated me well. She gave me potatoes and salt. Salt is more valuable than gold in Russia.

A far worse fate awaited Bonhoff, however:

One morning a large number of guards surrounded the prison camp and we were loaded up and sent to Svetlovsk, 2,000 kilometres east of Moscow in Russian Asia. There we were sent to the mines. There were three mines, 90, 120 and 180 metres deep, not, as they are in Germany, 2,000 metres deep. My God, it was primitive, really primitive. You'd have thought you were back in the nineteenth century or even the eighteenth. There were horses down there in the tunnels and home-made shovels, and as for the food, well, it was something else. We were given the sort of cabbage you usually give cows to eat, sour cabbage with large leaves, and some fish bones and the peelings from potatoes. Every morning we got a can full of tea made from pine needles, to prevent scurvy. We had to drink it, otherwise we'd get no food for the rest of the day.

Bonhoff had an accident in the mine and broke his foot. It was a fortunate, if painful, occurrence:

> With the Russians, if you couldn't work any more you could go home. They couldn't use you. Two thousand of us were gathered together in Svetlovsk and sent to Frankfurt an der Oder and when we arrived in Frankfurt an der Oder there were only 1,500 left. The rest had died on the way. They are all registered as missing to this day, but we know what happened to them.

Herr Räde became a prisoner of the Russians after they had retaken Sevastopol on May 9, 1944:

> I was captured near the Maxim Gorky coast, as it was called and we marched for three days without a single bite to eat, drinking filthy water from the puddles on the way. We were beaten, there were executions and suicides. Everything we had was stolen from us. Only a few Russian officers refrained from such outrages or tried to avoid them.
>
> I got to know a lad from the Balkans who could speak perfect Russian. That would be useful for escaping and he thought about escape a lot. He wanted me go with him. I answered that we were obliged to help the completely leaderless mass of our fellow prisoners and that we could only do that if we moulded ourselves to the existing circumstances, looked for support, won trust and in so doing, won the greatest chance for ourselves. He didn't agree and later he

was shot.

But because of him and because of my knowledge of Russian, the NKVD became suspicious of me. They interrogated me several times, at night. I pointed out to them that they could check which professors I had studied with at the German university in Prague and I told them their names. They must have checked up because they left me more or less alone after that.

Like Edmund Bonhoff, Räde was put to work in the mines, but with extra duties as a translator:

Whenever there was a public holiday in Russia, we had to produce twice as much as we did on ordinary days, just to honour this holiday. As a translator I had to report to the Russians about what was going on in the mines, what productivity was like. There was a wooden board that was freshly planed every day, and I wrote my entries on this board. There were beatings, the Russian workers lazed around, letting the prisoners do all the work, and they took credit for it. This was grossly unfair, and I thought about calling together the best leaders in the other mines in order to consider the formation of our own all-German mine. That would get rid of those layabout Russians. That is what happened. So, at the start of 1946, Mine 100 became our German mine. It was much better. We were permitted to write out our own work rotas, in shifts, and we got concessions about productivity because, as prisoners of war, we were working in the worst conditions and simply couldn't keep up a 100 per cent record. But we did that later.

There was just one Russian mine leader and I insisted on having a Russian mechanic. The dynamiters were young male and female Russians. They were in disgrace, because they had once worked in Germany and now had to work for five years in the mines as a punishment.

Through Räde's efforts at liaising with the Russians, conditions in the German mine gradually improved:

We had a much better chance of getting home alive, with our health intact. Productivity improved, too, and when it did, my men were given either 30 or 50 grams of bacon and additional soup. Later there was pocket money for the work we had done. We got only some it. The rest was credited to us, to stop us running away. The Russians reckoned we wouldn't want to leave our money behind!

In the outside world, the Cold War had begun and the Russians, now facing their erstwhile friends as enemies, began to seek a new alliance with the Germans. This had an effect in Räde's mine:

Our situation improved more and more, we were given fresh underwear once a week, and new suits, and by the beginning of 1947 there was even a small camp canteen where we men from the German mine could buy things with our money. Some of us were allowed outside the camp. They used to go to the local markets and brought things back with them into the camp, so that the food situation got better and better.

As for us, we had a new self-esteem. We were working for ourselves and willingly overproduced so that many of us were able to have 100 per cent productivity registered in our work papers.

We called our mine the "family mine", and, whenever special efforts were demanded, I demanded in return from the mine administration overalls and shoes for my people, which were delivered without further ado, simply because we overproduced and the director of the mine, or the directorship as a whole, received their state bonus for productivity over and above the norm. So everyone was happy.

Conditions were far worse in the other mines. In 1944 and 1945, Räde reckons, 10 corpses a day were carried out of the mining camps and buried outside. The Russians showed a particular lack of mercy to the Germans they considered deep-dyed criminals: the Waffen-SS, the police, members of security battalions, German marksmen and so on. By the beginning of 1949 Räde was a "trusty" and was given the task of training the Waffen-SS men in Mine 100:

They were going to be imprisoned for a much longer time. The

Russians intended to punish them very severely for what they had done in Russia during the war. There was a young Waffen-SS man, the son of a miller from the Hamburg area. He managed to escape four times and was captured each time. He was in very bad shape and looked deathly wretched. I got him healthy again, and gave him light work to do to help him recover. He was so grateful that he asked his parents via a sick comrade who had been released home, to help me when I returned to Hamburg.

I returned to Hamburg in March 1949, and the young man's parents helped me in a magnificent way. They gave me clothes and pocket money, and as Hamburg was totally strange to me, took care of my application to the school authorities for a job at a school. I had been a secondary-school teacher before the war.

Only six months later, in September, I was already employed by the school authorities. One of the friendly school directors said to me, "You were in the war and captivity, begin your work gradually." I taught the pre-school children initially and then went to the primary-school children. After that I was given back my post as a secondary-school teacher in Hamburg, and changed to the grammar school. There I became a senior master and by the time I retired, I was a school headmaster.

Walter Veitzen became a prisoner in 1945 when he was captured in Czechoslovakia by the Russians:

I was brought to Bruenn [Brno] as a prisoner of war and was guarded by the Russians at first. They weren't very good at it, and there was every chance for us to escape. The Russians were far more interested in our valuables, our watches and so on. I think they assumed that we wouldn't escape because the Czechs hated us for what Hitler had done to them before the war. They looked on the Russians as liberators, I suppose. I didn't escape, anyway, even though the Russians allowed us more or less free rein.

Eventually, at the end of May 1945, we were taken to a very unpleasant place: Auschwitz, in the concentration camp where internees had been incarcerated. We were put in there, there was plenty of room, there was space for hundreds of thousands of people. We stayed there roughly six to eight weeks, and were continuously sorted out according to our state of health. The older ones among us had to suffer most. It was easy for us young men, but not all that easy, considering where we were.

One day the word went round the camp that whoever wanted to work could leave Auschwitz and travel to Upper Silesia, in Poland. As I was one of the youngest there, and felt myself to be fairly strong, I said, "Good, this is the opportunity for you to get out of here, out of the camp. It was really terrible there, with hundreds of thousands of people living together, with little food and a lot of illness that could lead to epidemics.

So everyone who left the camp for work duty thought they had a good deal. But they hadn't. The offer of work with the harvest was a lie. We worked on the harvest all right, but not in Upper Silesia. We went on a six-week train journey and arrived in Chelyabinsk, in western Siberia. That's where the harvest was.

Several men died on the way there. There was not much to eat or drink and it was burning hot, something like 63 degrees [Celsius]. Around 50 people were locked in the carriages. The corpses were thrown out of the train each time it stopped. Many people came to the train to stare at us, but they were sorry afterwards. Once 20 or 30 corpses had been thrown out, the guards jumped out with their machine guns, screamed at the onlookers, "Stand still!" and surrounded them. The guards picked out an equivalent number to the corpses and put them into the carriages. So the quota was full, the number was right once more, and we arrived with roughly a full complement. Around 2,000 people arrived in the camp at Chelyabinsk. Poles, Ukrainians, different nationalities.

Life at the camp was extremely hard, there was little food and Veitzen and the other prisoners were made to do work simply for the sake of work:

During the first years in the camp we had to work hard, but no proper work was arranged for us. The Russians just made us work to make us work. I was glad when I suffered a minor accident, because this meant I didn't have to go to the stone quarry where I had been working. I was unable to work again for six weeks, though I was given jobs to do in the camp.

Maybe that's why I survived because the work in the quarry would have killed me. The conditions were too harsh. Next I went to a huge factory where tanks had been built during the war. It was reorganized and reconstructed and we were set to work building tractors instead. They were built on a conveyor belt, but they weren't very good tractors.

Veitzen worked alongside Russians, mainly young women, who had been sent to Germany as forced labour from the areas occupied by the armed forces in the first years of the war in Russia. They had been brought back to Russia, but only to work in forced-labour camps again:

We went to work in this huge factory with perhaps 1,500 people, a Russian soldier went in front of us, one followed behind – we had no chance of escape. It was practically impossible to get away from the place. The young Russian women walked in groups of roughly about 35 each, with at least three guards to each group who often had an extremely vicious dog with them. It was terrible. The Russians, these young women, were being treated worse than German prisoners of war.

Veitzen worked in the tractor factory until the end of his captivity in December 1949, but there were conditions about releasing the German prisoners:

The Russians demanded that we sign a declaration that when we went home – Germany had been divided into West and East Germany by this time – we would actively engage in pro-communist work here. Even though this would have given them their freedom, after five years in captivity some of the prisoners refused to sign. There were only about 20 or 30 of them, and they were punished for saying no. When we left the camp on December 8, 1949, they had to remain behind.

I knew one of them very well. Joachim Strobel, he had been a lieutenant in the Wehrmacht, the army. His family were looking for him and put his name in a journal that was supposed to help returnees get in touch. His name was still in the journal in 1954. He hadn't yet come home. I wrote to his brother to ask him to write to me when he returned, but I never heard anything. Maybe he never came home. Maybe he didn't want to write. I just don't know.

After the rest of us were released form the camp, on December 8, we spent 10 days travelling to Friedland, where all prisoners from the east were handed over to the Federal Republic – that is, West Germany.

Herr Senneberg was also housed in a former concentration camp, Maidanek, after he became a Russian prisoner. It was there that he learned of the appalling atrocities the Nazis had committed:

> The Russians took us in a gang to an assembly camp. We were not wearing the black SS uniforms. Our uniforms were field grey, but, like the SS, we had the Death's Head symbol on them. So, naturally, the Russians thought we were SS. They wanted to massacre us. They beat us up, tore off our shoulder epaulettes. Fortunately a Russian officer arrived and had our would-be murderers arrested. Otherwise we would have surely died there and then.
>
> We were sent to a big prisoner-of-war camp on what we called a "death march". It lasted a week. It was broiling hot, around 30 degrees [Celsius] in the shade. The sun beat down unbearably and more and more men collapsed the further we marched. There were perhaps 1,000 or 2,000 of us, and if someone collapsed, what did the Russians do? They grabbed hold of Polish farmers on the fields and stuffed them into our columns, so that the number was correct again. That's how they did it.
>
> Finally, at long last, we arrived at a camp and above the entrance was written: "Arbeit macht frei" – "Work makes you free." That puzzled me, I'd never seen anything like that. And then we learned our first POW camp was the concentration camp at Maidanek! We were the first German POWs to be put in there and there was a special purpose for it.

That evening the Russian commander, an officer called Bolkovnik, he read us the news of all the crimes that that Germans had committed in the concentration camps and other places. Some of us shouted at him, "It's all lies, it's not true, nothing like that happened at all." Bolkovnik didn't turn a hair. All he said was: "We will show it all to you tomorrow." The camp was cordoned off with a door to another camp and there were chimneys there, for the incinerators, barracks, stone barracks, very high. What I saw there, I've never seen anything like it, we would never have believed it possible. At Maidanek there were children, women, old people, who had been killed in the shower rooms and were put into the cremation ovens afterwards. That was described to us by former Konzentrationslager inmates, concentration-camp prisoners. They told us the whole story about what had happened, and we saw it in detail, everything that had happened there, it was absolutely appalling. Today the younger generation accuses us: "You must have known about it, that such things were going on." We didn't know about any of it. And certainly the soldiers at the front didn't.

When Fred Angerstein was a prisoner of the Russians, at Kalua, conditions were so bad that he and his fellow captives were reduced to eating cats and dogs. Bugs were everywhere:

Another prisoner and I used to share a piece of fur as a bed. Then we began to itch all over our bodies. It was the bugs. If you took your shirt off and lay it down, it ran off by itself. We were a filthy, ragged crowd and many of us were sick. Dogs and cats used to run away from us because they knew that otherwise they would be caught and eaten. Everyone grabbed hold of a cat and one evening another prisoner, called Albert, ate his cat. He didn't give me any, though. A couple of days later he became ill and couldn't eat anything, so I got his rations, such as they were. "That's the punishment," he said, "for not giving you anything of my cat." A good thing, too. That cat must have had some disease or infection.

The rats were terrible. They were everywhere. We had to hold our bread up so they wouldn't get it, but they ran over our heads. There were two planks set up at an angle and in the middle was an empty space and the rats ran around in there. Rats, bugs, lice, we had them all.

Death was commonplace in such conditions and Angerstein saw a great deal of it:

In Russia I only saw the many, many corpses. I was nearly one myself! Many men died from lung infections and from a build-up of fluid. One day I woke up on my plank bed and my face was swollen up, my legs were swollen up. I was certified as sick, but quite probably the Russians expected me to die. But I was lucky. A couple of prisoners knew something about medicinal herbs. One of them said, "I'll boil you some tea." Which he did, but after a fortnight of being swollen up, I thought: "Now you'll die, the old pump can't take it any more", because so much water pressed up against my heart. One night I had to go out and sat on the latrine and it ran and ran and ran and ran. God knows how many litres came out! The next day it was all over. I never got swellings again during the entire period in Russian captivity. Many colleagues got swollen feet over and over again and the body discharged it somehow, but I never got it again.

Some of the Russian guards Angerstein encountered were quite comradely, but there were others who were out-and-out sadists and thugs:

When we were herded from the main camp to the transports, they herded us on foot 100 kilometres each day for three days and the Russians who guarded us then were evil, evil thugs. If anyone could not walk any more and lagged behind, he was immediately shot. Shot immediately. And even the buckets of water that were put out along the road for us by the farmers' wives who took pity on us, these thugs kicked them over. So we didn't have anything to drink. That happened while we were being marched 300 kilometres to a train station in Romania. There were many, many deaths.

We arrived at the station, us survivors, and were then loaded up into small carriages, 50 men in each one. They were divided up like goods

shelves. The Russians put 12 men on the top shelf and 12 on the
bottom. Four carriages, that made 48 men. Two were left over and they
had to lie down beside the urine gully. During the journey, in winter,
they would always be urinated on. Then the urine froze. These men
often died. In the middle of the gully there was a funnel-like hole for
defecation. We travelled like that for three weeks through Russia,
with more or less nothing to eat, and we then came to a place 200 kilometres west of Moscow, where we were unloaded.

Angerstein had been a technical engineer in civilian life and he was
put to work on a lathe in a factory building steam engines. The working conditions were very difficult, mainly due to the extreme cold of the
Russian winter. It was the freezing cold that caused the accident in which
Angerstein was quite badly injured:

> I was supposed to cut pieces from a pipe and one always used water
> for lubrication, then came the sealant. I left the pipe in the machine
> overnight so that it could still move next day. But one night there was
> a terrible frost, and the pipe froze into the machine. The first thing I
> did next morning was to switch on the main switch so that the box
> would warm up. "Ah," I thought, "you left the pipe in there yesterday."
> I grasped hold of it with rags of wool and wanted to pull it out.
> Couldn't do it, because it was frozen solid. The glove twisted itself
> around my hand with the pipe because the machine was turning. I was
> hurled down on the floor and screamed for help. Then a very pretty
> nurse called Lydia arrived and switched off the main switch. When I
> took the glove off, I thought, "The thumb is still in there but it does-
> n't look right." It looks strange to this day. A Russian doctor operated
> on my hand. The operating table was a kitchen table, I think. He
> mixed an anaesthetic from a powder and water and put it on. He did
> the operation very well, sewed it up. There was only one bandage in
> the place and he bound my hand with that.

Herr Kosak was taken prisoner by the Russians near Luttenmensprey,
while he and his comrades were trying to get back to the German lines:

We were surrounded. We were exhausted, there were three of us, we had been sleeping in the woods, and I woke up because someone was shaking me, and there stood the Russians in front of me; they tried to take our watches, and the small handgun that I was carrying.

Fortunately these Russians were a bit more civilized. We weren't beaten or anything – well, I was hit once, but I suppose it was my own fault. I had been rebellious towards the guard, and he struck out with the butt of a rifle, but I was able to parry it, and he was then reprimanded by another guard.

The Russians made us march round continually. That's a Russian habit. If they don't know what to do with you, then they make you march around in a circle. We arrived in a camp in Sagan, where there were tens of thousands of men. The war had finished by that time, we heard that Hitler had, well, "fallen in battle" was how they described it. After Sagan we were taken to Oppeln in Upper Silesia, then on to the Volga near Stalingrad, a town called Volsk. Volsk was the centre or a centre of the Russian cement industry. The whole town was white with cement dust. We worked there. The food was very meagre.

I was starved just like the others, and had been very seriously ill. Fortunately I was naturally resistant. At such times the thin people, and I was always a thin person, have an easier time of it than the men with big muscles, they simply need more food than we did. Of the three million German prisoners of war in Russia, one million died, and they died mostly of starvation and illness rather than accidents while working. I can well remember that men lay down to sleep in the evening and simply didn't wake up again next morning because they were so weakened.

Later on, in 1949, Kosak was sentenced as a war criminal, but, he claims, he was nothing of the sort. It was all a ploy on the part of the Russians. They just wanted to preserve their workforce:

In 1949 the Russians wanted to keep hold of a certain number of people so there was this mass sentencing of German soldiers at Orel. There were 14 of us and we had to pass through the guardhouse attached to the detention centre in Orel. There was a Russian sergeant there, the duty guard, and as we passed through he said in Russian, "Fourteen times 25 years!" We understood him and knew that we were going to get 25 years' hard labour each. But because, according to this sergeant, we were all going to be given the same sentence, we didn't take it very seriously.

Russian officers said to us – we occasionally had contact with them and Russians can be very friendly – they said, "Oh, four or five years and then you'll be going home" – and that is virtually what happened. We were sent to southern Russia, or the Ukraine, to the Donetz Basin, there are two rivers, the Don and Donetz, a coal-mining and industrial area at the time, and there, in the main, we built factories. I worked mostly in the stone quarries, because as a school leaver I didn't have a trade. If you were a carpenter or stonemason you had a better trade, but I learned how to quarry stones well and also mastered the technique. It was still very hard work.

By this time conditions had improved in the Russian POW camps. They had become independent economic units, and prisoners were hired out to other companies as labourers and were paid for their services, as Kosak recalls: "From my camp, we were hired out most often to the Interior Ministry because we built roads, and the Ministry of the Interior was responsible for road building. They paid very badly, though. Other camps had better employers and the prisoners earned better money."

Kosak had a strange experience while he was in the prison camp. According to him, he met Hitler's nephew, who was a carbon copy of his famous uncle:

A new column arrived in the camp, and someone said, "Come with me and I'll show you Adolf Hitler." He led me around to the back where the new prisoners sat, they'd been given straw-filled sacks to sleep on, and were sewing them up, and right enough, I thought I was looking at Adolf Hitler. It was Hitler's nephew, and he was amazingly like him. He had the same moustache, the same hairstyle and those dark eyes and even moved in the same way. Adolf Hitler was able to fascinate people, and this nephew of his certainly fascinated me. He had been taken prisoner at Stalingrad.

Living through Russian captivity was a miracle of survival, for the Russians were determined to make the Germans they captured pay for all the depredations caused by the invasion of 1941. However, the Germans were more than just slave labourers. They were trophies for the Russian victors. In 1944 some 50,000 men captured during the collapse of Army Group Centre were paraded in triumph through Moscow, much as the Romans had once led their captives in chains through the streets of Rome in a flamboyant display of military power. Many of these Germans, and hundreds of thousands of thousands of others, would not survive to see home again. Their presumptions about Russian captivity had been all too accurate.

Generally speaking, so were the Germans' ideas about the superiority of British or American captivity. They were not always correct in this assumption, but the British and Americans were usually scrupulous in observing the provisions of the Geneva Convention on the treatment of prisoners. There was also a curious camaraderie of war in play, something civilians often find hard to understand. A British or American guard would look at a German prisoner and would know what he had been through. They may have been trying to kill each other. They may have been taught to hate each other, as many soldiers on both sides were, but they both knew what it was like being under fire. They both knew the fear of being killed. On a purely human-to-human basis, there was a certain empathy between them.

Herbert Beyer had the curious experience of becoming, in turn, a prisoner of the English, the Americans and the French. His war had been very short, only 13 months between arriving in the Western Desert of Africa and giving himself up:

> I became a prisoner of war on May 13, 1943 at 1300 hours, with 13 men, so the number 13 wasn't very lucky for me! That was in Tunis. I'd been with a maintenance company that had been set up in North Africa and first went there at the end of 1940. We marched the whole way back from El Alamein to Tunis, but though we reported our presence in Tunis, there was no one there to arrest us. So we saved the

English the trouble and gave ourselves up.

The camp we were put in was a field surrounded by rolls of barbed wire, but one evening all of it was trampled down during a little celebration we had with soldiers of the Eighth Army. They were there as our guards, but they were very friendly. In fact, the English envied us because for us the war was over, for them it would go on. They knew that their next battleground would be Sicily or Italy and that the fighting would be very hard.

Beyer was very glad that there would be no more fighting for him. He had never been very enthusiastic about the war: "I had never been an enthusiastic soldier and nothing bound me tightly to the regime of the time. On the contrary, I kept myself at a distance from them. Before the war I had to join the Hitler Youth, but I was kicked out in 1940 because I never went to the meetings and had no interest in them."

After a while Beyer was sent to a larger assembly camp in North Africa. It was there that the British handed their prisoners over to the Americans. The Americans treated Beyer and other prisoners very well. Then it was time to move on again:

We spent three weeks in a convoy of ships which sailed from Casablanca to America, to the harbour at Newport, where we were disembarked and de-loused because we were terribly infected with the creatures. There had been no facilities to wash properly on the ship or to clean ourselves and, for us, that being de-loused was a blessing. We were then taken by train on a two-day journey into the interior of the USA and arrived in Illinois, where we were put into a large POW camp.

We were the first German prisoners to come to America and people were very curious about us. When we arrived at the station in Illinois, hundreds of people were there to see the "Nazis", as they called us. The guards were told to watch us very carefully because the Nazis would jump away like rabbits. They had some fantastic ideas about us. Later we were told that the Americans had been told that the Nazis had horns and hooves. They believed it. So, when we were led out from the train, we heard children asking, "Where are the Nazis' horns and hooves?"

The treatment in the camp, where the Germans were housed in barracks, was very good. Angerstein and the others were told that they were there as guests, and as far as the food was concerned, they were treated as such:

> We were working guests, of course. We had to work because that was set down in the international conventions, and we then worked in a clothing warehouse for the American soldiers, and packed and sent things away that went overseas and elsewhere. Because we were in this clothing warehouse we were well clothed ourselves because we could take what we needed from the shelves. Americans used to take clothes, too, sometimes they stole them. We reported him and within a short time he wouldn't be there any more.
>
> The pay was 25 cents a day, which was paid once a month and we had a canteen where we could buy chewing gum or cigarettes or chocolate. There was beer as well and that was a little bit of comfort for us, and there was an orchestra set up in the camp, there were theatre groups, a cinema and a large sports ground on which we played football among other things, a small church. It was really marvellous.

Herbert Beyer was still in America when the war ended in 1945. After that, American attitudes towards the German prisoners changed, as the news of the Holocaust, the slaughter of six million Jews, the killing of the gypsies and other atrocities committed by the Nazis became known:

> I was only 20 years old and I'd never taken much notice of politics, so I didn't know too much about what went on in other places during the war. Of course, I knew that Jews were not liked in Germany, but I could never say anything bad about them. After all, I went to school with Jewish children. One day, though, they were suddenly no longer there. Where they were, I don't know. I heard from colleagues in 1939 or 1940 that there was a concentration camp somewhere, but no one could find out what it all meant. At the time we were told that the people with political opinions that didn't fit into the current framework

of Nazi Party thinking were sent there and they were isolated there. But I never knew what happened afterwards.

My mother worked for a Jewish family, cleaned for them and so on and my father was employed in a Jewish department store which was later "Aryanized", as the Nazi Party put it. The strange thing was that the Nazi Party bosses, dressed in civilian clothes, went to shop in these Jewish stores which existed in Berlin and were well treated. They received first-rate goods for their money. Everything that took place at the time was so absurd, there are just no words to describe it. But many Americans somehow thought that we prisoners were responsible, and they became rather cold towards us.

Beyer entered his third captivity in early 1946, when the German prisoners were sent to France. Their time in the United States had been luxurious by comparison:

The prison camp in France was in a very bad condition. It had rained and the ground was soft and small holes had been dug out and filled with straw to sleep on. It was cold and we had to lie around in damp, cold weather. The French camp was not very pleasant but the French at that time were in a terrible quandary. They didn't have much themselves, because the Germans had taken practically everything during the occupation. By the time we arrived, the French hadn't yet recovered from all that.

We were sent to work at first in an iron foundry in Lorraine, and afterwards, because it was such heavy work, I developed a hernia. I said, "I can't do this work any more", so I was sent to a camp in Metz, which was also in Lorraine. There I was sentenced to 30 days in prison because I had refused to work.

This camp was close to Germany and many of the German prisoners in France tried one way or another to escape and get home. So, this was some kind of a training school, where you learned everything you needed to know about escaping and staying free for when you wanted to make your own escape. But lots of these escapees made mistakes. They were caught and sent to another camp, where, I suppose, they attempted to escape again. I don't know whether they managed it or not.

Beyer did not escape from this particular camp, but remembered his "training" and took the opportunity, successfully, later on:

We were sent from there to a labour camp, also in Lorraine, which had originally been intended for coal miners. Luckily I didn't have to go to the mines, but worked outside in the open. The French guards were very lax. We had some civilians guarding us, but they stayed out of the way, enjoying their peace and quiet. They made it easy for us! We were in contact with people from Saarland, just across the border, and they helped us. I escaped with a comrade shortly before Christmas in 1946 and got right across the French-occupied zone into the American zone. The Americans sent me to Hanover and from there I crossed the Russian zone and travelled by train to Berlin. I arrived home on December 17.

Ulrich Bruss became a prisoner in Italy, but in dangerous circumstances. His first captors were Italian partisans. Fighting as they did outside the rules of war that governed the conduct of regular forces, they had a reputation for savagery., They proved it in 1945, when they executed Il Duce, Benito Mussolini, and his mistress, Claretta Petacci, and put their bodies on public view, hung upside down. Bruss was more fortunate. The partisans handed him over to the Americans:

I was in the Apennines, in the mountains for four months. We carried out communications work there, repaired the wires that were being continually shot away and so on. But we had to fight, too. We had to search for partisans. The mountain roads were under threat, so we had to guard them. To carry out this search, we had to clamber over rocky areas with mules and donkeys and go through water and rivers. And from wading through water I got a bad infection in a wound on my foot. I couldn't get to a doctor, because the roads were watched by Allied fighter-bombers, mostly American. The used to fire like hell at everyone when they came over. So I was unable to get treatment, until one day when there was heavy low cloud and the planes couldn't attack, I was driven to a field dressing station from where I was taken to a hospital at Cortina, where they found that my foot, the whole leg, was so badly damaged that it would probably have to be amputated. Fortunately I kept my leg and recovered. That was during the winter of 1944–45.

Not long afterwards the German front lines began to break up and Bruss found himself on the run:

The Americans landed on the nearby coast and we had to save our skins. We had no heavy weapons, no weapons at all. We travelled through Tuscany and hid ourselves anywhere, in churches and similar buildings, chapels, in schools as well, that would be lined with straw, where we spent the night. We tried to manage like that. It continued like that until April 1945. We had no orders. We simply wandered about.

The Americans were coming close, but we had no possibility of defending ourselves against them, so we retreated. A group of us moved into a hole in the ground that consisted of two openings, one on one side, the other several metres away on the other side. There were corridors in between, and a room. We crept in there.

The local Italian partisans probably thought that they would no longer be involved in the fighting, and we took the opportunity to stay there, very frightened, of course, and extremely nervous. We kept on thinking someone would come to find out who was in there. Maybe they would throw a hand grenade inside, and that would have been the end of us. We were in fear of our lives because of it.

The Italians came, but there were no hand grenades, thank God. They were partisans, we could tell that from the band they wore round their arms. We had wanted to be captured by the Americans because the Italians sometimes, shall I say, ignored the law, and let their hate out on us. We wanted to avoid that and be treated like proper prisoners of war.

Fortunately the partisans gave us to the Americans and so we got what we wanted. But what we didn't know was that it would not be a nice experience. The Americans took us away with our hands up, and made us march behind a jeep. American soldiers sat in the jeep with a machine gun, and we had to march for hours with our hands in the air, into captivity.

The camp was nothing more than an open field. The Americans had set up small, two-man tents and we spent the night in these two-man tents. There were 38,000 men meanwhile, Germans, and the camp was divided into cages, which consisted of 4,000 men in each one. The Americans did a lot for us. They put their rations at our disposal. With the help of black Americans, camp fires were quickly set up, large barrels like rubbish bins arrived and stew was prepared which we could eat.

But the regulations were severe. Each of us was given a tin and if someone got the clever idea to hold the tin out for a second time and he was caught, he had to stand in the searing summer heat until he collapsed. Sometimes there were stones piled up and he couldn't sit or lie down and he had to stand until he collapsed from the heat. The Americans liked to do that as a deterrent. They wanted to maintain absolute discipline.

I had the good fortune of getting into a bigger tent near the camp gate. One day American soldiers came and asked if anyone could speak English. Luckily I understood English, and said, "I have learned it at school." "OK, stay here," I was told. So I became an orderly. I was assigned to a tent with the soldiers who had taken a four-man tent and had to take care of everything that was needed. I used hand out Stars and Stripes, the US Army newspaper, clear the dining tables, keep the tents clean and so on. That was my job.

I was given cigarettes. I smoked in those days, and on August 10, 1945 it was my birthday. I was given a metal mirror by the Americans and matches and cigarettes, a comb and so on. As an orderly I had to iron uniforms, and I became really good at it. The Americans had the peculiar habit of ironing three horizontal folds into their shirts. That was difficult but I managed to do it.

On September 28, 1945 Bruss was sent away from the camp, ostensibly to be released. It was not as simple as that:

Because I came from Danzig, they told me that I couldn't be released. Danzig was disputed territory, so no one knew where I should go. So instead I was sent to the temporary camp at Bad Eibling [in Germany] and loaded into a caged-in lorry which was secured with barbed wire. We drove to France, where I was held in captivity for a long period of time. I worked at first in a mine, but the work was so hard that after a while I wasn't able to do it any more. A German doctor had to give me digitalis to help keep up my strength. I was so exhausted, I couldn't get up. He wanted to organize my return home but another doctor, who was French, said, "No! We can't do that, he is not in a condition to be moved." By that time, I weighed 80 pounds or less. I recovered, eventually, and worked for a French farmer for a while. Then I was sent back to the camp, and at long last I was released and came home to Hamburg.

Karl Born first became a prisoner of the Americans just after the end of the war in Europe. This, though, was not his only captivity. Back in Hamburg, he was arrested by the British for subversive activities:

I became a prisoner of war 10 days after the war ended. I was at Thüringen for a while and later in a camp at Babenhausen near Aschaffenburg. We called it a death camp. The Americans there were quite malicious, especially when it came to providing us with food. On the first day they sorted out the officers and NCOs, like me, which was permissible under the Geneva Convention because officers could not be forced to work. We were put into special quarters and got no food for seven days. The reason, we were told, was that we had bullied all the soldiers under our command into fighting the war for five years. It was stupid rubbish, but it was typical of the Americans at that time. They were somewhat inexperienced as far as events in Europe were concerned, they had strange conceptions. They were quite different from Europeans.

Born managed to escape from the prison camp and return to Hamburg. In Hamburg, however, he was soon in trouble again:

I got away in the night and somehow got through to Hamburg on a freight train. In Hamburg a group of us got together to oppose a meeting of the communist party. The English in Hamburg thought we were a German resistance movement, resistant, that is, to their authority. The English were occupiers and the military government, and it's true that we weren't very well disposed to them.

So, with a few hundred other Germans, we were arrested on April 20, 1946, Hitler's birthday. Initially we were sent to internment camp Number Six in Neuengamme, the former concentration camp. All manner of people were locked up there – top German commanders, anyone who had a civil service title, like "councillor" and so on.

The English put us on trial. We had to appear before a British War Tribunal in Ratzeburg. I was sentenced to 12 years for what the English called my "attempt to reconstruct a Nazi regime in Germany". It was total rubbish, but that was their standard speech at the time. On top of that I was condemned for disobedience towards the military government. Fortunately I didn't have to serve 12 years. After three or four years the Tribunal's judgements were rescinded. My sentence was reduced to five.

This was because there had been investigations and it was discovered that we had been badly treated after being arrested, especially by the British Secret Service. They found that the majority of statements they got from us had been made under duress. It was also very suspicious that, somehow or other, the files containing records of our trial had disappeared. So that's why the sentences were reduced.

Afterwards I sought to have my imprisonment recognized as time spent as a prisoner of war, which was in the end accepted by the Administrative Court of the Federal Republic of Germany, West Germany. During the proceedings the court wanted to have the files, but the English said they didn't know who I was. But fortunately I had some old charge sheets and indictments and so on. So I managed to prove my case. While I was in prison with the English at Neuengamme, we were treated correctly and were given what was due to us under the Land War Regulations. That was the same provisions that were due to the reserve troops. They rigorously adhered to them, so that was all right.

Clausdieter Oelschlagel, who had served on the U-boats, ended his war in port at Narvik, Norway, and eventually reached a prison camp at Butterly in central England, where he was very much aware of the differences the English made between their prisoners. His captivity of two years, however, helped him to make a fresh start in life. He eventually became a doctor and radiologist:

> In Butterly the conditions in Camp 18 were very good. There were three compounds each one for a different kind of prisoner. In Compound A were the active anti-fascists, in Compound B were the "grey" men, those the English weren't certain about, and in Compound C they kept the U-boat men, the SS and the prisoners from parachute regiments.
>
> We were a friendly group and we learned a lot in captivity. We were still so young and the war had prevented us from learning. There were three officers in the compound from university, lecturers, professors, and they opened up a sort of educational establishment. It was like going back to school. I spent two years there – that's what I got for serving on the U-boats. But it gave me the chance to study Latin and that helped me take up more studies when I was released and went to Bonn. It was difficult at first, because in the English military zone in 1947 an active officer like myself was not allowed to matriculate from a university. The rules were very strict at the start, but then they were eased a bit and I thought: "By the time they find out what I'm studying, it will all be over anyway."
>
> And that's what happened. I took my examination in 1952. I was a general practitioner at first, then studied radiology. Afterwards I was a radiologist in Hamburg for 32 years.

Herr Hesselbart, too, learned some valuable lessons in captivity:

> I was a prisoner of the Americans. I deserted from the army – it was hopeless, we could never have won – and was captured in France. By that time, in the middle of 1944, it was hopeless, we couldn't possibly have won the war. Of course, you didn't dare say so to anyone, you didn't know if they would tell your superior officers, and then they'll have you for betraying you country by talking about defeat. It was

possible that you would end up hanged. So no one spoke to anyone else about it.

But I remember very well the day that it was all made clear to me, the impossibility of Germany prevailing. It was July 26, 1944. There had been an air raid by 1,500 American "Flying Fortresses" [B-17 bombers] and I didn't see one Luftwaffe plane in the sky to challenge them. Of course, superior forces don't always win, but when the superiority is as enormous as that, there's nothing you can do. Close by us was the SS Tank Division Das Reich and contingents from the Hitler Youth. They were totally smashed from the air. They didn't even have the chance to show how brave they were. When that sort of thing happens, you know it must be the end.

The Americans had a lot of camps in England, not everyone was sent to America. I was in Buckinghamshire first and afterwards in Norfolk. It enabled me to get to know about the English way of life and about democracy, something we had never really known in Germany. I learned to speak English as well. Normally, if you are a prisoner of war, it's just wasted time in your life. But I made the best of it.

My life as a POW lasted from the summer of 1944 to the end of 1947. We were not mistreated at all, though there were some unfortunate times. One of my fellow prisoners drowned while swimming, and one died when he fell under a lorry. But those were accidents, they would have happened anyway.

I became due for release in late 1947. I had the chance to stay in England as a civilian labourer, so I did. I stayed for a year in order to get to know the country, the people and the language better. It was a good thing I did because things were very bad in Germany at that time. I managed to get an eight-pound bag of coffee to Leipzig, through an English friend. Coffee was like gold in Germany – very, very valuable. If I had gone home to Germany in 1947, I would probably have starved, just as they did. I think my life began all over again the day the Americans captured me!

Looking back in old age to the time when they were young and at war is, to some German veterans, much the same thing as wondering by what miracle or stroke of divine protection they managed to survive. Many are bitter at how easily they were seduced by the blandishments of the Nazi Party: for them, the foolishness of youth, normally a harmless stage in growing up, has an evil twist to it.

However, having escaped death when death and the risk of death were everywhere about them, most veterans find there is an extra joy to be had with their families. To them the simple fact of being alive, in old age, is reason enough to be glad. Some concentrate their memories on the pleasures of reunion with old comrades. Some are sad that, despite the war and its sufferings, the world has not changed.

Walter Veitzen puts his regrets in this way:

My worst experience of the war wasn't during the war. It's now. To this day nothing has been learned from what happened in that period. That is for me the worst experience of all. So much is written today, so much is discussed. But all the discussion, the writing, it doesn't help at all when there's no real understanding of what war means. We still have wars today, not so big, not worldwide, but even so, we who know how terrible war is cannot help wondering: what did we fight for in 1939–45?

Hundreds of thousands, if not millions, of people died. The Russians were just as deluded by Stalin and we were deluded by Hitler. I would put him on a par with Hitler because what that man had on his conscience has never and perhaps will never be known. I remember those people who afterwards were incarcerated in hundreds of thousands, who came back at the end of the war and who had done nothing criminal whatsoever. It has been proved that Stalin did not send the prisoners of war from Germany back home to their relatives after the war was over. How many died no one knows, and there were, besides, all those whom he executed. How could a human being do all that?

There is a touch of resentment in Edmund Bonhoff's view, but basically, like Veitzen, he regrets the lack of understanding he finds so common today:

Young people today simply don't understand. They have their own, new, ideas, but you can't apply them to a war that happened so many years ago, in a different time, a different world. Young people say, "Why did you not throw away your weapons? You should have surrendered." But at the time no one could do that. No one in their right mind, that is. These young people have no idea of what the Nazi regime was about. The Nazis would have thought nothing of shooting their own soldiers if they showed weakness, or failed to do what they were told. Throwing away our weapons, refusing to fight any more, was like we were committing suicide.

At the start, when our forces were so successful, yes, we believed in victory. But after Stalingrad we did not believe any more. To fight without belief was terrible.

Ernst Preuss has a more resigned view of the war:

It wasn't an adventure, it was forced upon us. We had to do our duty, there was no escape and we did it well. But basically, we fought for the sake of self-preservation. Sometimes, just sometimes, we'd think: "Perhaps it would be good to get taken prisoner and it will be over, we'll be out of it."

Once, during the war, I was happy when I contracted jaundice. I was in Riga for four weeks and was able to sleep peacefully at last in a clean, white bed. Only the sort of war we had to fight could make you glad to be ill.

Herr Poemüller began the war believing he had to do his duty, but as the war progressed, he began to have doubts:

We were standing up for Germany, not for Hitler, for Germany, for our homeland. And we felt solidarity, that it was our absolute duty. We had grown up in the Hitler Youth. We believed in the authorities, we knew that orders had to be carried out and every order had to be obeyed, there was nothing else to do. If you didn't, then you were in a bad way. There would be imprisonment for refusing to follow orders, punishment, even execution.

But later, when we were able to think back, we realized that we had been caught up in terrible evil. And we were tainted with it. God above, what did the Nazis do to all those people? They have been sent to their deaths. These crazy wars and battles that were fought and for what? Not for the good of the Fatherland, that's for sure. The Fatherland was destroyed.

Herbert Lange enjoys the comradeship of old warriors:

When I look back today, and during the years after the war, as a surviving crew we meet in a different place somewhere in Germany every two years. It always gives me enormous pleasure to see my old comrades again. Now and again we really let loose and celebrate and the U-boat comradeship has remained up to this day.

Werner Ritter von Voigtländer, too, still values the comradeship of war, but he has a proviso:

At our old comrades' meetings we clap one another on the shoulder and say, if only we could still get one of the old steamers and sail again together, wouldn't we just love to do that. But not in war. Forget it. Never again, never again. It was hard, but it was our job, there was nothing to be done about it at the time, so we did it. But never again!

One way or another, though, these and all the other veterans have been indelibly marked by their experiences in the Second World War. They saw horrors that made earth seem like hell. They experienced hardships no one should have to endure. Some of them still carry the physical evidence of the ordeal they went through. All have painful memories of men as young as themselves who died in the fiery cauldron of war before their lives had properly begun.

Edmund Bonhoff expressed it for all of them when he said, "I spent my youth fighting in the war. I never had a youth. When I returned, I was an old man."

Bibliography

Ailsby, Christopher: *Waffen SS* (Sidgwick and Jackson, 1999).

Brown, Eric and Green, G. William (Editor): *Wings of the Luftwaffe* (Airlife Books, 2000).

Bullock Alan: Hitler:*A Study in Tyranny* (Penguin Books, 1990).

Burleigh, Michael: *The Third Reich: A New History* (Macmillan, 2000).

Darman, Peter (editor) and Ripley, Tim: *SS Steel Storm: Waffen-SS Panzer Battles on the Eastern Front 1943-1945* (Motorbook International, 2000).

Fugate, Bryan I: *Operation Barbarossa* (Spa Books, 1989).

Hart, Stephen: *The Wehrmacht* (Fitzroy Dearbourn, 2001).

Kaufmann, J.E. and H. W.: *Hitler's Blitzkrieg Campaigns: The Invasion and Defense of Western Europe, 1939-1940* (Combined Books,1992).

Kershaw, Robert: *War Without Garlands: Operation Barbarossa 1941-42* (Sarpendon Publishers, 2000).

Kirk, Tim: *The Longman Companion to Nazi Germany* (Longman, 1996).

Lewis, Brenda Ralph: *Hitler Youth: The Hitlerjugend in War and Peace 1933-1945* (Spellmount Publishers, 2000).

Rauss, Erhard et al: *Fighting in Hell* (Greenhill Books, London 1995).

Snyder, Louis: *Encyclopedia of the Third Reich* (Robert Hale 1998).

Werner, Herbert A.: *Iron Coffins: A Personal Account of the German*

U-Boat Battles of World War II (Da Capo Press, 1998).

Wiggins, Melanie: *U-Boat Adventures*: *Firsthand Accounts from World War II* (Naval Institute Press, 1999).

Index

A

Abbeville, German bombing and capture of, 19–20, 22
Admiral Graf Spee, pocket battleship, 68
Admiral Hipper, heavy cruiser, 68, 97, 98
Admiral Scheer, pocket battleship, 97, 98
Alfonso XIII, King of Spain, 104
Allied Fifth Army, 173
Angerstein, Fred, 206–7, 243–5, 250
anti-aircraft batteries, German, 175–7
appeasement policy, Franco-British, 2
Archangel convoys, 94
Arctic waters, 129; U-boat campaign, 94–8; Luftwaffe attacks on convoys, 129, 131
Ardennes offensive (1944), 189, 208
Ark Royal, HMS, aircraft carrier, 99
Army NCO school, Potsdam-Reiche, xi
Arnim, Colonel-General Jürgen von, 171
ASDIC (sonar), 71, 79, 99, 139, 157
Athenia (British liner), sinking of, 71
Atlantic Ocean, 15, 69, 81, 87–8, 90–1, 94, 98, 136–7, 158
Augsburg, 180
Auschwitz concentration camp, 239–40
Australia, 2, 30
Austrian Anschluss (1938), 2
Axis (Germany, Italy, Japan), 27

B

Bad Eibling PoW camp, 255
Babenhausen PoW camp, 255
Barham, HMS, battleship, sinking of, 92–4, 100
Bari, Luftwaffe raid on, 173
Battle of Britain (1940), 104, 112, 113, 114–24, 138, 177
Bay of Biscay, 143
Belgium, 189, 189; German invasion of (1940), 17, 18, 19, 20, 35
Belgrade, 27; fall of (1941), 28
Benghazi, 124
Bense, Otto, 44–8
Benzing, Helmut, xiv, 136
Berlin, Allied air raids on, 175–8; battle for (1945), x, xiv, 208, 209, 210–20; and Russian storming of Reichstag, 220; German military capitulation in, 224
Beyer, Herbert, 248–52
Bismarck, battleship, 67–8
Blitzkrieg, 1–32, 105, 106, 126
Blücher, heavy cruiser, 12, 13–14
Bock, Field Marshal Fedor von, 40–1
Böhm, Herbert, 20
Bolkovnik, 243
Bonhoff, Edmund, xv, 37–9, 41–2, 235–6, 237, 259–60, 261
Born, Karl, x–xi, 102, 127–8, 255–6
Braun, Eva, 220
Bremen, German steamer, 89–90
Brest U-boat docks, 90, 91, 141, 143, 151
Britain, British, war declared on Germany (1939), 2, 10, 111; Norwegian campaign, 11, 12–13; Dunkirk evacuation (1940), 22–5, 112–13; Greek campaign, 28–30; invasion of Eritrea, 124; German prisoners of, 248–9, 255–7; *see also* convoys; Royal Air Force; Royal Navy
British Army: Eighth Army, 249; First British Airborne Division, 173
British Expeditionary Force (BEF), Dunkirk evacuation of, 22–5, 112
Bruss, Ulrich, 252–5
Bulgaria, 27–30
Bund Deutscher Mädel, 83
Bunke, Gunther, 43–4
Butterly PoW camp, 18, 257

C

Caen, 183
Canada, 140
Cape Bon (North Africa), 171
Cape Verde Islands, 154
Cardwell, Mrs Nora, 119–20
Caribbean, 140
Caucasus (Russia), 58, 132, 134; Kuban bridgehead, 168
Chamberlain, Neville, 111
Charles XII, King of Sweden, 35, 36
Chelyabinsk PoW camp, 240–2
Christian X, King of Denmark, 11
Chuikov, General Vasili, 134
Churchill, Winston, 25–6, 94
Cold War, 238
Condor Legion, 4; in Spain, 104–10, 111, 127; *see also* Luftwaffe
convoys, Allied, 15, 87–8, 90–1, 136–8, 156–8, 160, 249; American coastal, 140; Luftwaffe attacks on, 129–31 Murmansk and Archangel, 94–8; PQ-16: 95; PQ-17: 97–8; PQ-18: 95; *see also* U-boats
Courageous, HMS, aircraft carrier, sinking of, 72
Cranz, Otto, 60
Crete, German occupation of (1941), 30–1, 124–5
Crimea (Russia), 56, 63, 132, 199, 200

Croatia, 27
Czechoslovakia, xii, 2, 208, 211, 212, 220, 239; German occupation of (1939), 2, 6, 110

D

Daladier, Edouard, 111
Danish Royal Guard, 11
Danzig, 9, 204, 222, 234, 254
Daressalam, training ship, 69
deep-sea bunkers, 91
Demjansk pocket (Russia), 41–2, 43, 46–8
Denmark, 162; German invasion of (1940), 10–11, 112
depth bombs, airborne, 138
depth charges, 71, 76–7, 78, 79, 80, 81, 90, 92, 93, 96, 99, 138, 139, 141, 143, 147, 155, 156, 157
deserters, 205
Dietl, Colonel-General Eduard, 34
Dietrich, Sepp, 23
Difflüh, Willy, 78
Donetz Basin (Russia), 247
Dönitz, Grand Admiral Karl, 68, 87, 93, 144, 158, 160, 220
Dunkirk, evacuation of BEF from (1940), 22–5, 112–13

E

East Prussia, 200, 201–2, 204, 222, 235
Egypt, 124
Enigma code, 153–4, 193
Eritrea, British invasion of, 124
Estonia, 202, 222
Expositor, merchant ship, 95

F

Fairfield City, US freighter, 71–2
Finland, 208
First World War (1914–18, x, xii, xiii, 2, 3, 4, 5, 17, 21, 34, 101, 102, 103, 105, 108, 111
Fischl, Admiral, 110

Flieger-Hitlerjugend, 102
France, French, 10; war declared on Germany (1939), 2, 10, 111; German occupation of (1940), 17–26, 35, 37, 87, 112, 113; Allied invasion of (D-Day Normandy landings: 1944), 158, 183–8, 189; Allied landings in South of (1944), 188; German PoW camps in, 251–2
Franco, General Francisco, 104, 108, 110
Frauendorf, Heinz, 48–50, 195–6, 222–3
Friederich, Heinz, xiv
Fuchs, German NCO, 60
Fürth, 180

G

Galland, Adolf, 122, 183
Geneva Convention (1929), 226, 248, 255
German Air Sport Association, x
Germany, Allied bombing raids on, 174–83; Allied invasion of, and battle of Berlin, 189–90, 200–20; surrender of (1945), 160–2, 220, 224; *see also* Kriegsmarine; Luftwaffe; Wehrmacht
Gestapo, xiii, 208
Gibraltar, 98
gliders, 102, 183
Gneisenau, battle cruiser, 15–16, 67–8, 83
Goebbels, Josef, 3, 170, 220
Goering, Hermann, 102–4, 112, 113, 114, 117, 119, 121, 124, 163–4, 168, 169, 170, 177, 179–80
Goodall, HMS, destroyer, sinking of, 159–60
Greece, Greeks, 28–31; Italian invasion of (1940), 28; German occupation of (1941), 30–1, 124–5
Guderian, General Heinz, xiv, 5–6, 19, 20, 22, 23, 31, 39,

40, 192–3
Guernica, bombing of, 105–6
Guttmann, Rudolf, 76, 83–4, 87

H

Haakon VII, King of Norway, 11, 17
Hamburg, 223, 239, 255–6, 257; Allied raid on (1943), 179, 197
Harris, Air Chief Marshal Arthur "Bomber", 177
Hedgehog missiles, 138, 139
Heinemann, Anton, 119, 123–4, 180–2
Heinrici, Colonel-General Gotthard, 212
Henken, Ernst, 221
Herbert, John, 88–9
Hermann, Hajo, xii–xiii, 2–3, 14–15, 28–30, 103–4, 106–10, 111–13, 115, 125–6, 127, 129–30, 131, 171, 177–9, 186–7
Hesselbart, Herr, 257–8
HF/DF ("Huff Duff"), direction finder, 138
Hillary, Richard, 120–1
Hitler, Adolf, x, xii, xiii, xv, 2, 6, 7, 12, 23, 26, 31, 33–4, 35, 40, 41, 53, 55, 58, 59, 82, 101, 102, 103, 104, 110–11, 115, 124, 126, 127, 132, 163, 170, 171, 189, 192–3, 208, 209, 210, 211, 259; *Mein Kampf*, 26–7; assassination attempt on (1944), 202; suicide of (1945), 160, 217, 220–1; nephew of, 247
Hitler Youth (Hitlerjugend), x–xi, xii, xv, 102, 214, 249, 258, 260
Holdorf, Walter, 145, 146
Holocaust, 250
Horn, Gerhard, 145
Hungary, 27, 200, 223; German occupation of (1944), 200–1

I

Iceland, 94, 96, 97
Illinois, PoW camp, 249–50
Italian Air Force: C32: 109;
  Savoia Marchetti 81: 109
Italy, Italians, 27, 141, 171–4,
  209, 249; invasion of Greece
  (1940), 28; Allied invasion
  of (1943), 171–4; and sur-
  render to Allies of, 208;
  German prisoners in, 252–3

J

Japan, Japanese, 27, 225
Jodl, GeneralAlfred, 35
John Harvey, blowing up of, 173
Jordan, Lieutenant, 55, 56
Jungvolk, xi

K

Kalua PoW camp, 243
Kardell, Henning, 36, 55–6,
  62–4, 66, 221–2, 226–8, 229
Karsties, Werner, 73, 95, 98–9,
  137, 148, 149–51, 156
Kasserine Pass, battle of
  (1943), 126
Kearney, USS, 90
Kharkov, 132, 192, 193, 195–7
Kiel, 151, 152, 162, 223
Knight's Cross, 2, 83, 88, 227
Kosak, Herr, radio operator,
  196–7, 245–7; sentenced as
  war criminal (1949), 246–7
Kretschmer, Otto, 87–8
Kriegsmarine (German Navy, x,
  xiv, 25; *see also* U-boats
Kursk, battle of (1943), 170,
  192–5, 197, 198, 199

L

La Spezia shipyard, 141
Lange, Herbert, 68, 69–70, 74,
  77–8, 84–5, 91–2, 141, 142,
  261
Langsdorff, Captain Hans, 68
Latvia, 208, 222, 223, 228
Le Havre, 186
Lehmann, Hans, 3, 4, 7–10, 26,
  27, 32, 48

Lehrmann, Georg, 6, 18–19,
  21–2, 23, 26, 27, 39–40
Leipzig, German light cruiser,
  89
Leningrad, siege of, 35, 38, 41,
  44, 46, 62, 63–4, 66, 199,
  221, 222
Libya, 124
Lithuania, Lithuanians, 202,
  208, 222, 228, 234
Loch Ewe (Scotland), 94
London, Blitz on (1940),
  115–17
London Naval Agreement
  (1935), 71
"Lucy" spy network, Soviet,
  193
Lufthansa, 102
Luftwaffe (German Air Force),
  x, xii, 2, 4, 6–7, 11, 12, 13,
  14, 16, 18, 19–20, 21, 23–4,
  25, 28–30, 64, 90, 95, 97,
  98; and Allied invasion of
  Europe, 183–90; attacks on
  convoys, 129–31; Battle of
  Britain, 114–24, 138, 177;
  defeat of (1943–5), 163–90;
  defence of Germany,
  175–83; Italian campaign,
  171–4; Mediterranean campaign, 171–4; 1939–42:
  101–34; Russian campaign,
  126–9, 131–4, 163–71,
  193–4; Luftflotte 1: 127;
  Luftflotte 2: 113, 127;
  Luftflotte 3: 113–14;
  Luftflotte 4: 127; Luftflotte
  5: 114; Air Corps X, 124;
  BV-138 seaplane, 96; FW-
  190: 129, 167; FW-200
  patrol aircraft, 136; He-51
  fighter, 109, 111; He-111
  bomber, 65, 105, 127; HS-
  123: 128–9, 133; Ju-52
  bomber, 65, 105, 107, 109,
  168–9; Ju-87 "Stuka" dive-
  bomber, 4, 22, 105, 122,
  128, 194; Ju-88 bomber, 119,
  120, 173, 175, 182; Me-109
  fighter, 104, 114, 118, 119,

122, 127, 129, 174, 177; Me-
  110 fighter, 111, 119, 175;
  Me-262 turbojet fighter, 179,
  189; Me-323 Gigant troop
  transport, 172–3; *see also*
  Condor Legion
Lüttenmensprey, 105, 245
Lützow, pocket battleship, 97,
  98
Luxemburg, German invasion
  of, 17
Lvov, 222

M

Madrid, 108, 110
Maginot Line, 10, 17
Maidanek concentration camp,
  242–3
Malta, 98, 125; Luftwaffe raids
  on, 125–6
Manston, RAF, 121
Marschkompanie (German
  replacement company), 64–5
Mattowitz, Leo, xv, 50–4, 55,
  211–12, 221, 228–30
Meding, Karl, 56–8, 199
Mediterranean Sea, 77, 93, 94,
  125; sea war in, 98–100,
  143–6, 149–50, 156–8;
  Luftwaffe campaign in,
  171–4
Memel naval base, 69, 202
mines, minefields, 194
Mola, General, 110
Mosbach, Sergeant, 171
Moscow, 35, 38, 39, 41, 52,
  126, 132
Müller, Max von, 102
Munich Agreement (1938), xii,
  111
Murmansk, convoys to, 94–8,
  129, 137–8
Mussolini, Benito, 28, 124, 252

N

Naples-Cappodiccino airfield,
  172
Napoleon I Bonaparte,
  Emperor, 35, 36, 59
Narvik (Norway), 11, 15, 160,

257

Nazi-Soviet Non-Aggression Pact (1939), 55

Nebelwerfer ("smoke thrower"), 43

Netherlands, 189; German invasion of (1940), 17–18, 19, 35

Neuengamme internment camp Number Six, 256

Newfoundland, 158

New Zealand, 2, 30–1

Nichechieskaya (Russia), 165–6

Niessel, Gefreiter, 120

NKVD (Soviet secret police), 228, 232, 237

Normandy landings (D-Day: 1944), 158, 183–8, 209, 231

North Africa, 124, 126, 171, 172, 193, 248, 249; Allied landings in (1942), 143

Norway, Norwegians, 161–2; German occupation of (1940), 10–11, 12–17, 87, 89, 97, 98, 112

Nürnberg, light cruiser, 89

O

Oelkers, Rudolf, xiii–xiv, 197–9

Oelschlagel, Clausdieter, 72–4, 75, 80–1, 84, 85–6, 96, 142, 153, 159–61, 256–7

Ohrt, Karl, 74, 79–80, 82–3, 140–1, 142–6, 156

Ollech, Ulf, 214–17

O'Neill, James, 88–9

Operation Barbarossa (German invasion of Russia), 33, 39; *see also* Russia

Operation Citadel (battle of Kursk), 192–5, 197, 199

Operation Dynamo, British (Dunkirk evacuation), 22–5

Operation Sea Lion (German planned invasion of Britain), 36, 123

Operation Torch (Allied landings in North Africa), 143

Oppeln PoW camp, 246

Oran, 143, 146

Orel (Russia), 193, 194, 195, 198, 199; mass sentencing of German soldiers at, 246–7

Oslo, German occupation of, 14, 15, 112

P

Pakovnik, Colonel, 227

Panzerfaust/Faustpatrone (anti-tank weapon), 214

Paris, German occupation of, 26

partisans, Italian, 252–3; Lithuanian, 228; Russian, 59–60, 197–8

Paul, Prince, Regent of Yugoslavia, 27

Paulus, General, 165, 166, 170, 191

Peenemünde, RAF bombing of, 179

Penelope Barker, convoy ship, sinking of, 95

periscope: air or "knee-bend", 159–60; attack, 159, 160

Petacci, Claretta, 252

Peter II, king of Yugoslavia, 27, 28

Philip, Heinz, 175, 179–80, 187–8, 189–90

Phoney War (Sitzkrieg), 10

"pill thrower", 79–80

Pitomnik supply field, 169

Poemüller, Herr, 209–10, 260–1

Poland, xii, 240; German occupation of (1939), xii–xiii, 1–10, 27, 31, 35, 106, 111; Russian advance into (1944), 200, 208

Potbolkovnik, Russian officer, 229–30

Poznan (Posen), 205

Preuss, Ernst, 32, 218, 220–1, 260

Prien, Captain Günther, 72, 88

prisoners (PoWs), 225–61; Geneva Convention on treatment of (1929), 226, 248, 255; in Russian camps, 225–48; in Allied camps, 248–58

Q

Queen Elizabeth, HMS, battleship, 92, 94

Quisling, Vidkun, 11, 15

R

radar, 122–3, 138, 143–4, 147, 152, 153, 154, 175

Radbruch, Detlef, x, 168, 169–70, 172–3

Räde, Herr, 200, 236–9

Rall, Günther, 122

Ramsey, Vice-Admiral Bertram, 24

Ramstetter, Horst, 122–3, 128–9, 132–4, 164–7, 170, 174

"ratch-boom" (Russian gun), 44–5, 50

Ratzeburg, British War Tribunal in, 256

Rauss, General Erhard, 33, 226

Red Army, Soviet, 211, 215, 217; Central Front, 192, 194; First Ukrainian Front, 208; First Belorussian Front, 208; Voronezh Front, 192; 62nd Army, 134; *see also* Russia

Regensburg, 180

Reiners, Heinz, x, 72, 83, 86–7, 95, 147–8

Reinhardt, Wolfgang, xi–xii, 36–7, 42–3, 58–9, 205–6

Remagen, Ludendorff Bridge at, 189–90

Reuben James, USS, 90

Reuhs, Werner, 200–1, 223–4

Reykjavik (Iceland), 94

Rhineland, German re-occupation of (1936), 2, 10

Richthofen, Baron Manfred von ("Red Baron"), 102, 103

Richthofen, General Baron Wolfram von, 169

Richthofen Squadron, 103

Riga (Latvia), 62

Rittau, Hannau, x, 175–7, 212–14
River Bzura, Battle of the (1939), 2
Roger, Alan Stuart, 19–20
Röhde, Ernst Günther, 68–9
Röhm, Ernst, 103
Romania, Romanians, 27, 55, 64, 165, 200, 244; USAAF bombing of Ploesti oilfields, 179; German occupation of (1944), 201, 202; surrender to Allies (1944), 208
Rommel, Field Marshal Erwin, 92, 93, 124, 126, 171
Rönner, Herr, 192
Rostov, 132, 192
Royal Air Force (RAF), 11, 12–13, 16, 25, 92, 98, 112, 113, 114, 117, 124, 125, 142, 171, 175; Battle of Britain, 117–24; Bomber Command, 180; Fighter Command, 117; Hurrican fighter, 113, 118, 122; Lancaster bomber, 175; Mosquito fighter, 178–9; Polish Fighter Wing, 172; raids on Germany, 104, 175–9, 180–2; Short Sunderland flying boat, 91, 152; Spitfire fighter, 118, 119, 121, 122, 183
Royal Navy, 25, 68, 72, 89–90, 92–4, 98, 112, 114, 138–9, 153, 171; British Home Fleet, 97; see also convoys; submarines; U-boats
Royal Oak, HMS, battleship, sinking of, 72
Royal Yugoslav Army, 27–8
Rûnde, Reinhold, 10, 11–13, 15–17
Russia/Soviet Union, 6, 27, 221; German campaign in x, xv, 31–66, 126–9, 131–4, 163–71, 172, 191–200; Poland occupied by (1939), 2, 7; Rasputitza (season of mud), 39–41, 132; Allied

convoys to, 94–8, 129, 137–8; in Spanish Civil War, 106–7; partisans, 59–60, 197–8; advance into Germany and battle for Berlin, 200–20, 222–4; German prisoners of, 225–48, 259; women soldiers, 232
Russian/Soviet Air Force, 127–8, 131, 168, 169; Polikarpov 1–16 Rata, 106–7, 127
Russian/Soviet Army see Red Army

S

SA (Sturmabteilung), 103
Sagan PoW camp, 246
Salmon, HM submarine, 89–90
Sarastone, Welsh collier, 88–9
Sardinia, 172, 173
Scapa Flow, British naval base, 72
Scharnhorst, German battle cruiser, 15–16, 67
Schmidt, Heinrich, 92–4, 137–8, 139
Schörner, Field Marshal, 211, 212
Schweinfurt, 179
Senneberg, Herr, 64–6, 194–5, 242–3
Sevastopol, 63, 132, 199, 200, 236
Siberia, 229, 240–2
Sicily, 124, 249; Allied invasion of (1943), 171–2, 173, 193
Sieb, Benedikt, xiii, 60–2
Sinclair, Sir Archibald, 125
Slovakia, 27
Smolensk, 233
snipers, Russian, 45–6
snorkel, 147, 161
Somaliland, Italian invasion of (1940), 124
sonar, 71, 79, 99, 139, 147, 154
Soviet Union see Russia
Spanish Civil War (1936–39), 104–10, 111, 127

Spanish Republicans, 105, 106, 108, 109, 110
Speer, Albert, 111, 179
spotted fever, 52–3, 54
Squid missiles, 138–9
SS (Schutzstaffeln), 41, 47, 200, 209, 212, 219, 223, 224, 228–9, 234, 235, 242, 258; see also Waffen-SS
Stahl, Unteroffizier Peter, 115
Stalin, Josef, 52, 55, 170, 193, 259
"Stalin Organs" (Katyusha rockets), 43, 50, 192, 203
Stalingrad, Battle of, 58–9, 63, 64–6, 129, 134, 163–70, 1911, 193, 197, 218, 222, 260
Starzynski, M. Lord Mayor of Warsaw, 8
Steiner, SS Lieutenant-General Felix, 211
Steinhilper, Ulrich, 121
Stelbe, Eduard, 231–5
Strasosky, Eckhart, xii, 202–5
Strobel, Joachim, 242
Stuttgart, 180
submarines, British, 89, 92; Italian, 92, 160; see also U-boats
Sudetanland, xii, 2
Suez Canal, 124
Svetlovsk (Russia), 235–6
Sweden, Swedish, 14, 223

T

tanks, German, 4–5, 20, 21, 22, 23, 193, 200, 203; Russian T-34: 42–3, 44, 47, 169, 192, 203, 215
Tedder, Air Chief Marshal Sir Arthur, 224
Tirpitz, battleship, 97, 98
Todt Organization, 211
torpedoes, 69, 74, 75, 76, 90, 93, 100, 139, 142; LUT, 75; Type 5 acoustic, 159
Toulon, bombing raid on, 84
Trafkin, Colonel Alexander, 227

Trondheim, 90, 160
Tunisia, 171, 248
Turinsk PoW camp (Urals), 233–4
"turnip" technique (Schtekrübe), 129–30

U

U-boats (German submarines), x, 25; days of success (1939–42), 67–100; diving, 78, 85–6, 96; days of failure (1943–5), 135–62; "wolf pack" technique, 136–7, 139–40, 153; closing the hatch, 148–9, 154; Type VII class, 91–2; Type 9 (supply vessels), 142; Type 21: 149, 152; First U-boat Flotilla, 90, 151; U-23: 87; U-28: 69; U-29: 72; U-36: 89; U-47: 72; U-81: 100; U-88: 95; U-99: 87, 88; U-331: 92–4, 100; U-415: 151, 154–6; U-457: 95; U-505: 154; U-589: 95; U-595: 140, 143–6; U-952: 77; U-968: 96
Udet, Ernst, 102, 119
Ukraine, 65, 128, 192, 247
United States, 90, 140; Operation Torch, 143; invasion of Sicily, 171–2; German prisoners of, 248, 249, 251, 253–5, 257–8
US Army, 219; Seventh Army, 189; Ninth Armoured Division, 189
USAAF (US Army Air Force), Eighth Air Force, 182; 15th Air Force, 173; Flying Fortresses (B-17 bombers), 175, 182, 184, 258; Liberators, 152, 153, 172, 184; Mustang fighter-bombers, 171–2; P-51 Mustang fighters, 180,

182–3; raids on Germany, 175–8, 179, 180–3; Thunderbolts, 184, 185
US Navy, 97

V

V1 and V2 weapons, 179
Valiant, HMS, battleship, 92, 93, 94
Valletta (Malta), 125–6
Veitzen, Walter, 239–42, 259
Versailles, Treaty of (1919), xii, xiii, 2, 101, 103
Vitebsk (Russia), 57
Voigtländer, Werner Ritter von, 75, 78–9, 82, 148–9, 151–2, 154–6, 158–9, 161–2, 261
Volkhov (Russia), 41, 42, 199
Volsk PoW camp, 246
Volkssturm (citizens' militia), 214, 215
Voss, Werner, 102

W

Waffen-SS, xiv, 23, 238–9; Liebstandarte Adolf Hitler, 23; *see also* Wehrmacht
Wagner, Alfred, 102, 129, 183–6, 219
Warsaw, German occupation of, 2, 8–9
Wehling, Kurt, 70–1, 76, 143, 152–3, 156–8
Wehrmacht (German Army), xii, 11, 14; Army Group A, 208; Army Group Africa, 171; Army Group Centre, 39, 40, 248; Army Group North, 208; Army Group South, 166; Army Group Vistula, 212; Third Panzer Army, 34; Fourth Panzer Army, 34, 134, 194; Sixth Army (at Stalingrad), 134, 163, 165, 166, 168, 170, 191, 193; Ninth Army, 194,

212; Afrika Korps, 125, 126, 171, 193; Second Panzer Group, 39; Group Steiner, 211; XI Airborne Corps, 124–5; 2nd Panzer Division, 30; 3rd Tank Division, 200; 7th German Flieger Division, 30; 18th Panzer Division, 198–9; 18th Tank Division, xiv; Division Hermann Goering, 172; Grossdeutschland Division, 202, 203; SS Tank Division Das Reich, 258; Infantry Regiment, 630: 36; tank-infantry battalion 125: 65; AR20 (Horse-Drawn Artillery), 39; *see also* SS; tanks; Waffen-SS
"Wild Boar" (night–fighter technique), 104
Wilhelm II, Kaiser, 27
Wilhelmshaven, 68, 82, RAF bombing of, 179
Woldag, Captain Heinrich, 13
"wolf pack" technique, 136–7, 138, 139–40, 153

Y

Yugoslavia, xii; German occupation of (1941), 27–8, 30

Y

Zeitzler, Colonel-General Kurt, 193
Ziemer, Werner, 71, 72, 74, 75, 81, 83, 89, 90–1, 148